THIRD EDITION

Web Scraping with Python
Data Extraction from the Modern Web

Ryan Mitchell

Beijing · Boston · Farnham · Sebastopol · Tokyo

Web Scraping with Python

by Ryan Mitchell

Published by O'Reilly Media, Inc., 1005 Gravenstein Highway North, Sebastopol, CA 95472.

O'Reilly books may be purchased for educational, business, or sales promotional use. Online editions are also available for most titles (*http://oreilly.com*). For more information, contact our corporate/institutional sales department: 800-998-9938 or *corporate@oreilly.com*.

Acquisitions Editor: Amanda Quinn	**Indexer:** nSight, Inc
Development Editor: Sara Hunter	**Interior Designer:** David Futato
Production Editor: Aleeya Rahman	**Cover Designer:** Karen Montgomery
Copyeditor: Sonia Saruba	**Illustrator:** Kate Dullea
Proofreader: Piper Editorial Consulting, LLC	

July 2015:	First Edition
April 2018:	Second Edition
February 2024:	Third Edition

Revision History for the Third Edition

2024-02-14:   First Release

See *http://oreilly.com/catalog/errata.csp?isbn=9781098145354* for release details.

978-1-098-14535-4

[LSI]

Table of Contents

Part II. Advanced Scraping

Preface

To those who have not developed the skill, computer programming can seem like a kind of magic. If programming is magic, *web scraping* is wizardry: the application of magic for particularly impressive and useful—yet surprisingly effortless—feats.

In my years as a software engineer, I've found that few programming practices capture the excitement of both programmers and laypeople alike quite like web scraping. The ability to write a simple bot that collects data and streams it down a terminal or stores it in a database, while not difficult, never fails to provide a certain thrill and sense of possibility, no matter how many times you might have done it before.

Unfortunately, when I speak to other programmers about web scraping, there's a lot of misunderstanding and confusion about the practice. Some people aren't sure it's legal (it is), or how to handle problems like JavaScript-heavy pages or required logins. Many are confused about how to start a large web scraping project, or even where to find the data they're looking for. This book seeks to put an end to many of these common questions and misconceptions about web scraping, while providing a comprehensive guide to most common web scraping tasks.

Web scraping is a diverse and fast-changing field, and I've tried to provide both high-level concepts and concrete examples to cover just about any data collection project you're likely to encounter. Throughout the book, code samples are provided to demonstrate these concepts and allow you to try them out. The code samples themselves can be used and modified with or without attribution (although acknowledgment is always appreciated). All code samples are available on GitHub (*https://github.com/REMitchell/python-scraping*) for viewing and downloading.

What Is Web Scraping?

The automated gathering of data from the internet is nearly as old as the internet itself. Although *web scraping* is not a new term, in years past the practice has been more commonly known as *screen scraping*, *data mining*, *web harvesting*, or similar variations. General consensus today seems to favor *web scraping*, so that is the term I use throughout the book, although I also refer to programs that specifically traverse multiple pages as *web crawlers* or refer to the web scraping programs themselves as *bots*.

In theory, web scraping is the practice of gathering data through any means other than a program interacting with an API (or, obviously, through a human using a web browser). This is most commonly accomplished by writing an automated program that queries a web server, requests data (usually in the form of HTML and other files that compose web pages), and then parses that data to extract needed information.

In practice, web scraping encompasses a wide variety of programming techniques and technologies, such as data analysis, natural language parsing, and information security. Because the scope of the field is so broad, this book covers the fundamental basics of web scraping and crawling in Part I and delves into advanced topics in Part II. I suggest that all readers carefully study the first part and delve into the more specific in the second part as needed.

Why Web Scraping?

If the only way you access the internet is through a browser, you're missing out on a huge range of possibilities. Although browsers are handy for executing JavaScript, displaying images, and arranging objects in a more human-readable format (among other things), web scrapers are excellent at gathering and processing large amounts of data quickly. Rather than viewing one page at a time through the narrow window of a monitor, you can view databases spanning thousands or even millions of pages at once.

In addition, web scrapers can go places that traditional search engines cannot. A Google search for "cheapest flights to Boston" will result in a slew of advertisements and popular flight search sites. Google knows only what these websites say on their content pages, not the exact results of various queries entered into a flight search application. However, a well-developed web scraper can chart the cost of a flight to Boston over time, across a variety of websites, and tell you the best time to buy your ticket.

You might be asking: "Isn't data gathering what APIs are for?" (If you're unfamiliar with APIs, see Chapter 15.) Well, APIs can be fantastic, if you find one that suits your purposes. They are designed to provide a convenient stream of well-formatted data from one computer program to another. You can find an API for many types of data you might want to use, such as Twitter posts or Wikipedia pages. In general, it is preferable to use an API (if one exists), rather than build a bot to get the same data. However, an API might not exist or be useful for your purposes for several reasons:

- You are gathering relatively small, finite sets of data across a large collection of websites without a cohesive API.

- The data you want is fairly small or uncommon, and the creator did not think it warranted an API.

- The source does not have the infrastructure or technical ability to create an API.

- The data is valuable and/or protected and not intended to be spread widely.

Even when an API *does* exist, the request volume and rate limits, the types of data, or the format of data that it provides might be insufficient for your purposes.

This is where web scraping steps in. With few exceptions, if you can view data in your browser, you can access it via a Python script. If you can access it in a script, you can store it in a database. And if you can store it in a database, you can do virtually anything with that data.

There are obviously many extremely practical applications of having access to nearly unlimited data: market forecasting, machine-language translation, and even medical diagnostics have benefited tremendously from the ability to retrieve and analyze data from news sites, translated texts, and health forums, respectively.

Even in the art world, web scraping has opened up new frontiers for creation. The 2006 project "We Feel Fine" (*http://wefeelfine.org/*) by Jonathan Harris and Sep Kamvar scraped a variety of English-language blog sites for phrases starting with "I feel" or "I am feeling." This led to a popular data visualization, describing how the world was feeling day by day and minute by minute.

Regardless of your field, web scraping almost always provides a way to guide business practices more effectively, improve productivity, or even branch off into a brand-new field entirely.

About This Book

This book is designed to serve not only as an introduction to web scraping but also as a comprehensive guide to collecting, transforming, and using data from uncooperative sources. Although it uses the Python programming language and covers many Python basics, it should not be used as an introduction to the language.

If you don't know any Python at all, this book might be a bit of a challenge. Please do not use it as an introductory Python text. With that said, I've tried to keep all concepts and code samples at a beginning-to-intermediate Python programming level in order to make the content accessible to a wide range of readers. To this end, there are occasional explanations of more advanced Python programming and general computer science topics where appropriate. If you are a more advanced reader, feel free to skim these parts!

If you're looking for a more comprehensive Python resource, *Introducing Python* by Bill Lubanovic (O'Reilly) is a good, if lengthy, guide. For those with shorter attention spans, the video series *Introduction to Python* by Jessica McKellar (O'Reilly) is an excellent resource. I've also enjoyed *Think Python* by a former professor of mine, Allen Downey (O'Reilly). This last book in particular is ideal for those new to programming, and teaches computer science and software engineering concepts along with the Python language.

Technical books often focus on a single language or technology, but web scraping is a relatively disparate subject, with practices that require the use of databases, web servers, HTTP, HTML, internet security, image processing, data science, and other tools. This book attempts to cover all of these, and other topics, from the perspective of "data gathering." It should not be used as a complete treatment of any of these subjects, but I believe they are covered in enough detail to get you started writing web scrapers!

Part I covers the subject of web scraping and web crawling in depth, with a strong focus on a small handful of libraries used throughout the book. Part I can easily be used as a comprehensive reference for these libraries and techniques (with certain exceptions, where additional references will be provided). The skills taught in the first part will likely be useful for everyone writing a web scraper, regardless of their particular target or application.

Part II covers additional subjects that the reader might find useful when writing web scrapers, but that might not be useful for all scrapers all the time. These subjects are, unfortunately, too broad to be neatly wrapped up in a single chapter. Because of this, frequent references are made to other resources for additional information.

The structure of this book enables you to easily jump around among chapters to find only the web scraping technique or information that you are looking for. When a concept or piece of code builds on another mentioned in a previous chapter, I explicitly reference the section that it was addressed in.

Conventions Used in This Book

The following typographical conventions are used in this book:

Italic
> Indicates new terms, URLs, email addresses, filenames, and file extensions.

`Constant width`
> Used for program listings, as well as within paragraphs to refer to program elements such as variable or function names, databases, data types, environment variables, statements, and keywords.

Constant width bold

Shows commands or other text that should be typed by the user.

Constant width italic

Shows text that should be replaced with user-supplied values or by values determined by context.

 This element signifies a tip or suggestion.

 This element signifies a general note.

 This element indicates a warning or caution.

Using Code Examples

Supplemental material (code examples, exercises, etc.) is available for download at *https://github.com/REMitchell/python-scraping*.

This book is here to help you get your job done. If the example code in this book is useful to you, you may use it in your programs and documentation. You do not need to contact us for permission unless you're reproducing a significant portion of the code. For example, writing a program that uses several chunks of code from this book does not require permission. Selling or distributing a CD-ROM of examples from O'Reilly books does require permission. Answering a question by citing this book and quoting example code does not require permission. Incorporating a significant amount of example code from this book into your product's documentation does require permission.

We appreciate, but do not require, attribution. An attribution usually includes the title, author, publisher, and ISBN. For example: "*Web Scraping with Python*, Third Edition, by Ryan Mitchell (O'Reilly). Copyright 2024 Ryan Mitchell, 978-1-098-14535-4."

If you feel your use of code examples falls outside fair use or the permission given here, feel free to contact us at *permissions@oreilly.com*.

Unfortunately, printed books are difficult to keep up-to-date. With web scraping, this provides an added challenge, as the many libraries and websites that the book references and that the code often depends on may occasionally be modified, and code samples may fail or produce unexpected results. If you choose to run the code samples, please run them from the GitHub repository rather than copying from the book directly. I, and readers of this book who choose to contribute (including, perhaps, you!), will strive to keep the repository up-to-date with required modifications.

In addition to code samples, terminal commands are often provided to illustrate how to install and run software. In general, these commands are geared toward Linux-based operating systems but will usually be applicable for Windows users with a properly configured Python environment and pip installation. When this is not the case, I have provided instructions for all major operating systems, or external references for Windows users to accomplish the task.

O'Reilly Online Learning

 For more than 40 years, *O'Reilly Media* has provided technology and business training, knowledge, and insight to help companies succeed.

Our unique network of experts and innovators share their knowledge and expertise through books, articles, and our online learning platform. O'Reilly's online learning platform gives you on-demand access to live training courses, in-depth learning paths, interactive coding environments, and a vast collection of text and video from O'Reilly and 200+ other publishers. For more information, visit *https://oreilly.com*.

How to Contact Us

Please address comments and questions concerning this book to the publisher:

O'Reilly Media, Inc.
1005 Gravenstein Highway North
Sebastopol, CA 95472
800-889-8969 (in the United States or Canada)
707-829-7019 (international or local)
707-829-0104 (fax)
support@oreilly.com
https://www.oreilly.com/about/contact.html

We have a web page for this book, where we list errata, examples, and any additional information. You can access this page at *https://oreil.ly/web_scraping_with_python*.

For news and information about our books and courses, visit *https://oreilly.com*.

Find us on LinkedIn: *https://linkedin.com/company/oreilly-media*

Follow us on Twitter: *https://twitter.com/oreillymedia*

Watch us on YouTube: *https://youtube.com/oreillymedia*

Acknowledgments

Just as some of the best products arise out of a sea of user feedback, this book never could have existed in any useful form without the help of many collaborators, cheerleaders, and editors. Thank you to the O'Reilly staff and their amazing support for this somewhat unconventional subject; to my friends and family who have offered advice and put up with impromptu readings; and to my coworkers at the Gerson Lehrman Group, whom I now likely owe many hours of work.

Thank you to my editors: Sara Hunter, John Obelenus, and Tracey Larvenz. Their feedback, guidance, and occasional tough love were invaluable. Quite a few sections and code samples were written as a direct result of their suggestions.

The inspiration for the first two chapters, as well as many new inclusions throughout the third edition, are thanks to Bryan Specht. The legacy he left is more broad and vast than even he knew, but the hole he left to be filled by that legacy is even bigger.

Finally, thanks to Jim Waldo, who started this whole project many years ago when he mailed a Linux box and *The Art and Science of C* by Eric Roberts (Addison-Wesley) to a young, impressionable teenager.

## PART I

Building Scrapers

This first part of this book focuses on the basic mechanics of web scraping: how to use Python to request information from a web server, how to perform basic handling of the server's response, and how to begin interacting with a website in an automated fashion. By the end, you'll be cruising around the internet with ease, building scrapers that can hop from one domain to another, gather information, and store that information for later use.

To be honest, web scraping is a fantastic field to get into if you want a huge payout for relatively little up-front investment. In all likelihood, 90% of web scraping projects you'll encounter will draw on techniques used in just the next 6 chapters. This section covers what the general (albeit technically savvy) public tends to think of when they think of "web scrapers":

- Retrieving HTML data from a domain name
- Parsing that data for target information
- Storing the target information
- Optionally, moving to another page to repeat the process

This will give you a solid foundation before moving on to more complex projects in Part II. Don't be fooled into thinking that this first section isn't as important as some of the more advanced projects in the second half. You will use nearly all the information in the first half of this book on a daily basis while writing web scrapers!

## CHAPTER 1

How the Internet Works

I have met very few people in my life who truly know how the internet works, and I am certainly not one of them.

The vast majority of us are making do with a set of mental abstractions that allow us to use the internet just as much as we need to. Even for programmers, these abstractions might extend only as far as what was required for them to solve a particularly tricky problem once in their career.

Due to limitations in page count and the knowledge of the author, this chapter must also rely on these sorts of abstractions. It describes the mechanics of the internet and web applications, to the extent needed to scrape the web (and then, perhaps a little more).

This chapter, in a sense, describes the world in which web scrapers operate: the customs, practices, protocols, and standards that will be revisited throughout the book.

When you type a URL into the address bar of your web browser and hit Enter, interactive text, images, and media spring up as if by magic. This same magic is happening for billions of other people every day. They're visiting the same websites, using the same applications—often getting media and text customized just for them.

And these billions of people are all using different types of devices and software applications, written by different developers at different (often competing!) companies.

Amazingly, there is no all-powerful governing body regulating the internet and coordinating its development with any sort of legal force. Instead, different parts of the internet are governed by several different organizations that evolved over time on a somewhat ad hoc and opt-in basis.

Of course, choosing *not* to opt into the standards that these organizations publish may result in your contributions to the internet simply...not working. If your website can't be displayed in popular web browsers, people likely aren't going to visit it. If the data your router is sending can't be interpreted by any other router, that data will be ignored.

Web scraping is, essentially, the practice of substituting a web browser for an application of your own design. Because of this, it's important to understand the standards and frameworks that web browsers are built on. As a web scraper, you must both mimic and, at times, subvert the expected internet customs and practices.

Networking

In the early days of the telephone system, each telephone was connected by a physical wire to a central switchboard. If you wanted to make a call to a nearby friend, you picked up the phone, asked the switchboard operator to connect you, and the switchboard operator physically created (via plugs and jacks) a dedicated connection between your phone and your friend's phone.

Long-distance calls were expensive and could take minutes to connect. Placing a long-distance call from Boston to Seattle would result in the coordination of switchboard operators across the United States creating a single enormous length of wire directly connecting your phone to the recipient's.

Today, rather than make a telephone call over a temporary dedicated connection, we can make a video call from our house to anywhere in the world across a persistent web of wires. The wire doesn't tell the data where to go, the data guides itself, in a process called *packet switching*. Although many technologies over the years contributed to what we think of as "the internet," packet switching is really the technology that single-handedly started it all.

In a packet-switched network, the message to be sent is divided into discrete ordered packets, each with its own sender and destination address. These packets are routed dynamically to any destination on the network, based on that address. Rather than being forced to blindly traverse the single dedicated connection from receiver to sender, the packets can take any path the network chooses. In fact, packets in the same message transmission might take different routes across the network and be reordered by the receiving computer when they arrive.

If the old phone networks were like a zip line—taking passengers from a single destination at the top of a hill to a single destination at the bottom—then packet-switched networks are like a highway system, where cars going to and from multiple destinations are all able to use the same roads.

A modern packet-switching network is usually described using the Open Systems Interconnection (OSI) model, which is composed of seven layers of routing, encoding, and error handling:

1. Physical layer
2. Data link layer
3. Network layer
4. Transport layer
5. Session layer
6. Presentation layer
7. Application layer

Most web application developers spend their days entirely in layer 7, the application layer. This is also the layer where the most time is spent in this book. However, it is important to have at least conceptual knowledge of the other layers when scraping the web. For example, TLS fingerprinting, discussed in Chapter 17, is a web scraping detection method that involves the transport layer.

In addition, knowing about all of the layers of data encapsulation and transmission can help troubleshoot errors in your web applications and web scrapers.

Physical Layer

The *physical layer* specifies how information is physically transmitted with electricity over the Ethernet wire in your house (or on any local network). It defines things like the voltage levels that encode 1's and 0's, and how fast those voltages can be pulsed. It also defines how radio waves over Bluetooth and WiFi are interpreted.

This layer does not involve any programming or digital instructions but is based purely on physics and electrical standards.

Data Link Layer

The *data link layer* specifies how information is transmitted between two nodes in a local network, for example, between your computer and a router. It defines the beginning and ending of a single transmission and provides for error correction if the transmission is lost or garbled.

At this layer, the packets are wrapped in an additional "digital envelope" containing routing information and are referred to as *frames*. When the information in the frame is no longer needed, it is unwrapped and sent across the network as a packet.

It's important to note that, at the data link layer, all devices on a network are receiving the same data at all times—there's no actual "switching" or control over where the data is going. However, devices that the data is not addressed to will generally ignore the data and wait until they get something that's meant for them.

Network Layer

The *network layer* is where packet switching, and therefore "the internet," happens. This is the layer that allows packets from your computer to be forwarded by a router and reach devices beyond their immediate network.

The network layer involves the Internet Protocol (IP) part of the Transmission Control Protocol/Internet Protocol (TCP/IP). IP is where we get IP addresses from. For instance, my IP address on the global internet is currently 173.48.178.92. This allows any computer in the world to send data to me and for me to send data to any other address from my own address.

Transport Layer

Layer 4, the *transport layer*, concerns itself with connecting a specific service or application running on a computer to a specific application running on another computer, rather than just connecting the computers themselves. It's also responsible for any error correction or retrying needed in the stream of data.

TCP, for example, is very picky and will keep requesting any missing packets until all of them are correctly received. TCP is often used for file transfers, where all packets must be correctly received in the right order for the file to work.

In contrast, the User Datagram Protocol (UDP) will happily skip over missing packets in order to keep the data streaming in. It's often used for videoconferencing or audioconferencing, where a temporary drop in transmission quality is preferable to a lag in the conversation.

Because different applications on your computer can have different data reliability needs at the same time (for instance, making a phone call while downloading a file), the transport layer is also where the port number comes in. The operating system assigns each application or service running on your computer to a specific port, from where it sends and receives data.

This port is often written as a number after the IP address, separated by a colon. For example, 71.245.238.173:8080 indicates the application assigned by the operating system to port 8080 on the computer assigned by the network at IP address 71.245.238.173.

Session Layer

The *session layer* is responsible for opening and closing a session between two applications. This session allows stateful information about what data has and hasn't been sent, and who the computer is communicating with. The session generally stays open for as long as it takes to complete the data request, and then closes.

The session layer allows for retrying a transmission in case of a brief crash or disconnect.

Sessions Versus Sessions

Sessions in the session layer of the OSI model are different from sessions and session data that web developers usually talk about. Session variables in a web application are a concept in the application layer that are implemented by the web browser software.

Session variables, in the application layer, stay in the browser for as long as they need to or until the user closes the browser window. In the session layer of the OSI model, the session usually only lasts for as long as it takes to transmit a single file!

Presentation Layer

The *presentation layer* transforms incoming data from character strings into a format that the application can understand and use. It is also responsible for character encoding and data compression. The presentation layer cares about whether incoming data received by the application represents a PNG file or an HTML file, and hands this file to the application layer accordingly.

Application Layer

The *application layer* interprets the data encoded by the presentation layer and uses it appropriately for the application. I like to think of the presentation layer as being concerned with transforming and identifying things, while the application layer is concerned with "doing" things. For instance, HTTP with its methods and statuses is an application layer protocol. The more banal JSON and HTML (because they are file types that define how data is encoded) are presentation layer protocols.

HTML

The primary function of a web browser is to display HTML (HyperText Markup Language) documents. HTML documents are files that end in *.html* or, less frequently, *.htm*.

Like text files, HTML files are encoded with plain-text characters, usually ASCII (see "Text Encoding and the Global Internet" on page 147). This means that they can be opened and read with any text editor.

This is an example of a simple HTML file:

```
<html>
  <head>
    <title>A Simple Webpage</title>
  </head>
  <body>
    <!-- This comment text is not displayed in the browser -->
    <h1>Hello, World!</h1>
  </body>
</html>
```

HTML files are a special type of XML (Extensible Markup Language) files. Each string beginning with a < and ending with a > is called a *tag*.

The XML standard defines the concept of opening or *starting tags* like <html> and closing or *ending tags* that begin with a </, like </html>. Between the starting and ending tags is the *content* of the tags.

In the case where it's unnecessary for tags to have any content at all, you may see a tag that acts as its own closing tag. This is called an empty element tag or a self-closing tag and looks like:

```
<p />
```

Tags can also have attributes in the form of attributeKey="attribute value", for example:

```
<div class="content">
  Lorem ipsum dolor sit amet, consectetur adipiscing elit
</div>
```

Here, the div tag has the attribute class which has the value main-content.

An HTML *element* has a starting tag with some optional attributes, some content, and a closing tag. An element can also contain multiple other elements, in which case they are *nested* elements.

While XML defines these basic concepts of tags, content, attributes, and values, HTML defines what those tags can and can't be, what they can and cannot contain, and how they must be interpreted and displayed by the browser.

For example, the HTML standard defines the usage of the class *attribute* and the id *attribute*, which are often used to organize and control the display of HTML elements:

```
<h1 id="main-title">Some Title</h1>
<div class="content">
  Lorem ipsum dolor sit amet, consectetur adipiscing elit
</div>
```

As a rule, multiple elements on the page can contain the same `class` value; however, any value in the `id` field must be unique on that page. So multiple elements could have the `class content`, but there can only be one element with the `id main-title`.

How the elements in an HTML document are displayed in the web browser is entirely dependent on how the web browser, as a piece of software, is programmed. If one web browser is programmed to display an element differently than another web browser, this will result in inconsistent experiences for users of different web browsers.

For this reason, it's important to coordinate exactly what the HTML tags are supposed to do and codify this into a single standard. The HTML standard is currently controlled by the World Wide Web Consortium (W3C). The current specification for all HTML tags can be found at *https://html.spec.whatwg.org/multipage/*.

However, the formal W3C HTML standard is probably not the best place to learn HTML if you've never encountered it. A large part of web scraping involves reading and interpreting raw HTML files found on the web. If you've never dealt with HTML before, I highly recommend a book like *HTML & CSS: The Good Parts* to get familiar with some of the more common HTML tags.

CSS

Cascading Style Sheets (CSS) define the appearance of HTML elements on a web page. CSS defines things like layout, colors, position, size, and other properties that transform a boring HTML page with browser-defined default styles into something more appealing for a modern web viewer.

Using the HTML example from earlier:

```
<html>
  <head>
    <title>A Simple Webpage</title>
  </head>
  <body>
    <!-- This comment text is not displayed in the browser -->
    <h1>Hello, World!</h1>
  </body>
</html>
```

some corresponding CSS might be:

```
h1 {
  font-size: 20px;
  color: green;
}
```

This CSS will set the h1 tag's content font size to be 20 pixels and display it in green text.

The h1 part of this CSS is called the *selector* or the CSS selector. This CSS selector indicates that the CSS inside the curly braces will be applied to the content of any h1 tags.

CSS selectors can also be written to apply only to elements with certain class or id attributes. For example, using the HTML:

```
<h1 id="main-title">Some Title</h1>
<div class="content">
  Lorem ipsum dolor sit amet, consectetur adipiscing elit
</div>
```

the corresponding CSS might be:

```
h1#main-title {
  font-size: 20px;
}

div.content {
  color: green;
}
```

A # is used to indicate the value of an id attribute, and a . is used to indicate the value of a class attribute.

If it's unimportant what the value of the tag is, the tag name can be omitted entirely. For instance, this CSS would turn the contents of any element having the class content green:

```
.content {
  color: green;
}
```

CSS data can be contained either in the HTML itself or in a separate CSS file with a *.css* file extension. CSS in the HTML file is placed inside <style> tags in the head of the HTML document:

```
<html>
  <head>
    <style>
      .content {
        color: green;
      }
    </style>
...
```

More commonly, you'll see CSS being imported in the head of the document using the link tag:

```
<html>
  <head>
    <link rel="stylesheet" href="mystyle.css">
...
```

As a web scraper, you won't often find yourself writing style sheets to make the HTML pretty. However, it is important to be able to read and recognize how an HTML page is being transformed by the CSS in order to relate what you're seeing in your web browser to what you're seeing in code.

For instance, you may be confused when an HTML element doesn't appear on the page. When you read the element's applied CSS, you see:

```
.mystery-element {
    display: none;
}
```

This sets the display attribute of the element to none, hiding it from the page.

If you've never encountered CSS before, you likely won't need to study it in any depth in order to scrape the web, but you should be comfortable with its syntax and note the CSS rules that are mentioned in this book.

JavaScript

When a client makes a request to a web server for a particular web page, the web server executes some code to create the web page that it sends back. This code, called *server-side code*, can be as simple as retrieving a static HTML file and sending it on. Or, it can be a complex application written in Python (the best language), Java, PHP, or any number of common server-side programming languages.

Ultimately, this server-side code creates some sort of stream of data that gets sent to the browser and displayed. But what if you want some type of interaction or behavior—a text change or a drag-and-drop element, for example—to happen without going back to the server to run more code? For this, you use *client-side code*.

Client-side code is any code that is sent over by a web server but actually executed by the client's browser. In the olden days of the internet (pre-mid-2000s), client-side code was written in a number of languages. You may remember Java applets and Flash applications, for example. But JavaScript emerged as the lone option for client-side code for a simple reason: it was the only language supported by the browsers themselves, without the need to download and update separate software (like Adobe Flash Player) in order to run the programs.

JavaScript originated in the mid-90s as a new feature in Netscape Navigator. It was quickly adopted by Internet Explorer, making it the standard for both major web browsers at the time.

Despite the name, JavaScript has almost nothing to do with Java, the server-side programming language. Aside from a small handful of superficial syntactic similarities, they are extremely dissimilar languages.

In 1996, Netscape (the creator of JavaScript) and Sun Microsystems (the creator of Java) did a license agreement allowing Netscape to use the name "JavaScript," anticipating some further collaboration between the two languages (*https://www.info world.com/article/2653798/javascript-creator-ponders-past--future.html*). However, this collaboration never happened, and it's been a confusing misnomer ever since.

Although it had an uncertain start as a scripting language for a now-defunct web browser, JavaScript is now the most popular programming language in the world. This popularity is boosted by the fact that it can also be used server-side, using Node.js. But its popularity is certainly cemented by the fact that it's the only client-side programming language available.

JavaScript is embedded into HTML pages using the `<script>` tag. The JavaScript code can be inserted as content:

```
<script>
  alert('Hello, world!');
</script>
```

Or it can be referenced in a separate file using the `src` attribute:

```
<script src="someprogram.js"></script>
```

Unlike HTML and CSS, you likely won't need to read or write JavaScript while scraping the web, but it is handy to at least get a feel for what it looks like. It can sometimes contain useful data. For example:

```
<script>
  const data = '{"some": 1, "data": 2, "here": 3}';
</script>
```

Here, a JavaScript variable is being declared with the keyword `const` (which stands for "constant") and is being set to a JSON-formatted string containing some data, which can be parsed by a web scraper directly.

JSON (JavaScript Object Notation) is a text format that contains human-readable data, is easily parsed by web scrapers, and is ubiquitous on the web. I will discuss it further in Chapter 15.

You may also see JavaScript making a request to a different source entirely for data:

```
<script>
  fetch('http://example.com/data.json')
    .then((response) => {
      console.log(response.json());
    });
</script>
```

Here, JavaScript is creating a request to `http://example.com/data.json` and, after the response is received, logging it to the console (more about the "console" in the next section).

JavaScript was originally created to provide dynamic interactivity and animation in an otherwise static web. However, today, not all dynamic behavior is created by Java-Script. HTML and CSS also have some features that allow them to change the content on the page.

For example, CSS keyframe animation can allow elements to move, change color, change size, or undergo other transformations when the user clicks on or hovers over that element.

Recognizing how the (often literally) moving parts of a website are put together can help you avoid wild goose chases when you're trying to locate data.

Watching Websites with Developer Tools

Like a jeweler's loupe or a cardiologist's stethoscope, your browser's *developer tools* are essential to the practice of web scraping. To collect data from a website, you have to know how it's put together. The developer tools show you just that.

Throughout this book, I will use developer tools as shown in Google Chrome. However, the developer tools in Firefox, Microsoft Edge, and other browsers are all very similar to each other.

To access the developer tools in your browser's menu, use the following instructions:

Chrome

View→ Developer → Developer Tools

Safari

Safari → Preferences → Advanced → Check "Show Develop menu in menu bar"

Then, using the Develop menu: Develop → Show web inspector

Microsoft Edge

Using the menu: Tools → Developer → Developer Tools

Firefox

Tools → Browser Tools → Web Developer Tools

Across all browsers, the keyboard shortcut for opening the developer tools is the same, and depending on your operating system.

Mac

Option + Command + I

Windows

CTRL + Shift + I

When web scraping, you'll likely spend most of your time in the Network tab (shown in Figure 1-1) and the Elements tab.

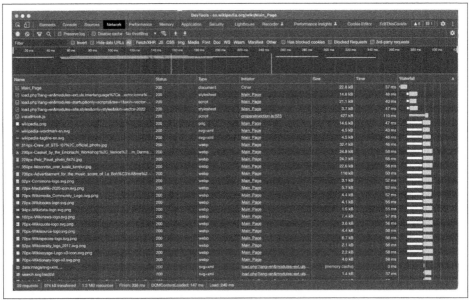

Figure 1-1. The Chrome Developer tools showing a page load from Wikipedia

The Network tab shows all of the requests made by the page as the page is loading. If you've never used it before, you might be in for a surprise! It's common for complex pages to make dozens or even hundreds of requests for assets as they're loading. In some cases, the pages may even continue to make steady streams of requests for the duration of your stay on them. For instance, they may be sending data to action tracking software, or polling for updates.

Don't See Anything in the Network Tab?

Note that the developer tools must be open *while* the page is making its requests in order for those requests to be captured. If you load a page without having the developer tab open, and then decide to inspect it by opening the developer tools, you may want to refresh the page to reload it and see the requests it is making.

If you click on a single network request in the Network tab, you'll see all of the data associated with that request. The layout of this network request inspection tool differs slightly from browser to browser, but generally allows you to see:

- The URL the request was sent to
- The HTTP method used
- The response status
- All headers and cookies associated with the request
- The payload
- The response

This information is useful for writing web scrapers that replicate these requests in order to fetch the same data the page is fetching.

The Elements tab (see Figures 1-2 and 1-3) is used to examine the structure and contents of HTML files. It's extremely handy for examining specific pieces of data on a page in order to locate the HTML tags surrounding that data and write scrapers to grab it.

As you hover over the text of each HTML element in the Elements tab, you'll see the corresponding element on the page visually highlight in the browser. Using this tool is a great way to explore the pages and develop a deeper understanding of how they're constructed (Figure 1-3).

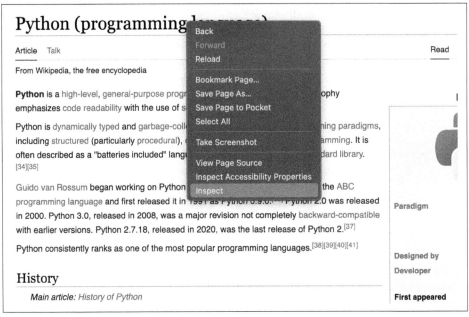

Figure 1-2. Right-click on any piece of text or data and select Inspect to view the elements surrounding that data in the Elements tab

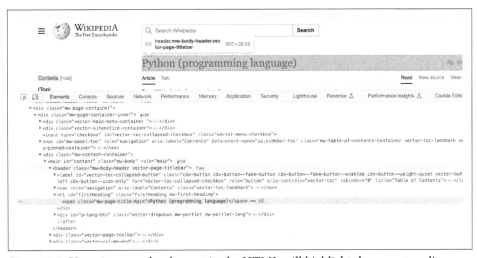

Figure 1-3. Hovering over the element in the HTML will highlight the corresponding structure on the page

You don't need to be an expert on the internet, networking, or even programming to begin scraping the web. However, having a basic understanding of how the pieces fit together, and how your browser's developer tools show those pieces, is essential.

## CHAPTER 2

The Legalities and Ethics of Web Scraping

In 2010, software engineer Pete Warden built a web crawler to gather data from Facebook. He collected data from approximately 200 million Facebook users—names, location information, friends, and interests. Of course, Facebook noticed and sent him cease and desist letters, which he obeyed. When asked why he complied with the cease and desist, he said: "Big data? Cheap. Lawyers? Not so cheap."

In this chapter, you'll look at US laws (and some international ones) that are relevant to web scraping and learn how to analyze the legality and ethics of a given web scraping situation.

Before you read the following section, consider the obvious: I am a software engineer, not a lawyer. Do not interpret anything you read here or in any other chapter of the book as professional legal advice or act on it accordingly. Although I believe I'm able to discuss the legalities and ethics of web scraping knowledgeably, you should consult a lawyer (not a software engineer) before undertaking any legally ambiguous web scraping projects.

The goal of this chapter is to provide you with a framework for being able to understand and discuss various aspects of web scraping legalities, such as intellectual property, unauthorized computer access, and server usage, but this should not be a substitute for actual legal advice.

Trademarks, Copyrights, Patents, Oh My!

It's time for a crash course in intellectual property! There are three basic types of intellectual property: trademarks (indicated by a ™ or ® symbol), copyrights (the ubiquitous ©), and patents (sometimes indicated by text noting that the invention is patent protected or a patent number but often by nothing at all).

Patents are used to declare ownership over inventions only. You cannot patent images, text, or any information itself. Although some patents, such as software patents, are less tangible than what we think of as "inventions," keep in mind that it is the *thing* (or technique) that is patented—not the data that comprises the software. Unless you are either building things from scraped diagrams, or someone patents a method of web scraping, you are unlikely to inadvertently infringe on a patent by scraping the web.

Trademarks also are unlikely to be an issue but still something that must be considered. According to the US Patent and Trademark Office:

> A *trademark* is a word, phrase, symbol, and/or design that identifies and distinguishes the source of the goods of one party from those of others. A *service mark* is a word, phrase, symbol, and/or design that identifies and distinguishes the source of a service rather than goods. The term "trademark" is often used to refer to both trademarks and service marks.

In addition to the words and symbols that come to mind when you think of trademarks, other descriptive attributes can be trademarked. This includes, for example, the shape of a container (like Coca-Cola bottles) or even a color (most notably, the pink color of Owens Corning's Pink Panther fiberglass insulation).

Unlike with patents, the ownership of a trademark depends heavily on the context in which it is used. For example, if I wish to publish a blog post with an accompanying picture of the Coca-Cola logo, I could do that, as long as I wasn't implying that my blog post was sponsored by, or published by, Coca-Cola. If I wanted to manufacture a new soft drink with the same Coca-Cola logo displayed on the packaging, that would clearly be a trademark infringement. Similarly, although I could package my new soft drink in Pink Panther pink, I could not use that same color to create a home insulation product.

This brings us to the topic of "fair use," which is often discussed in the context of copyright law but also applies to trademarks. Storing or displaying a trademark as a reference to the brand it represents is fine. Using a trademark in a way that might mislead the consumer is not. The concept of "fair use" does not apply to patents, however. For example, a patented invention in one industry cannot be applied to another industry without an agreement with the patent holder.

Copyright Law

Both trademarks and patents have something in common in that they have to be formally registered in order to be recognized. Contrary to popular belief, this is not true with copyrighted material. What makes images, text, music, etc., copyrighted? It's not the All Rights Reserved warning at the bottom of the page or anything special about "published" versus "unpublished" material. Every piece of material you create is automatically subject to copyright law as soon as you bring it into existence.

The Berne Convention for the Protection of Literary and Artistic Works, named after Berne, Switzerland, where it was first adopted in 1886, is the international standard for copyright. This convention says, in essence, that all member countries must recognize the copyright protection of the works of citizens of other member countries as if they were citizens of their own country. In practice, this means that, as a US citizen, you can be held accountable in the United States for violating the copyright of material written by someone in, say, France (and vice versa).

Copyright Registration

While it's true that copyright protections apply automatically and do not require any sort of registration, it is also possible to formally register a copyright with the US government. This is often done for valuable creative works, such as major motion pictures, in order to make any litigation easier later on and create a strong paper trail about who owns the work. However, do not let the existence of this copyright registration confuse you—all creative works, unless specifically part of the public domain, are copyrighted!

Obviously, copyright is more of a concern for web scrapers than trademarks or patents. If I scrape content from someone's blog and publish it on my own blog, I could very well be opening myself up to a lawsuit. Fortunately, I have several layers of protection that might make my blog-scraping project defensible, depending on how it functions.

First, copyright protection extends to creative works only. It does not cover statistics or facts. Fortunately, much of what web scrapers are after *are* statistics and facts.

A web scraper that gathers poetry from around the web and displays that poetry on your own website might be violating copyright law; however, a web scraper that gathers information on the frequency of poetry postings over time is not. The poetry, in its raw form, is a creative work. The average word count of poems published on a website by month is factual data and not a creative work.

Content that is posted verbatim (as opposed to aggregated/calculated content from raw scraped data) might not be violating copyright law if that data is prices, names of company executives, or some other factual piece of information.

Even copyrighted content can be used directly, within reason, under the Digital Millennium Copyright Act of 1988. The DMCA outlines some rules for the automated handling of copyrighted material. The DMCA is long, with many specific rules governing everything from ebooks to telephones. However, two main points may be of particular relevance to web scraping:

- Under the "safe harbor" protection, if you scrape material from a source that you are led to believe contains only copyright-free material, but a user has submitted copyright material to, you are protected as long as you removed the copyrighted material when notified.

- You cannot circumvent security measures (such as password protection) in order to gather content.

In addition, the DMCA also acknowledges that fair use under 17 U.S. Code § 107 applies, and that take-down notices may not be issued according to the safe harbor protection if the use of the copyrighted material falls under fair use.

In short, you should never directly publish copyrighted material without permission from the original author or copyright holder. If you are storing copyrighted material that you have free access to in your own nonpublic database for the purposes of analysis, that is fine. If you are publishing that database to your website for viewing or download, that is not fine. If you are analyzing that database and publishing statistics about word counts, a list of authors by prolificacy, or some other meta-analysis of the data, that is fine. If you are accompanying that meta-analysis with a few select quotes, or brief samples of data to make your point, that is likely also fine, but you might want to examine the fair-use clause in the US Code to make sure.

Copyright and artificial intelligence

Generative artificial intelligence, or AI programs that generate new "creative" works based on a corpus of existing creative works, present unique challenges for copyright law.

If the output of the generative AI program resembles an existing work, there may be a copyright issue. Many cases have been used as precedent to guide what the word "resembles" means here, but, according to the Congressional Research Service:[1]

> The substantial similarity test is difficult to define and varies across U.S. courts. Courts have variously described the test as requiring, for example, that the works have "a substantially similar total concept and feel" or "overall look and feel" or that "the ordinary reasonable person would fail to differentiate between the two works."

The problem with modern complex algorithms is that it can be impossible to automatically determine if your AI has produced an exciting and novel mash-up or something more...directly derivative. The AI may have no way of labeling its output as "substantially similar" to a particular input, or even identifying which of the inputs it

---

[1] For the full analysis see "Generative Artificial Intelligence and Copyright Law" (*https://crsreports.congress.gov/product/pdf/LSB/LSB10922*), Legal Sidebar, Congressional Research Service. 29 September 2023.

used to generate its creation at all! The first indication that anything is wrong at all may come in the form of a cease and desist letter or a court summons.

Beyond the issues of copyright infringement over the output of generative AI, upcoming court cases are testing whether the training process itself might infringe on a copyright holder's rights.

To train these systems, it is almost always necessary to download, store, and reproduce the copyrighted work. While it might not seem like a big deal to download a copyrighted image or text, this isn't much different from downloading a copyrighted movie—and you wouldn't download a movie, would you?

Some claim that this constitutes fair use, and they are not publishing or using the content in a way that would impact its market.

As of this writing, OpenAI is arguing before the United States Patent and Trademark Office that its use of large volumes of copyrighted material constitutes fair use.[2] While this argument is primarily in the context of AI generative algorithms, I suspect that its outcome will be applicable to web scrapers built for a variety of purposes.

Trespass to Chattels

Trespass to chattels is fundamentally different from what we think of as "trespassing laws" in that it applies not to real estate or land but to movable property, or *chattels* in legal parlance. It applies when your property is interfered with in some way that does not allow you to access or use it.

In this era of cloud computing, it's tempting not to think of web servers as real, tangible resources. However, not only do servers consist of expensive components, but they also need to be stored, monitored, cooled, cleaned, and supplied with vast amounts of electricity. By some estimates, 10% of global electricity usage is consumed by computers.[3] If a survey of your own electronics doesn't convince you, consider Google's vast server farms, all of which need to be connected to large power stations.

Although servers are expensive resources, they're interesting from a legal perspective in that webmasters generally *want* people to consume their resources (i.e., access their websites); they just don't want them to consume their resources *too much*. Checking out a website via your browser is fine; launching a full-scale Distributed Denial of Service (DDOS) attack against it obviously is not.

---

2 See "Comment Regarding Request for Comments on Intellectual Property Protection for Artificial Intelligence Innovation." (*https://www.uspto.gov/sites/default/files/documents/OpenAI_RFC-84-FR-58141.pdf*) Docket No. PTO-C-2019-0038, U.S. Patents and Trademark Office.

3 Bryan Walsh, "The Surprisingly Large Energy Footprint of the Digital Economy [UPDATE]" (*http://ti.me/2IFOF3F*), TIME.com, August 14, 2013.

Three criteria need to be met for a web scraper to violate trespass to chattels:

Lack of consent
> Because web servers are open to everyone, they are generally "giving consent" to web scrapers as well. However, many websites' Terms of Service agreements specifically prohibit the use of scrapers. In addition, any cease and desist notices delivered to you may revoke this consent.

Actual harm
> Servers are costly. In addition to server costs, if your scrapers take a website down, or limit its ability to serve other users, this can add to the "harm" you cause.

Intentionality
> If you're writing the code, you know what it does! Arguing a lack of intention would likely not go well when defending your web scraper.

You must meet all three of these criteria for trespass to chattels to apply. However, if you are violating a Terms of Service agreement, but not causing actual harm, don't think that you're immune from legal action. You might very well be violating copyright law, the DMCA, the Computer Fraud and Abuse Act (more on that later in this chapter), or one of the other myriad of laws that apply to web scrapers.

Throttling Your Bots

Back in the olden days, web servers were far more powerful than personal computers. In fact, part of the definition of *server* was *big computer*. Now, the tables have turned somewhat. My personal computer, for instance, has a 3.5 GHz processor and 32 GB of RAM. An AWS medium instance, in contrast, has 4 GB of RAM and about 3 GHz of processing capacity.

With a decent internet connection and a dedicated machine, even a single personal computer can place a heavy load on many websites, even crippling them or taking them down completely. Unless there's a medical emergency and the only cure is aggregating all the data from Joe Schmo's website in two seconds flat, there's really no reason to hammer a site.

A watched bot never completes. Sometimes it's better to leave crawlers running overnight than in the middle of the afternoon or evening for a few reasons:

- If you have about 8 hours, even at the glacial pace of 2 seconds per page, you can crawl over 14,000 pages. When time is less of an issue, you're not tempted to push the speed of your crawlers.

- Assuming the target audience of the website is in your general location (adjust accordingly for remote target audiences), the website's traffic load is probably far

---

lower during the night, meaning that your crawling will not be compounding peak traffic hour congestion.

- You save time by sleeping, instead of constantly checking your logs for new information. Think of how excited you'll be to wake up in the morning to brand-new data!

Consider the following scenarios:

- You have a web crawler that traverses Joe Schmo's website, aggregating some or all of its data.
- You have a web crawler that traverses hundreds of small websites, aggregating some or all of their data.
- You have a web crawler that traverses a very large site, such as Wikipedia.

In the first scenario, it's best to leave the bot running slowly and during the night.

In the second scenario, it's best to crawl each website in a round-robin fashion, rather than crawling them slowly, one at a time. Depending on how many websites you're crawling, this means that you can collect data as fast as your internet connection and machine can manage, yet the load is reasonable for each individual remote server. You can accomplish this programmatically, either using multiple threads (where each individual thread crawls a single site and pauses its own execution), or using Python lists to keep track of sites.

In the third scenario, the load your internet connection and home machine can place on a site like Wikipedia is unlikely to be noticed or cared much about. However, if you're using a distributed network of machines, this is obviously a different matter. Use caution, and ask a company representative whenever possible.

The Computer Fraud and Abuse Act

In the early 1980s, computers started moving out of academia and into the business world. For the first time, viruses and worms were seen as more than an inconvenience (or even a fun hobby) and as a serious criminal matter that could cause monetary damages. In 1983, the movie *War Games*, starring Matthew Broderick, also brought this issue to the public eye and to the eye of President Ronald Reagan.[4] In response, the Computer Fraud and Abuse Act (CFAA) was created in 1986.

Although you might think that the CFAA applies to only a stereotypical version of a malicious hacker unleashing viruses, the act has strong implications for web scrapers

---

4 See "'WarGames' and Cybersecurity's Debt to a Hollywood Hack," *https://oreil.ly/nBCMT*, and "Disloyal Computer Use and the Computer Fraud and Abuse Act: Narrowing the Scope," *https://oreil.ly/6TWJq*.

as well. Imagine a scraper that scans the web looking for login forms with easy-to-guess passwords, or collects government secrets accidentally left in a hidden but public location. All of these activities are illegal (and rightly so) under the CFAA.

The act defines seven main criminal offenses, which can be summarized as follows:

- The knowing unauthorized access of computers owned by the US government and obtaining information from those computers.
- The knowing unauthorized access of a computer, obtaining financial information.
- The knowing unauthorized access of a computer owned by the US government, affecting the use of that computer by the government.
- Knowingly accessing any protected computer with the attempt to defraud.
- Knowingly accessing a computer without authorization and causing damage to that computer.
- Sharing or trafficking passwords or authorization information for computers used by the US government or computers that affect interstate or foreign commerce.
- Attempts to extort money or "anything of value" by causing damage, or threatening to cause damage, to any protected computer.

In short: stay away from protected computers, do not access computers (including web servers) that you are not given access to, and especially, stay away from government or financial computers.

robots.txt and Terms of Service

A website's terms of service and *robots.txt* files are in interesting territory, legally speaking. If a website is publicly accessible, the webmaster's right to declare what software can and cannot access it is debatable. Saying that "it is fine if you use your browser to view this site, but not if you use a program you wrote to view it" is tricky.

Most sites have a link to their Terms of Service (TOS) in the footer on every page. The TOS contains more than just the rules for web crawlers and automated access; it often has information about what kind of information the website collects, what it does with it, and usually a legal disclaimer that the services provided by the website come without any express or implied warranty.

If you are interested in search engine optimization (SEO) or search engine technology, you've probably heard of the *robots.txt* file. If you go to just about any large website and look for its *robots.txt* file, you will find it in the root web folder: *http://website.com/robots.txt*.

The syntax for *robots.txt* files was developed in 1994 during the initial boom of web search engine technology. It was about this time that search engines scouring the entire internet, such as AltaVista and DogPile, started competing in earnest with simple lists of sites organized by subject, such as the one curated by Yahoo! This growth of search across the internet meant an explosion not only in the number of web crawlers but also in the availability of information collected by those web crawlers to the average citizen.

While we might take this sort of availability for granted today, some webmasters were shocked when information they published deep in the file structure of their website became available on the front page of search results in major search engines. In response, the syntax for *robots.txt* files, called the Robots Exclusion Protocol, was developed.

Unlike the terms of service, which often talks about web crawlers in broad terms and in very human language, *robots.txt* can be parsed and used by automated programs extremely easily. Although it might seem like the perfect system to solve the problem of unwanted bots once and for all, keep in mind that:

- There is no official governing body for the syntax of *robots.txt*. It is a commonly used and generally well-followed convention, but there is nothing to stop anyone from creating their own version of a *robots.txt* file (apart from the fact that no bot will recognize or obey it until it gets popular). That being said, it is a widely accepted convention, mostly because it is relatively straightforward, and there is no incentive for companies to invent their own standard or try to improve on it.

- There is no way to legally or technically enforce a *robots.txt* file. It is merely a sign that says "Please don't go to these parts of the site." Many web scraping libraries are available that obey *robots.txt*—although this is usually a default setting that can be overridden. Library defaults aside, writing a web crawler that obeys *robots.txt* is actually more technically challenging than writing one that ignores it altogether. After all, you need to read, parse, and apply the contents of *robots.txt* to your code logic.

The Robot Exclusion Protocol syntax is fairly straightforward. As in Python (and many other languages), comments begin with a # symbol, end with a newline, and can be used anywhere in the file.

The first line of the file, apart from any comments, is started with `User-agent:`, which specifies the user to which of the following rules apply. This is followed by a set of rules, either `Allow:` or `Disallow:`, depending on whether the bot is allowed on that section of the site. An asterisk (*) indicates a wildcard and can be used to describe either a `User-agent` or a URL.

If a rule follows a rule that it seems to contradict, the last rule takes precedence. For example:

```
#Welcome to my robots.txt file!
User-agent: *
Disallow: *

User-agent: Googlebot
Allow: *
Disallow: /private
```

In this case, all bots are disallowed from anywhere on the site, except for the Googlebot, which is allowed anywhere except for the */private* directory.

The *robots.txt* file of Twitter (also branded as "X") has explicit instructions for the bots of Google, Yahoo!, Yandex (a popular Russian search engine), Microsoft, and other bots or search engines not covered by any of the preceding categories. The Google section (which looks identical to the permissions allowed to all other categories of bots) looks like this:

```
#Google Search Engine Robot
User-agent: Googlebot
Allow: /?_escaped_fragment_

Allow: /?lang=
Allow: /hashtag/*?src=
Allow: /search?q=%23
Disallow: /search/realtime
Disallow: /search/users
Disallow: /search/*/grid

Disallow: /*?
Disallow: /*/followers
Disallow: /*/following
```

Notice that Twitter restricts access to the portions of its site for which it has an API in place. Because Twitter has a well-regulated API (and one that it can make money off of by licensing), it is in the company's best interest to disallow any "home-brewed APIs" that gather information by independently crawling its site.

Although a file telling your crawler where it can't go might seem restrictive at first, it can be a blessing in disguise for web crawler development. If you find a *robots.txt* file that disallows crawling in a particular section of the site, the webmaster is saying, essentially, that they are fine with crawlers in all other sections of the site. After all, if they weren't fine with it, they would have restricted access when they were writing *robots.txt* in the first place.

For example, the section of Wikipedia's *robots.txt* file that applies to general web scrapers (as opposed to search engines) is wonderfully permissive. It even goes as far as containing human-readable text to welcome bots (that's us!) and blocks access to only a few pages, such as the login page, search page, and "random article" page:

```
#
# Friendly, low-speed bots are welcome viewing article pages, but not
# dynamically generated pages please.
#
# Inktomi's "Slurp" can read a minimum delay between hits; if your bot supports
# such a thing using the 'Crawl-delay' or another instruction, please let us
# know.
#
# There is a special exception for API mobileview to allow dynamic mobile web &
# app views to load section content.
# These views aren't HTTP-cached but use parser cache aggressively and don't
# expose special: pages etc.
#
User-agent: *
Allow: /w/api.php?action=mobileview&
Disallow: /w/
Disallow: /trap/
Disallow: /wiki/Especial:Search
Disallow: /wiki/Especial%3ASearch
Disallow: /wiki/Special:Collection
Disallow: /wiki/Spezial:Sammlung
Disallow: /wiki/Special:Random
Disallow: /wiki/Special%3ARandom
Disallow: /wiki/Special:Search
Disallow: /wiki/Special%3ASearch
Disallow: /wiki/Spesial:Search
Disallow: /wiki/Spesial%3ASearch
Disallow: /wiki/Spezial:Search
Disallow: /wiki/Spezial%3ASearch
Disallow: /wiki/Specjalna:Search
Disallow: /wiki/Specjalna%3ASearch
Disallow: /wiki/Speciaal:Search
Disallow: /wiki/Speciaal%3ASearch
Disallow: /wiki/Speciaal:Random
Disallow: /wiki/Speciaal%3ARandom
Disallow: /wiki/Speciel:Search
Disallow: /wiki/Speciel%3ASearch
Disallow: /wiki/Speciale:Search
Disallow: /wiki/Speciale%3ASearch
Disallow: /wiki/Istimewa:Search
Disallow: /wiki/Istimewa%3ASearch
Disallow: /wiki/Toiminnot:Search
Disallow: /wiki/Toiminnot%3ASearch
```

Whether you choose to write web crawlers that obey *robots.txt* is up to you, but I highly recommend it, particularly if you have crawlers that indiscriminately crawl the web.

Three Web Scrapers

Because web scraping is such a limitless field, there are a staggering number of ways to land yourself in legal hot water. This section presents three cases that touched on some form of law that generally applies to web scrapers, and how it was used in that case.

eBay v. Bidder's Edge and Trespass to Chattels

In 1997, the Beanie Baby market was booming, the tech sector was bubbling, and online auction houses were the hot new thing on the internet. A company called Bidder's Edge formed and created a new kind of meta-auction site. Rather than force you to go from auction site to auction site, comparing prices, it would aggregate data from all current auctions for a specific product (say, a hot new Furby doll or a copy of *Spice World*) and point you to the site that had the lowest price.

Bidder's Edge accomplished this with an army of web scrapers, constantly making requests to the web servers of the various auction sites to get price and product information. Of all the auction sites, eBay was the largest, and Bidder's Edge hit eBay's servers about 100,000 times a day. Even by today's standards, this is a lot of traffic. According to eBay, this was 1.53% of its total internet traffic at the time, and it certainly wasn't happy about it.

eBay sent Bidder's Edge a cease and desist letter, coupled with an offer to license its data. However, negotiations for this licensing failed, and Bidder's Edge continued to crawl eBay's site.

eBay tried blocking IP addresses used by Bidder's Edge, blocking 169 IP addresses—although Bidder's Edge was able to get around this by using proxy servers (servers that forward requests on behalf of another machine but using the proxy server's own IP address). As I'm sure you can imagine, this was a frustrating and unsustainable solution for both parties—Bidder's Edge was constantly trying to find new proxy servers and buy new IP addresses while old ones were blocked, and eBay was forced to maintain large firewall lists (and adding computationally expensive IP address-comparing overhead to each packet check).

Finally, in December 1999, eBay sued Bidder's Edge under trespass to chattels.

Because eBay's servers were real, tangible resources that it owned, and it didn't appreciate Bidder's Edge's abnormal use of them, trespass to chattels seemed like the ideal law to use. In fact, in modern times, trespass to chattels goes hand in hand with web-scraping lawsuits and is most often thought of as an IT law.

The courts ruled that for eBay to win its case using trespass to chattels, eBay had to show two things:

- Bidder's Edge knew it was explicitly disallowed from using eBay's resources.
- eBay suffered financial loss as a result of Bidder's Edge's actions.

Given the record of eBay's cease and desist letters, coupled with IT records showing server usage and actual costs associated with the servers, this was relatively easy for eBay to do. Of course, no large court battles end easily: countersuits were filed, many lawyers were paid, and the matter was eventually settled out of court for an undisclosed sum in March 2001.

So does this mean that any unauthorized use of another person's server is automatically a violation of trespass to chattels? Not necessarily. Bidder's Edge was an extreme case; it was using so many of eBay's resources that the company had to buy additional servers, pay more for electricity, and perhaps hire additional personnel. Although the 1.53% increase might not seem like a lot, in large companies, it can add up to a significant amount.

In 2003, the California Supreme Court ruled on another case, Intel Corp versus Hamidi, in which a former Intel employee (Hamidi) sent emails Intel didn't like, across Intel's servers, to Intel employees. The court said:

> Intel's claim fails not because e-mail transmitted through the internet enjoys unique immunity, but because the trespass to chattels tort—unlike the causes of action just mentioned—may not, in California, be proved without evidence of an injury to the plaintiff's personal property or legal interest therein.

Essentially, Intel had failed to prove that the costs of transmitting the six emails sent by Hamidi to all employees (each one, interestingly enough, with an option to be removed from Hamidi's mailing list—at least he was polite!) contributed to any financial injury for Intel. It did not deprive Intel of any property or use of its property.

United States v. Auernheimer and the Computer Fraud and Abuse Act

If information is readily accessible on the internet to a human using a web browser, it's unlikely that accessing the same exact information in an automated fashion would land you in hot water with the Feds. However, as easy as it can be for a sufficiently curious person to find a small security leak, that small security leak can quickly become a much larger and much more dangerous one when automated scrapers enter the picture.

In 2010, Andrew Auernheimer and Daniel Spitler noticed a nice feature of iPads: when you visited AT&T's website on them, AT&T would redirect you to a URL containing your iPad's unique ID number:

```
https://dcp2.att.com/OEPClient/openPage?ICCID=<idNumber>&IMEI=
```

This page would contain a login form, with the email address of the user whose ID number was in the URL. This allowed users to gain access to their accounts simply by entering their password.

Although there were a large number of potential iPad ID numbers, it was possible, with a web scraper, to iterate through the possible numbers, gathering email addresses along the way. By providing users with this convenient login feature, AT&T, in essence, made its customer email addresses public to the web.

Auernheimer and Spitler created a scraper that collected 114,000 of these email addresses, among them the private email addresses of celebrities, CEOs, and government officials. Auernheimer (but not Spitler) then sent the list, and information about how it was obtained, to Gawker Media, which published the story (but not the list) under the headline: "Apple's Worst Security Breach: 114,000 iPad Owners Exposed."

In June 2011, Auernheimer's home was raided by the FBI in connection with the email address collection, although they ended up arresting him on drug charges. In November 2012, he was found guilty of identity fraud and conspiracy to access a computer without authorization and later sentenced to 41 months in federal prison and ordered to pay $73,000 in restitution.

His case caught the attention of civil rights lawyer Orin Kerr, who joined his legal team and appealed the case to the Third Circuit Court of Appeals. On April 11, 2014 (these legal processes can take quite a while), they made the argument:

> Auernheimer's conviction on Count 1 must be overturned because visiting a publicly available website is not unauthorized access under the Computer Fraud and Abuse Act, 18 U.S.C. § 1030(a)(2)(C). AT&T chose not to employ passwords or any other protective measures to control access to the e-mail addresses of its customers. It is irrelevant that AT&T subjectively wished that outsiders would not stumble across the data or that Auernheimer hyperbolically characterized the access as a "theft." The company configured its servers to make the information available to everyone and thereby authorized the general public to view the information. Accessing the e-mail addresses through AT&T's public website was authorized under the CFAA and therefore was not a crime.

Although Auernheimer's conviction was only overturned on appeal due to lack of venue, the Third Circuit Court did seem amenable to this argument in a footnote they wrote in their decision:

Although we need not resolve whether Auernheimer's conduct involved such a breach, no evidence was advanced at trial that the account slurper ever breached any password gate or other code-based barrier. The account slurper simply accessed the publicly facing portion of the login screen and scraped information that AT&T unintentionally published.

While Auernheimer ultimately was not convicted under the Computer Fraud and Abuse Act, he had his house raided by the FBI, spent many thousands of dollars in legal fees, and spent three years in and out of courtrooms and prisons.

As web scrapers, what lessons can we take away from this to avoid similar situations? Perhaps a good start is: don't be a jerk.

Scraping any sort of sensitive information, whether it's personal data (in this case, email addresses), trade secrets, or government secrets, is probably not something you want to do without having a lawyer on speed dial. Even if it's publicly available, think: "Would the average computer user be able to easily access this information if they wanted to see it?" or "Is this something the company wants users to see?"

I have on many occasions called companies to report security vulnerabilities in their web applications. This line works wonders: "Hi, I'm a security professional who discovered a potential vulnerability on your website. Could you direct me to someone so that I can report it and get the issue resolved?" In addition to the immediate satisfaction of recognition for your (white hat) hacking genius, you might be able to get free subscriptions, cash rewards, and other goodies out of it!

In addition, Auernheimer's release of the information to Gawker Media (before notifying AT&T) and his showboating around the exploit of the vulnerability also made him an especially attractive target for AT&T's lawyers.

If you find security vulnerabilities in a site, the best thing to do is to alert the owners of the site, not the media. You might be tempted to write up a blog post and announce it to the world, especially if a fix to the problem is not put in place immediately. However, you need to remember that it is the company's responsibility, not yours. The best thing you can do is take your web scrapers (and, if applicable, your business) away from the site!

Field v. Google: Copyright and robots.txt

Blake Field, an attorney, filed a lawsuit against Google on the basis that its site-caching feature violated copyright law by displaying a copy of his book after he had removed it from his website. Copyright law allows the creator of an original creative work to have control over the distribution of that work. Field's argument was that Google's caching (after he had removed it from his website) removed his ability to control its distribution.

The Google Web Cache

When Google web scrapers (also known as *Googlebots*) crawl websites, they make a copy of the site and host it on the internet. Anyone can access this cache, using the URL format:

> *http://webcache.googleusercontent.com/search?q=cache:http://pythonscraping.com*

If a website you are searching for, or scraping, is unavailable, you might want to check there to see if a usable copy exists!

Knowing about Google's caching feature and not taking action did not help Field's case. After all, he could have prevented the Googlebots from caching his website simply by adding the *robots.txt* file, with simple directives about which pages should and should not be scraped.

More important, the court found that the DMCA Safe Harbor provision allowed Google to legally cache and display sites such as Field's: "[a] service provider shall not be liable for monetary relief...for infringement of copyright by reason of the intermediate and temporary storage of material on a system or network controlled or operated by or for the service provider."

## CHAPTER 3

Applications of Web Scraping

While web scrapers can help almost any business, often the real trick is figuring out *how*. Like artificial intelligence, or really, programming in general, you can't just wave a magic wand and expect it to improve your bottom line.

Applying the practice of web scraping to your business takes real strategy and careful planning in order to use it effectively. You need to identify specific problems, figure out what data you need to fix those problems, and then outline the inputs, outputs, and algorithms that will allow your web scrapers to create that data.

Classifying Projects

When planning a web scraping project, you should think about how it fits into one of several categories.

Is your web scraper "broad" or "targeted"? You can write templates to instruct a targeted web scraper but need different techniques for a broad one:

- Will you be scraping a single website or perhaps even a fixed set of pages within that website? If so, this is an extremely targeted web scraping project.

- Do you need to scrape a fixed number of known websites? This is still a fairly targeted scraper, but you may need to write a small amount of custom code for each website and invest a little more time into the architecture of your web scraper.

- Are you scraping a large number of unknown websites and discovering new targets dynamically? Will you build a crawler that must automatically detect and make assumptions about the structure of the websites? You may be writing a broad or untargeted scraper.

Do you need to run the scraper just one time or will this be an ongoing job that re-fetches the data or is constantly on the lookout for new pages to scrape?

- A one-time web scraping project can be quick and cheap to write. The code doesn't have to be pretty! The end result of this project is the data itself—you might hand off an Excel or CSV file to business, and they're happy. The code goes in the trash when you're done.

- Any project that involves monitoring, re-scanning for new data, or updating data, will require more robust code that is able to be maintained. It may also need its own monitoring infrastructure to detect when it encounters an error, fails to run, or uses more time or resources than expected.

Is the collected data your end product or is more in-depth analysis or manipulation required?

- In cases of simple data collection, the web scraper deposits data into the database exactly as it finds it, or perhaps with a few lines of simple cleaning (e.g., stripping dollar signs from product prices).

- When more advanced analysis is required, you may not even know what data will be important. Here too, you must put more thought into the architecture of your scraper.

I encourage you to consider which categories each of these projects might fall into, and how the scope of that project might need to be modified to fit the needs of your business.

E-commerce

Although I've written web scrapers that have collected all sorts of interesting data from the web, the most popular request I get is to collect product and pricing data from e-commerce sites.

Generally, these requests come from people who own a competing e-commerce site or are doing research, planning to launch a new product or market. The first metric you might think of in e-commerce is "pricing." You want to find out how your price compares with the competition. However, there's a huge space of other possibilities and data you may want to collect.

Many, but not all, products come in a variety of sizes, colors, and styles. These variations can be associated with different costs and availabilities. It may be helpful to keep track of every variation available for each product, as well as each major product listing. Note that for each variation you can likely find a unique SKU (stock-keeping unit) identification code, which is unique to a single product variation and e-commerce website (Target will have a different SKU than Walmart for each product variation, but the SKUs will remain the same if you go back and check later). Even if the SKU isn't immediately visible on the website, you'll likely find it hidden in the page's HTML somewhere, or in a JavaScript API that populates the website's product data.

While scraping e-commerce sites, it might also be important to record how many units of the product are available. Like SKUs, units might not be immediately visible on the website. You may find this information hidden in the HTML or APIs that the website uses. Make sure to also track when products are out of stock! This can be useful for gauging market demand and perhaps even influencing the pricing of your own products if you have them in stock.

When a product is on sale, you'll generally find the sale price and original price clearly marked on the website. Make sure to record both prices separately. By tracking sales over time, you can analyze your competitor's promotion and discount strategies.

Product reviews and ratings are another useful piece of information to capture. Of course, you cannot directly display the text of product reviews from competitors' websites on your own site. However, analyzing the raw data from these reviews can be useful to see which products are popular or trending.

Marketing

Online brand management and marketing often involve the aggregation of large amounts of data. Rather than scrolling through social media or spending hours searching for a company's name, you can let web scrapers do all the heavy lifting!

Web scrapers can be used by malicious attackers to essentially "copy" a website with the aim of selling counterfeit goods or defrauding would-be customers. Fortunately, web scrapers can also assist in combating this by scanning search engine results for fraudulent or improper use of a company's trademarks and other IP. Some companies, such as MarqVision, also sell these web scrapers as a service, allowing brands to outsource the process of scraping the web, detecting fraud, and issuing takedown notices.

On the other hand, not all use of a brand's trademarks is infringing. If your company is mentioned for the purpose of commentary or review, you'll probably want to know about it! Web scrapers can aggregate and track public sentiment and perceptions about a company and its brand.

While you're tracking your brand across the web, don't forget about your competitors! You might consider scraping the information of people who have reviewed competing products, or talk about competitors' brands, in order to offer them discounts or introductory promotions.

Of course, when it comes to marketing and the internet, the first thing that often comes to mind is "social media." The benefit of scraping social media is that there are usually only a handful of large sites that allow you to write targeted scrapers. These sites contain millions of well-formatted posts with similar data and attributes (such as likes, shares, and comments) that easily can be compared across sites.

The downside to social media is that there may be roadblocks to obtaining the data. Some sites, like Twitter, provide APIs, either available for free or for a fee. Other social media sites protect their data with both technology and lawyers. I recommend that you consult with your company's legal representation before scraping websites like Facebook and LinkedIn, especially.

Tracking metrics (likes, shares, and comments) of posts about topics relevant to your brand can help to identify trending topics or opportunities for engagement. Tracking popularity against attributes such as content length, inclusion of images/media, and language usage can also identify what tends to resonate best with your target audience.

If getting your product sponsored by someone with hundreds of millions of followers is outside of your company's budget, you might consider "micro-influencers" or "nano-influencers"—users with smaller social media presences who may not even consider themselves to be influencers! Building a web scraper to find and target accounts that frequently post about relevant topics to your brand would be helpful here.

Academic Research

While most of the examples in this chapter ultimately serve to grease the wheels of capitalism, web scrapers are also used in the pursuit of knowledge. Web scrapers are commonly used in medical, sociological, and psychological research, among many other fields.

For example, Rutgers University offers a course called "Computational Social Science" which teaches students web scraping to collect data for research projects. Some university courses, such as the University of Oslo's "Collecting and Analyzing Big Data" even feature this book on the syllabus!

In 2017, a project supported by the National Institutes of Health scraped the records of jail inmates in US prisons to estimate the number of inmates infected with HIV.[1] This project precipitated an extensive ethical analysis, weighing the benefits of this

---

[1] Stuart Rennie, Mara Buchbinder, and Eric Juengst, "Scraping the Web for Public Health Gains: Ethical Considerations from a 'Big Data' Research Project on HIV and Incarceration," *National Library of Medicine* 13(1): April 2020, https://www.ncbi.nlm.nih.gov/pmc/articles/PMC7392638/.

research with the risk to privacy of the inmate population. Ultimately, the research continued, but I recommend examining the ethics of your project before using web scraping for research, particularly in the medical field.

Another health research study scraped hundreds of comments from news articles in *The Guardian* about obesity and analyzed the rhetoric of those comments.[2] Although smaller in scale than other research projects, it's worth considering that web scrapers can be used for projects that require "small data" and qualitative analysis as well.

Here's another example of a niche research project that utilized web scraping. In 2016, a comprehensive study was done to scrape and perform qualitative analysis on marketing materials for every Canadian community college. [3] Researchers determined that modern facilities and "unconventional organizational symbols" are most popularly promoted.

In economics research, the Bank of Japan published a paper[4] about their use of web scraping to obtain "alternative data." That is, data outside of what banks normally use, such as GDP statistics and corporate financial reports. In this paper, they revealed that one source of alternative data is web scrapers, which they use to adjust price indices.

Product Building

Do you have a business idea and just need a database of relatively public, common-knowledge information to get it off the ground? Can't seem to find a reasonably-priced and convenient source of this information just lying around? You may need a web scraper.

Web scrapers can quickly provide data that will get you a minimum viable product for launch. Here are a few situations in which a web scraper may be the best solution:

A travel site with a list of popular tourist destinations and activities
> In this case, a database of simple geographic information won't cut it. You want to know that people are going to view Cristo Redentor, not simply visit Rio de Janeiro, Brazil. A directory of businesses won't quite work either. While people might be very interested in the British Museum, the Sainsbury's down the street

---

2 Philip Brooker et al., "Doing Stigma: Online Commentary Around Weight-Related News Media." *New Media & Society* 20(9): 1—22, December 2017.

3 Roger Pizarro Milian, "Modern Campuses, Local Connections, and Unconventional Symbols: Promotional Practises in the Canadian Community College Sector," *Tertiary Education and Management* 22:218-30, September 2016, *https://link.springer.com/article/10.1080/13583883.2016.1193764.*

4 Seisaku Kameda, "Use of Alternative Data in the Bank of Japan's Research Activities," *Bank of Japan Review* 2022-E-1, January 2022, *https://www.boj.or.jp/en/research/wps_rev/rev_2022/data/rev22e01.pdf.*

doesn't have the same appeal. However, there are many travel review sites that already contain information about popular tourist destinations.

A product review blog
Scrape a list of product names and keywords or descriptions and use your favorite generative chat AI to fill in the rest.

Speaking of artificial intelligence, those models require data—often, a lot of it! Whether you're looking to predict trends or generate realistic natural language, web scraping is often the best way to get a training dataset for your product.

Many business services products require having closely guarded industry knowledge that may be expensive or difficult to obtain, such as a list of industrial materials suppliers, contact information for experts in niche fields, or open employment positions by company. A web scraper can aggregate bits of this information found in various locations online, allowing you to build a comprehensive database with relatively little up-front cost.

Travel

Whether you're looking to start a travel-based business or are very enthusiastic about saving money on your next vacation, the travel industry deserves special recognition for the myriad of web scraping applications it provides.

Hotels, airlines, and car rentals all have very little product differentiation and many competitors within their respective markets. This means that prices are generally very similar to each other, with frequent fluctuations over time as they respond to market conditions.

While websites like Kayak and Trivago may now be large and powerful enough that they can pay for, or be provided with, APIs, all companies have to start somewhere. A web scraper can be a great way to start a new travel aggregation site that finds users the best deals from across the web.

Even if you're not looking to start a new business, have you flown on an airplane or anticipate doing so in the future? If you're looking for ideas for testing the skills in this book, I highly recommend writing a travel site scraper as a good first project. The sheer volume of data and the chronological fluctuations in that data make for some interesting engineering challenges.

Travel sites are also a good middle ground when it comes to anti-scraper defenses. They want to be crawled and indexed by search engines, and they want to make their data user-friendly and accessible to all. However, they're in strong competition with other travel sites, which may require using some of the more advanced techniques later in this book. Paying attention to your browser headers and cookies is a good first step.

If you do find yourself blocked by a particular travel site and aren't sure how to access its content via Python, rest assured that there's probably another travel site with the exact same data that you can try.

Sales

Web scrapers are an ideal tool for getting sales leads. If you know of a website with sources of contact information for people in your target market, the rest is easy. It doesn't matter how niche your area is. In my work with sales clients, I've scraped lists of youth sports team coaches, fitness gym owners, skin care vendors, and many other types of target audiences for sales purposes.

The recruiting industry (which I think of as a subset of sales) often takes advantage of web scrapers on both sides. Both candidate profiles and job listings are scraped. Because of LinkedIn's strong anti-scraping policies, plug-ins, such as Instant Data Scraper or Dux-Soup, are often used scrape candidate profiles as they're manually visited in a browser. This gives recruiters the advantage of being able to give candidates a quick glance to make sure they're suitable for the job description before scraping the page.

Directories like Yelp can help tailor searches of brick-and-mortar businesses on attributes like "expensiveness," whether or not they accept credit cards, offer delivery or catering, or serve alcohol. Although Yelp is mostly known for its restaurant reviews, it also has detailed information about local carpenters, retail stores, accountants, auto repair shops, and more.

Sites like Yelp do more than just advertise the businesses to customers—the contact information can also be used to make a sales introduction. Again, the detailed filtering tools will help tailor your target market.

Scraping employee directories or career sites can also be a valuable source of employee names and contact information that will help make more personal sales introductions. Checking for Google's structured data tags (see the next section, "SERP Scraping") is a good strategy for building a broad web scraper that can target many websites while scraping reliable, well-formatted contact information.

Nearly all the examples in this book are about scraping the "content" of websites—the human-readable information they present. However, even the underlying code of the website can be revealing. What content management system is it using? Are there any clues about what server-side stack it might have? What kind of customer chatbot or analytics system, if any, is present?

Knowing what technologies a potential customer might already have, or might need, can be valuable for sales and marketing.

SERP Scraping

SERP, or *search engine results page* scraping, is the practice of scraping useful data directly from search engine results without going to the linked pages themselves. Search engine results have the benefit of having a known, consistent format. The pages that search engines link to have varied and unknown formats—dealing with those is a messy business that's best avoided if possible.

Search engine companies have dedicated staff whose entire job is to use metadata analysis, clever programming, and AI tools to extract page summaries, statistics, and keywords from websites. By using their results, rather than trying to replicate them in-house, you can save a lot of time and money.

For example, if you want the standings for every major American sports league for the past 40 years, you might find various sources of that information. *http://nhl.com* has hockey standings in one format, while *http://nfl.com* has the standings in another format. However, searching Google for "nba standings 2008" or "mlb standings 2004" will provide consistently formatted results, with drill downs available into individual game scores and players for that season.

You might also want information about the existence and positioning of the search results themselves, for instance, tracking which websites appear, and in which order, for certain search terms. This can help to monitor your brand and keep an eye out for competitors.

If you're running a search engine ad campaign, or interested in launching one, you can monitor just the ads rather than all search results. Again, you track which ads appear, in what order, and perhaps how those results change over time.

Make sure you're not limiting yourself to the main search results page. Google, for example, has Google Maps, Google Images, Google Shopping, Google Flights, Google News, etc. All of these are essentially search engines for different types of content that may be relevant to your project.

Even if you're not scraping data from the search engine itself, it may be helpful to learn more about how search engines find and tag the data that they display in special search result features and enhancements. Search engines don't play a lot of guessing games to figure out how to display data; they request that web developers format the content specifically for display by third parties like themselves.

The documentation for Google's structured data can be found here (*https://develop ers.google.com/search/docs/appearance/structured-data*). If you encounter this data while scraping the web, now you'll know how to use it.

## CHAPTER 4

Writing Your First Web Scraper

Once you start web scraping, you start to appreciate all the little things that browsers do for you. The web, without its layers of HTML formatting, CSS styling, JavaScript execution, and image rendering, can look a little intimidating at first. In this chapter, we'll begin to look at how to format and interpret this bare data without the help of a web browser.

This chapter starts with the basics of sending a GET request (a request to fetch, or "get," the content of a web page) to a web server for a specific page, reading the HTML output from that page, and doing some simple data extraction in order to isolate the content you are looking for.

Installing and Using Jupyter

The code for this course can be found at *https://github.com/REMitchell/python-scraping*. In most cases, code samples are in the form of Jupyter Notebook files, with an *.ipynb* extension.

If you haven't used them already, Jupyter Notebooks are an excellent way to organize and work with many small but related pieces of Python code, as shown in Figure 4-1.

```
jupyter  Chapter04_FirstWebScraper Last Checkpoint: a few seconds ago (autosaved)        Logout

File    Edit    View    Insert    Cell    Kernel    Widgets    Help              Trusted | Python 3 (ipykernel) O

+  ✂  ⎘ ⎘  ↑  ↓  ▶ Run  ■ C ⟫  Code          ∨  ▦


Writing Your First Web Scraper

In [1]: from urllib.request import urlopen

        html = urlopen('http://pythonscraping.com/pages/page1.html')
        print(html.read())

        b'<html>\n<head>\n<title>A Useful Page</title>\n</head>\n<body>\n<h1>An Interesting Title</h1>\n<div>\nLorem ipsum do
        lor sit amet, consectetur adipisicing elit, sed do eiusmod tempor incididunt ut labore et dolore magna aliqua. Ut eni
        m ad minim veniam, quis nostrud exercitation ullamco laboris nisi ut aliquip ex ea commodo consequat. Duis aute irure
        dolor in reprehenderit in voluptate velit esse cillum dolore eu fugiat nulla pariatur. Excepteur sint occaecat cupida
        tat non proident, sunt in culpa qui officia deserunt mollit anim id est laborum.\n</div>\n</body>\n</html>\n'

In [1]: from urllib.request import urlopen
        from bs4 import BeautifulSoup

        html = urlopen('http://www.pythonscraping.com/pages/page1.html')
        bs = BeautifulSoup(html.read(), 'html.parser')
        print(bs.h1)

        <h1>An Interesting Title</h1>

In [2]: from urllib.request import urlopen
        from urllib.error import HTTPError
        from urllib.error import URLError

        try:
            html = urlopen("https://pythonscrapingthisurldoesnotexist.com")
        except HTTPError as e:
            print("The server returned an HTTP error")
        except URLError as e:
            print("The server could not be found!")
        else:
            print(html.read())

        The server could not be found!
```

Figure 4-1. A Jupyter Notebook running in the browser

Each piece of code is contained in a box called a *cell*. The code within each cell can be run by typing Shift + Enter, or by clicking the Run button at the top of the page.

Project Jupyter began as a spin-off project from the IPython (Interactive Python) project in 2014. These notebooks were designed to run Python code in the browser in an accessible and interactive way that would lend itself to teaching and presenting.

To install Jupyter Notebooks:

```
$ pip install notebook
```

After installation, you should have access to the `jupyter` command, which will allow you to start the web server. Navigate to the directory containing the downloaded exercise files for this book, and run:

```
$ jupyter notebook
```

This will start the web server on port 8888. If you have a web browser running, a new tab should open automatically. If it doesn't, copy the URL shown in the terminal, with the provided token, to your web browser.

Connecting

In the first section of this book, we took a deep dive into how the internet sends packets of data across wires from a browser to a web server and back again. When you open a browser, type in **google.com**, and hit Enter, that's exactly what's happening—data, in the form of an HTTP request, is being transferred from your computer, and Google's web server is responding with an HTML file that represents the data at the root of *google.com*.

But where, in this exchange of packets and frames, does the web browser actually come into play? Absolutely nowhere. In fact, ARPANET (the first public packet-switched network) predated the first web browser, Nexus, by at least 20 years.

Yes, the web browser is a useful application for creating these packets of information, telling your operating system to send them off and interpreting the data you get back as pretty pictures, sounds, videos, and text. However, a web browser is just code, and code can be taken apart, broken into its basic components, rewritten, reused, and made to do anything you want. A web browser can tell the processor to send data to the application that handles your wireless (or wired) interface, but you can do the same thing in Python with just three lines of code:

```
from urllib.request import urlopen

html = urlopen('http://pythonscraping.com/pages/page1.html')
print(html.read())
```

To run this, you can use the IPython notebook (*https://github.com/REMitchell/python-scraping/blob/master/Chapter01_BeginningToScrape.ipynb*) for Chapter 1 in the GitHub repository, or you can save it locally as *scrapetest.py* and run it in your terminal by using this command:

```
$ python scrapetest.py
```

Note that if you also have Python 2.x installed on your machine and are running both versions of Python side by side, you may need to explicitly call Python 3.x by running the command this way:

```
$ python3 scrapetest.py
```

This command outputs the complete HTML code for *page1* located at the URL *http://pythonscraping.com/pages/page1.html*. More accurately, this outputs the HTML file *page1.html*, found in the directory *<web root>/pages*, on the server located at the domain name *http://pythonscraping.com*.

Why is it important to start thinking of these addresses as "files" rather than "pages"? Most modern web pages have many resource files associated with them. These could be image files, JavaScript files, CSS files, or any other content that the page you are requesting is linked to. When a web browser hits a tag such as `<img src="cute`

`Kitten.jpg">`, the browser knows that it needs to make another request to the server to get the data at the location *cuteKitten.jpg* in order to fully render the page for the user.

Of course, your Python script doesn't have the logic to go back and request multiple files (yet); it can read only the single HTML file that you've directly requested.

```
from urllib.request import urlopen
```

means what it looks like it means: it looks at the Python module request (found within the *urllib* library) and imports only the function `urlopen`.

urllib is a standard Python library (meaning you don't have to install anything extra to run this example) and contains functions for requesting data across the web, handling cookies, and even changing metadata such as headers and your user agent. We will be using urllib extensively throughout the book, so I recommend you read the Python documentation for the library (*https://docs.python.org/3/library/urllib.html*).

`urlopen` is used to open a remote object across a network and read it. Because it is a fairly generic function (it can read HTML files, image files, or any other file stream with ease), we will be using it quite frequently throughout the book.

An Introduction to BeautifulSoup

> Beautiful Soup, so rich and green,
> Waiting in a hot tureen!
> Who for such dainties would not stoop?
> Soup of the evening, beautiful Soup!

The *BeautifulSoup* library was named after a Lewis Carroll poem of the same name in *Alice's Adventures in Wonderland*. In the story, this poem is sung by a character called the Mock Turtle (itself a pun on the popular Victorian dish Mock Turtle Soup made not of turtle but of cow).

Like its Wonderland namesake, BeautifulSoup tries to make sense of the nonsensical; it helps format and organize the messy web by fixing bad HTML and presenting us with easily traversable Python objects representing XML structures.

Installing BeautifulSoup

Because the BeautifulSoup library is not a default Python library, it must be installed. If you're already experienced at installing Python libraries, please use your favorite installer and skip ahead to the next section, "Running BeautifulSoup" on page 46.

For those who have not installed Python libraries (or need a refresher), this general method will be used for installing multiple libraries throughout the book, so you may want to reference this section in the future.

We will be using the BeautifulSoup 4 library (also known as BS4) throughout this book. The complete documentation, as well as installation instructions, for BeautifulSoup 4 can be found at Crummy.com (*https://www.crummy.com/software/Beauti fulSoup/bs4/doc/*).

If you've spent much time writing Python, you've probably used the package installer for Python (pip (*https://pypi.org/project/pip/*)). If you haven't, I highly recommend that you install pip in order to install BeautifulSoup and other Python packages used throughout this book.

Depending on the Python installer you used, pip may already be installed on your computer. To check, try:

```
$ pip
```

This command should result in the pip help text being printed to your terminal. If the command isn't recognized, you may need to install pip. Pip can be installed in a variety of ways, such as with `apt-get` on Linux or `brew` on macOS. Regardless of your operating system, you can also download the pip bootstrap file at *https://boot strap.pypa.io/get-pip.py*, save this file as *get-pip.py*, and run it with Python:

```
$ python get-pip.py
```

Again, note that if you have both Python 2.x and 3.x installed on your machine, you might need to call `python3` explicitly:

```
$ python3 get-pip.py
```

Finally, use pip to install BeautifulSoup:

```
$ pip install bs4
```

If you have two versions of Python, along with two versions of pip, you may need to call `pip3` to install the Python 3.x versions of packages:

```
$ pip3 install bs4
```

And that's it! BeautifulSoup will now be recognized as a Python library on your machine. You can test this by opening a Python terminal and importing it:

```
$ python
> from bs4 import BeautifulSoup
```

The import should complete without errors.

Keeping Libraries Straight with Virtual Environments

If you intend to work on multiple Python projects, or you need a way to easily bundle projects with all associated libraries, or you're worried about potential conflicts between installed libraries, you can install a Python virtual environment to keep everything separated and easy to manage.

When you install a Python library without a virtual environment, you are installing it *globally*. This usually requires that you be an administrator, or run as root, and that the Python library exists for every user and every project on the machine. Fortunately, creating a virtual environment is easy:

```
$ virtualenv scrapingEnv
```

This creates a new environment called scrapingEnv, which you must activate to use:

```
$ cd scrapingEnv/
$ source bin/activate
```

After you have activated the environment, you will see that environment's name in your command-line prompt, reminding you that you're currently working with it. Any libraries you install or scripts you run will be under that virtual environment only.

Working in the newly created scrapingEnv environment, you can install and use BeautifulSoup; for instance:

```
(scrapingEnv)ryan$ pip install beautifulsoup4
(scrapingEnv)ryan$ python
> from bs4 import BeautifulSoup
>
```

You can leave the environment with the deactivate command, after which you can no longer access any libraries that were installed inside the virtual environment:

```
(scrapingEnv)ryan$ deactivate
ryan$ python
> from bs4 import BeautifulSoup
Traceback (most recent call last):
  File "<stdin>", line 1, in <module>
ImportError: No module named 'bs4'
```

Keeping all your libraries separated by project also makes it easy to zip up the entire environment folder and send it to someone else. As long as they have the same version of Python installed on their machine, your code will work from the virtual environment without requiring them to install any libraries themselves.

Although I won't explicitly instruct you to use a virtual environment in all of this book's examples, keep in mind that you can apply a virtual environment anytime simply by activating it beforehand.

Running BeautifulSoup

The most commonly used object in the BeautifulSoup library is, appropriately, the BeautifulSoup object. Let's take a look at it in action, modifying the example found in the beginning of this chapter:

```
from urllib.request import urlopen
from bs4 import BeautifulSoup

html = urlopen('http://www.pythonscraping.com/pages/page1.html')
bs = BeautifulSoup(html.read(), 'html.parser')
print(bs.h1)
```

The output is as follows:

```
<h1>An Interesting Title</h1>
```

Note that this returns only the first instance of the h1 tag found on the page. By convention, only one h1 tag should be used on a single page, but conventions are often
broken on the web, so you should be aware that this will retrieve only the first
instance of the tag, and not necessarily the one that you're looking for.

As in previous web scraping examples, you are importing the urlopen function and
calling html.read() to get the HTML content of the page. In addition to the text
string, BeautifulSoup can use the file object directly returned by urlopen, without
needing to call .read() first:

```
bs = BeautifulSoup(html, 'html.parser')
```

This HTML content is then transformed into a BeautifulSoup object with the following structure:

- **html** → *<html><head>...</head><body>...</body></html>*
  - **head** → *<head><title>A Useful Page<title></head>*
    - **title** → *<title>A Useful Page</title>*
  - **body** → *<body><h1>An Int...</h1> Lorem ip... </body>*
    - **h1** → *<h1>An Interesting Title</h1>*
    - **div** → *<div>Lorem Ipsum dolor...</div>*

Note that the h1 tag that you extract from the page is nested two layers deep into your
BeautifulSoup object structure (html → body → h1). However, when you actually
fetch it from the object, you call the h1 tag directly:

```
bs.h1
```

In fact, any of the following function calls would produce the same output:

```
bs.html.body.h1
bs.body.h1
bs.html.h1
```

When you create a BeautifulSoup object, two arguments are passed in:

```
bs = BeautifulSoup(html.read(), 'html.parser')
```

The first is the HTML string that the object is based on, and the second specifies the parser that you want BeautifulSoup to use to create that object. In the majority of cases, it makes no difference which parser you choose.

`html.parser` is a parser that is included with Python 3 and requires no extra installations to use. Except where required, we will use this parser throughout the book.

Another popular parser is `lxml` (*http://lxml.de/parsing.html*). This can be installed through pip:

```
$ pip install lxml
```

`lxml` can be used with BeautifulSoup by changing the parser string provided:

```
bs = BeautifulSoup(html.read(), 'lxml')
```

`lxml` has some advantages over `html.parser` in that it is generally better at parsing "messy" or malformed HTML code. It is forgiving and fixes problems like unclosed tags, tags that are improperly nested, and missing head or body tags.

`lxml` is also somewhat faster than `html.parser`, although speed is not necessarily an advantage in web scraping, given that the speed of the network itself will almost always be your largest bottleneck.

Avoid Over-Optimizing Web Scraping Code

Elegant algorithms are lovely to behold, but when it comes to web scraping, they may not have a practical impact. A few microseconds of processing time will likely be dwarfed by the—sometimes *actual*—seconds of network latency that a network request takes.

Good web scraping code generally focuses on robust and easily readable implementations, rather than clever processing optimizations.

One of the disadvantages of `lxml` is that it needs to be installed separately and depends on third-party C libraries to function. This can cause problems for portability and ease of use, compared to `html.parser`.

Another popular HTML parser is `html5lib`. Like `lxml`, `html5lib` is an extremely forgiving parser that takes even more initiative with correcting broken HTML. It also depends on an external dependency and is slower than both `lxml` and `html.parser`. Despite this, it may be a good choice if you are working with messy or handwritten HTML sites.

It can be used by installing and passing the string `html5lib` to the BeautifulSoup object:

```
bs = BeautifulSoup(html.read(), 'html5lib')
```

I hope this small taste of BeautifulSoup has given you an idea of the power and simplicity of this library. Virtually any information can be extracted from any HTML (or XML) file, as long as it has an identifying tag surrounding it or near it. Chapter 5 delves more deeply into more-complex BeautifulSoup function calls and presents regular expressions and how they can be used with BeautifulSoup in order to extract information from websites.

Connecting Reliably and Handling Exceptions

The web is messy. Data is poorly formatted, websites go down, and closing tags go missing. One of the most frustrating experiences in web scraping is to go to sleep with a scraper running, dreaming of all the data you'll have in your database the next day—only to find that the scraper hit an error on some unexpected data format and stopped execution shortly after you stopped looking at the screen.

In situations like these, you might be tempted to curse the name of the developer who created the website (and the oddly formatted data), but the person you should really be kicking is yourself for not anticipating the exception in the first place!

Let's look at the first line of our scraper, after the import statements, and figure out how to handle any exceptions this might throw:

```
html = urlopen('http://www.pythonscraping.com/pages/page1.html')
```

Two main things can go wrong in this line:

- The page is not found on the server (or there was an error in retrieving it).
- The server is not found at all.

In the first situation, an HTTP error will be returned. This HTTP error may be "404 Page Not Found," "500 Internal Server Error," and so forth. In all of these cases, the urlopen function will throw the generic exception HTTPError. You can handle this exception in the following way:

```
from urllib.request import urlopen
from urllib.error import HTTPError

try:
    html = urlopen('http://www.pythonscraping.com/pages/page1.html')
except HTTPError as e:
    print(e)
    # return null, break, or do some other "Plan B"
else:
    # program continues. Note: If you return or break in the
    # exception catch, you do not need to use the "else" statement
```

If an HTTP error code is returned, the program now prints the error and does not execute the rest of the program under the else statement.

If the server is not found at all (if, for example, *http://www.pythonscraping.com* is down, or the URL is mistyped), urlopen will throw an URLError. This indicates that no server could be reached at all, and, because the remote server is responsible for returning HTTP status codes, an HTTPError cannot be thrown, and the more serious URLError must be caught. You can add a check to see whether this is the case:

```
from urllib.request import urlopen
from urllib.error import HTTPError
from urllib.error import URLError

try:
    html = urlopen('https://pythonscrapingthisurldoesnotexist.com')
except HTTPError as e:
    print(e)
except URLError as e:
    print('The server could not be found!')
else:
    print('It Worked!')
```

Of course, if the page is retrieved successfully from the server, there is still the issue of the content on the page not being quite what you expected. Every time you access a tag in a BeautifulSoup object, it's smart to add a check to make sure the tag actually exists. If you attempt to access a tag that does not exist, BeautifulSoup will return a None object. The problem is, attempting to access a tag on a None object itself will result in an AttributeError being thrown.

The following line (where nonExistentTag is a made-up tag, not the name of a real BeautifulSoup function):

```
print(bs.nonExistentTag)
```

returns a None object. This object is perfectly reasonable to handle and check for. The trouble comes if you don't check for it but instead go on and try to call another function on the None object, as illustrated here:

```
print(bs.nonExistentTag.someTag)
```

This returns an exception:

```
AttributeError: 'NoneType' object has no attribute 'someTag'
```

So how can you guard against these two situations? The easiest way is to explicitly check for both situations:

```
try:
    badContent = bs.nonExistingTag.anotherTag
except AttributeError as e:
    print('Tag was not found')
```

```
    else:
        if badContent == None:
            print ('Tag was not found')
        else:
            print(badContent)
```

This checking and handling of every error does seem laborious at first, but it's easy to add a little reorganization to this code to make it less difficult to write (and, more important, much less difficult to read). This code, for example, is our same scraper written in a slightly different way:

```
from urllib.request import urlopen
from urllib.error import HTTPError
from bs4 import BeautifulSoup

def getTitle(url):
    try:
        html = urlopen(url)
    except HTTPError as e:
        return None
    try:
        bs = BeautifulSoup(html.read(), 'html.parser')
        title = bs.body.h1
    except AttributeError as e:
        return None
    return title

title = getTitle('http://www.pythonscraping.com/pages/page1.html')
if title == None:
    print('Title could not be found')
else:
    print(title)
```

In this example, you're creating a function getTitle, which returns either the title of the page, or a None object if there was a problem retrieving it. Inside getTitle, you check for an HTTPError, as in the previous example, and encapsulate two of the Beautiful Soup lines inside one try statement. An AttributeError might be thrown from either of these lines (if the server did not exist, html would be a None object, and html.read() would throw an AttributeError). You could, in fact, encompass as many lines as you want inside one try statement or call another function entirely, which can throw an AttributeError at any point.

When writing scrapers, it's important to think about the overall pattern of your code in order to handle exceptions and make it readable at the same time. You'll also likely want to heavily reuse code. Having generic functions such as getSiteHTML and getTitle (complete with thorough exception handling) makes it easy to quickly—and reliably—scrape the web.

## CHAPTER 5

Advanced HTML Parsing

When Michelangelo was asked how he could sculpt a work of art as masterful as his *David*, he is famously reported to have said, "It is easy. You just chip away the stone that doesn't look like David."

Although web scraping is unlike marble sculpting in most other respects, you must take a similar attitude when it comes to extracting the information you're seeking from complicated web pages. In this chapter, we'll explore various techniques to chip away any content that doesn't look like content you want, until you arrive at the information you're seeking. Complicated HTML pages may be look intimidating at first, but just keep chipping!

Another Serving of BeautifulSoup

In Chapter 4, you took a quick look at installing and running BeautifulSoup, as well as selecting objects one at a time. In this section, we'll discuss searching for tags by attributes, working with lists of tags, and navigating parse trees.

Nearly every website you encounter contains stylesheets. Stylesheets are created so that web browsers can render HTML into colorful and aesthetically pleasing designs for humans. You might think of this styling layer as, at the very least, perfectly ignorable for web scrapers—but not so fast! CSS is, in fact, a huge boon for web scrapers because it requires the differentiation of HTML elements in order to style them differently.

CSS provides an incentive for web developers to add tags to HTML elements they might have otherwise left with the exact same markup. Some tags might look like this:

```
<span class="green"></span>
```

Others look like this:

```
<span class="red"></span>
```

Web scrapers can easily separate these two tags based on their class; for example, they might use BeautifulSoup to grab all the red text but none of the green text. Because CSS relies on these identifying attributes to style sites appropriately, you are almost guaranteed that these class and id attributes will be plentiful on most modern websites.

Let's create an example web scraper that scrapes the page located at *http://www.pythonscraping.com/pages/warandpeace.html*.

On this page, the lines spoken by characters in the story are in red, whereas the names of characters are in green. You can see the span tags, which reference the appropriate CSS classes, in the following sample of the page's source code:

```
<span class="red">Heavens! what a virulent attack!</span> replied
<span class="green">the prince</span>, not in the least disconcerted
by this reception.
```

You can grab the entire page and create a BeautifulSoup object with it by using a program similar to the one used in Chapter 4:

```
from urllib.request import urlopen
from bs4 import BeautifulSoup

html = urlopen('http://www.pythonscraping.com/pages/warandpeace.html')
bs = BeautifulSoup(html.read(), 'html.parser')
```

Using this BeautifulSoup object, you can use the find_all function to extract a Python list of proper nouns found by selecting only the text within <span class="green"></span> tags (find_all is an extremely flexible function you'll be using a lot later in this book):

```
nameList = bs.find_all('span', {'class':'green'})
for name in nameList:
    print(name.get_text())
```

When run, it should list all the proper nouns in the text, in the order they appear in *War and Peace*. How does it work? Previously, you've called bs.tagName to get the first occurrence of that tag on the page. Now, you're calling bs.find_all(tagName, tagAttributes) to get a list of all of the tags on the page, rather than just the first.

After getting a list of names, the program iterates through all names in the list and prints name.get_text() in order to separate the content from the tags.

When to get_text() and When to Preserve Tags

`.get_text()` strips all tags from the document you are working with and returns a Unicode string containing the text only. For example, if you are working with a large block of text that contains many hyperlinks, paragraphs, and other tags, all those will be stripped away, and you'll be left with a tagless block of text.

Keep in mind that it's much easier to find what you're looking for in a BeautifulSoup object than in a block of text. Calling `.get_text()` should always be the last thing you do, immediately before you print, store, or manipulate your final data. In general, you should try to preserve the tag structure of a document as long as possible.

find() and find_all() with BeautifulSoup

BeautifulSoup's `find()` and `find_all()` are the two functions you will likely use the most. With them, you can easily filter HTML pages to find lists of desired tags, or a single tag, based on their various attributes.

The two functions are extremely similar, as evidenced by their definitions in the BeautifulSoup documentation:

```
find_all(tag, attrs, recursive, text, limit, **kwargs)
find(tag, attrs, recursive, text, **kwargs)
```

In all likelihood, 95% of the time you will need to use only the first two arguments: `tag` and `attrs`. However, let's take a look at all the parameters in greater detail.

The `tag` parameter is one that you've seen before; you can pass a string name of a tag or even a Python list of string tag names. For example, the following returns a list of all the header tags in a document:[1]

```
.find_all(['h1','h2','h3','h4','h5','h6'])
```

Unlike the `tag` parameter, which can be either a string or an iterable, the `attrs` parameter must be a Python dictionary of attributes and values. It matches tags that contain any one of those attributes. For example, the following function would return *both* the green and red `span` tags in the HTML document:

```
.find_all('span', {'class': ['green', 'red']})
```

The `recursive` parameter is a boolean. How deeply into the document do you want to go? If `recursive` is set to `True`, the `find_all` function looks into children, and

---

1 If you're looking to get a list of all h<*some_level*> tags in the document, there are more succinct ways of writing this code to accomplish the same thing. We'll take a look at other ways of approaching these types of problems in the section "Regular Expressions and BeautifulSoup".

children's children, etc., for tags that match the parameters. If it is `False`, it will look only at the top-level tags in your document. By default, `find_all` works recursively (`recursive` is set to `True`). In general, it's a good idea to leave this as is, unless you really know what you need to do and performance is an issue.

The `text` parameter is unusual in that it matches based on the text content of the tags, rather than properties of the tags themselves. For instance, if you want to find the number of times "the prince" is surrounded by tags on the example page, you could replace your `.find_all()` function in the previous example with the following lines:

```
nameList = bs.find_all(text='the prince')
print(len(nameList))
```

The output of this is 7.

The `limit` parameter, of course, is used only in the `find_all` method; `find` is equivalent to the same `find_all` call, with a limit of 1. You might set this if you're interested in retrieving only the first *x* items from the page. Be aware that this gives you the first items on the page in the order they occur in the document, not necessarily the first ones you want.

The additional `kwargs` parameter allows you to pass any additional named arguments you want into the method. Any extra arguments that `find` or `find_all` doesn't recognize will be used as tag attribute matchers. For example:

```
title = bs.find_all(id='title', class_='text')
```

This returns the first tag with the word "text" in the `class` attribute and "title" in the `id` attribute. Note that, by convention, each value for an `id` should be used only once on the page. Therefore, in practice, a line like this may not be particularly useful and should be equivalent to using the `find` function:

```
title = bs.find(id='title')
```

Keyword Arguments and Class

`class` is a reserved word in Python that cannot be used as a variable or argument name. For example, if you try the following call, you'll get a syntax error due to the nonstandard use of `class`:

```
bs.find_all(class='green')
```

For this reason, BeautifulSoup requires that you use the keyword argument `_class` instead of `class`.

You might have noticed that BeautifulSoup already has a way to find tags based on their attributes and values: the `attr` parameter. Indeed, the following two lines are identical:

```
bs.find(id='text')
bs.find(attrs={'id':'text'})
```

However, the syntax of the first line is shorter and arguably easier to work with for quick filters where you need tags by a particular attribute. When filters get more complex, or when you need to pass attribute value options as a list in the arguments, you may want to use the `attrs` parameter:

```
bs.find(attrs={'class':['red', 'blue', 'green']})
```

Other BeautifulSoup Objects

So far in the book, you've seen two types of objects in the BeautifulSoup library:

`BeautifulSoup` *objects*
Instances seen in previous code examples as the variable `bs`

`Tag` *objects*
Retrieved in lists, or retrieved individually by calling `find` and `find_all` on a `BeautifulSoup` object, or drilling down:
```
bs.div.h1
```

However, two more objects in the library, although less commonly used, are still important to know about:

`NavigableString` *objects*
Used to represent text within tags, rather than the tags themselves (some functions operate on and produce `NavigableStrings`, rather than tag objects).

`Comment` *object*
Used to find HTML comments in comment tags, `<!--like this one-->`.

These are the only four objects in the BeautifulSoup package at the time of this writing. These were also the only four objects in the BeautifulSoup package when it was released in 2004, so the number of available objects is unlikely to change in the near future.

Navigating Trees

The `find_all` function is responsible for finding tags based on their name and attributes. But what if you need to find a tag based on its location in a document? That's where tree navigation comes in handy. In Chapter 4, you looked at navigating a BeautifulSoup tree in a single direction:

```
bs.tag.subTag.anotherSubTag
```

Now let's look at navigating up, across, and diagonally through HTML trees. You'll use our highly questionable online shopping site at *http://www.pythonscraping.com/pages/page3.html* as an example page for scraping, as shown in Figure 5-1.

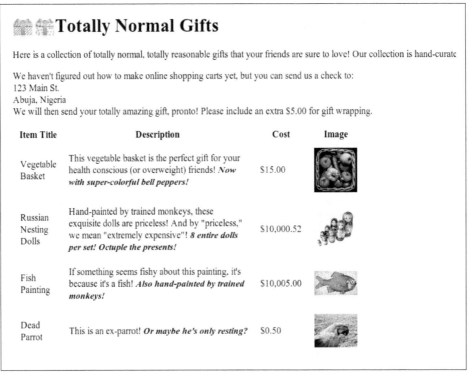

Figure 5-1. Screenshot from http://www.pythonscraping.com/pages/page3.html

The HTML for this page, mapped out as a tree (with some tags omitted for brevity), looks like this:

- HTML
  — body
    — div.wrapper
      — h1
      — div.content
      — table#giftList
        — tr
          — th
          — th
          — th
          — th
        — tr.gift#gift1
          — td
          — td
            — span.excitingNote
          — td
          — td
            — img
        — ...table rows continue...
    — div.footer

You will use this same HTML structure as an example in the next few sections.

Dealing with children and other descendants

In computer science and some branches of mathematics, you often hear about horrible things done to children: moving them, storing them, removing them, and even killing them. Fortunately, this section focuses only on selecting them!

In the BeautifulSoup library, as well as many other libraries, there is a distinction drawn between *children* and *descendants*: much like in a human family tree, children are always exactly one tag below a parent, whereas descendants can be at any level in the tree below a parent. For example, the tr tags are children of the table tag, whereas tr, th, td, img, and span are all descendants of the table tag (at least in our example page). All children are descendants, but not all descendants are children.

In general, BeautifulSoup functions always deal with the descendants of the current tag selected. For instance, bs.body.h1 selects the first h1 tag that is a descendant of the body tag. It will not find tags located outside the body.

Similarly, bs.div.find_all('img') will find the first div tag in the document, and then retrieve a list of all img tags that are descendants of that div tag.

If you want to find only descendants that are children, you can use the .children tag:

```
from urllib.request import urlopen
from bs4 import BeautifulSoup

html = urlopen('http://www.pythonscraping.com/pages/page3.html')
bs = BeautifulSoup(html, 'html.parser')

for child in bs.find('table',{'id':'giftList'}).children:
    print(child)
```

This code prints the list of product rows in the giftList table, including the initial row of column labels. If you were to write it using the descendants() function instead of the children() function, about two dozen tags would be found within the table and printed, including img tags, span tags, and individual td tags. It's definitely important to differentiate between children and descendants!

Dealing with siblings

The BeautifulSoup next_siblings() function makes it trivial to collect data from tables, especially ones with title rows:

```
from urllib.request import urlopen
from bs4 import BeautifulSoup

html = urlopen('http://www.pythonscraping.com/pages/page3.html')
bs = BeautifulSoup(html, 'html.parser')

for sibling in bs.find('table', {'id':'giftList'}).tr.next_siblings:
    print(sibling)
```

The output of this code is to print all rows of products from the product table, except for the first title row. Why does the title row get skipped? Objects cannot be siblings with themselves. Anytime you get siblings of an object, the object itself will not be included in the list. As the name of the function implies, it calls *next* siblings only. If you were to select a row in the middle of the list, for example, and call next_siblings on it, only the subsequent siblings would be returned. So, by selecting the title row and calling `next_siblings`, you can select all the rows in the table without selecting the title row itself.

Make Selections Specific

The preceding code will work just as well if you select `bs.table.tr` or even just `bs.tr` to select the first row of the table. However, in the code, I go to the trouble of writing everything out in a longer form:

```
bs.find('table',{'id':'giftList'}).tr
```

Even if it looks like there's just one table (or other target tag) on the page, it's easy to miss things. In addition, page layouts change all the time. What was once the first of its kind on the page might someday be the second or third tag of that type found on the page. To make your scrapers more robust, it's best to be as specific as possible when making tag selections. Take advantage of tag attributes when they are available.

As a complement to `next_siblings`, the `previous_siblings` function often can be helpful if there is an easily selectable tag at the end of a list of sibling tags that you would like to get.

And, of course, there are the `next_sibling` and `previous_sibling` functions, which perform nearly the same function as `next_siblings` and `previous_siblings`, except they return a single tag rather than a list of them.

Dealing with parents

When scraping pages, you will likely discover that you need to find parents of tags less frequently than you need to find their children or siblings. Typically, when you look at HTML pages with the goal of crawling them, you start by looking at the top layer of tags, and then figure out how to drill your way down into the exact piece of data that you want. Occasionally, however, you can find yourself in odd situations that require BeautifulSoup's parent-finding functions, `.parent` and `.parents`. For example:

```
from urllib.request import urlopen
from bs4 import BeautifulSoup

html = urlopen('http://www.pythonscraping.com/pages/page3.html')
bs = BeautifulSoup(html, 'html.parser')
print(bs.find('img',
              {'src':'../img/gifts/img1.jpg'})
       .parent.previous_sibling.get_text())
```

This code will print the price of the object represented by the image at the location *../img/gifts/img1.jpg* (in this case, the price is $15.00).

How does this work? The following diagram represents the tree structure of the portion of the HTML page you are working with, with numbered steps:

- `<tr>`
  - — `td`
  - — `td`
  - — `td` ❸
    - — `"$15.00"` ❹
  - — `td` ❷
    - — `<img src="../img/gifts/img1.jpg">` ❶

❶ The image tag where `src="../img/gifts/img1.jpg"` is first selected.

❷ You select the parent of that tag (in this case, the `td` tag).

❸ You select the `previous_sibling` of the `td` tag (in this case, the `td` tag that contains the dollar value of the product).

❹ You select the text within that tag `"$15.00"`.

Regular Expressions

As the old computer science joke goes: "Let's say you have a problem, and you decide to solve it with regular expressions. Well, now you have two problems."

Unfortunately, regular expressions (often shortened to *regex*) are often taught using large tables of random symbols, strung together to look like a lot of nonsense. This tends to drive people away, and later they get out into the workforce and write needlessly complicated searching and filtering functions in order to avoid regex.

Regular expressions are an invaluable tool when it comes to web scraping. Fortunately for you, regular expressions are not all that difficult to get up and running with quickly, and they can be learned by looking at and experimenting with a few simple examples.

Regular expressions are so called because they are used to identify strings belonging to a *regular language*. The word "language" here doesn't mean a language in the sense of a programming language or even a natural language (like English or French). Instead it is the mathematical sense meaning "a set of strings that follow some rules."

A regular language is the set of strings that can be generated by a set of linear rules that can be followed simply while moving along the candidate string and matching it to the rules as you go.[2] For example:

1. Write the letter *a* at least once.
2. Append the letter *b* exactly five times.
3. Append to this the letter *c* an even number of times.
4. Write either the letter *d* or *e* at the end.

A regular expression can definitively determine: "Yes, this string you've given me follows the rules," or "This string does not follow the rules." This can be exceptionally handy for quickly scanning large documents to look for strings that look like phone numbers or email addresses.

Strings that follow the rules above are strings like *aaaabbbbbcccd*, *aabbbbbcce*, and so on. There are, mathematically speaking, an infinite number of strings matching this pattern.

Regular expressions are merely a shorthand way of expressing these sets of rules. For instance, here's the regular expression for the series of steps just described:

```
aa*bbbbb(cc)*(d|e)
```

This string might seem a little daunting at first, but it becomes clearer when you break it into its components:

*aa**

The letter *a* is written, followed by *a** (read as *a star*), which means "any number of a's, including 0 of them." In this way, you can guarantee that the letter *a* is written at least once.

bbbbb

No special effects here—just five b's in a row.

(cc)*

Any even number of things can be grouped into pairs, so to enforce this rule about even things, you can write two c's, surround them with parentheses, and write an asterisk after it, meaning that you can have any number of *pairs* of c's (note that this can mean zero pairs, as well).

---

2 You might be asking yourself, "Are there 'irregular' languages and irregular expressions?" Nonregular expressions are beyond the scope of this book, but they encompass strings such as "write a prime number of a's, followed by exactly twice that number of b's" or "write a palindrome." It's impossible to identify strings of this type with a regular expression. Fortunately, I've never been in a situation where my web scraper needed to identify these kinds of strings.

(d|e)

Adding a bar in the middle of two expressions means that it can be "this thing *or* that thing." In this case, you are saying "add a *d* or an *e*." In this way, you can guarantee that there is exactly one of either of these two characters.

Experimenting with RegEx

When learning how to write regular expressions, it's critical to play around with them and get a feel for how they work. If you don't feel like firing up a code editor, writing a few lines, and running your program to see whether a regular expression works as expected, you can go to a website such as RegEx Pal (*http://regex pal.com/*) and test your regular expressions on the fly.

Table 5-1 lists commonly used regular expression symbols, with brief explanations and examples. This list is by no means complete, and, as mentioned before, you might encounter slight variations from language to language. However, these 12 symbols are the most commonly used regular expressions in Python and can be used to find and collect almost any string type.

Table 5-1. Commonly used regular expression symbols

Symbol(s)	Meaning	Example	Example matches
*	Matches the preceding character, subexpression, or bracketed character, 0 or more times.	a*b*	aaaaaaaa, aaabbbbb, bbbbbb
+	Matches the preceding character, subexpression, or bracketed character, 1 or more times.	a+b+	aaaaaaaab, aaabbbbb, abbbbbb
[]	Matches any character within the brackets (i.e., "Pick any one of these things").	[A-Z]*	APPLE, CAPITALS, QWERTY
()	A grouped subexpression (these are evaluated first, in the "order of operations" of regular expressions).	(a*b)*	aaabaab, abaaab, ababaaaab
{m, n}	Matches the preceding character, subexpression, or bracketed character between *m* and *n* times (inclusive).	a{2,3}b{2,3}	aabbb, aaabbb, aabb
[^]	Matches any single character that is *not* in the brackets.	[^A-Z]*	apple, lowercase, qwerty
|	Matches any character, string of characters, or subexpression separated by the I (note that this is a vertical bar, or *pipe*, not a capital i).	b(a|i|e)d	bad, bid, bed
.	Matches any single character (including symbols, numbers, a space, etc.).	b.d	bad, bzd, b$d, b d
^	Indicates that a character or subexpression occurs at the beginning of a string.	^a	apple, asdf, a

Symbol(s)	Meaning	Example	Example matches
\	An escape character (this allows you to use special characters as their literal meanings).	\^ | \\	^ | \
$	Often used at the end of a regular expression, it means "match this up to the end of the string." Without it, every regular expression has a de facto ".*" at the end of it, accepting strings where only the first part of the string matches. This can be thought of as analogous to the ^ symbol.	[A-Z]*[a-z]*$	ABCabc, zzzyx, Bob
?!	"Does not contain." This odd pairing of symbols, immediately preceding a character (or regular expression), indicates that that character should not be found in that specific place in the larger string. This can be tricky to use; after all, the character might be found in a different part of the string. If trying to eliminate a character entirely, use in conjunction with a ^ and $ at either end.	^((?![A-Z]).)*$	no-caps-here, $ymb0ls a4e f!ne

One classic example of regular expressions can be found in the practice of identifying email addresses. Although the exact rules governing email addresses vary slightly from mail server to mail server, we can create a few general rules. The corresponding regular expression for each of these rules is shown in the second column:

Rule 1

    The first part of an email address contains at least one of the following: uppercase letters, lowercase letters, the numbers 0–9, periods (.), plus signs (+), or underscores (_).

[A-Za-z0-9._+]+

    The regular expression shorthand is pretty smart. For example, it knows that "A-Z" means "any uppercase letter, A through Z." By putting all these possible sequences and symbols in brackets (as opposed to parentheses), you are saying, "This symbol can be any one of these things we've listed in the brackets." Note also that the + sign means "these characters can occur as many times as they want to but must occur at least once."

Rule 2

    After this, the email address contains the @ symbol.

@

    This is fairly straightforward: the @ symbol must occur in the middle, and it must occur exactly once.

Rule 3

    The email address then must contain at least one uppercase or lowercase letter.

[A-Za-z]+

    You may use only letters in the first part of the domain name, after the @ symbol. Also, there must be at least one character.

Rule 4

    This is followed by a period (.).

.

    You must include a period (.) before the top-level domain.

Rule 5	(com|org|edu|net)
Finally, the email address ends with *com*, *org*, *edu*, or *net* (in reality, there are many possible top-level domains, but these four should suffice for the sake of example).	This lists the possible sequences of letters that can occur after the period in the second part of an email address.

By concatenating all of the rules, you arrive at this regular expression:

```
[A-Za-z0-9._+]+@[A-Za-z]+.(com|org|edu|net)
```

When attempting to write any regular expression from scratch, it's best to first make a list of steps that concretely outlines what your target string looks like. Pay attention to edge cases. For instance, if you're identifying phone numbers, are you considering country codes and extensions?

Regular Expressions: Not Always Regular!

The standard version of regular expressions (the one covered in this book and used by Python and BeautifulSoup) is based on syntax used by Perl. Most modern programming languages use this or one similar to it. Be aware, however, that if you are using regular expressions in another language, you might encounter problems. Even some modern languages, such as Java, have slight differences in the way they handle regular expressions. When in doubt, read the docs!

Regular Expressions and BeautifulSoup

If the previous section on regular expressions seemed a little disjointed from the mission of this book, here's where it all ties together. BeautifulSoup and regular expressions go hand in hand when it comes to scraping the web. In fact, most functions that take in a string argument (e.g., find(id="aTagIdHere")) will also take in a regular expression just as well.

Let's take a look at some examples, scraping the page found at *http://www.python-scraping.com/pages/page3.html*.

Notice that the site has many product images, which take the following form:

```
<img src="../img/gifts/img3.jpg">
```

If you wanted to grab URLs of all of the product images, it might seem fairly straightforward at first: just grab all the image tags by using .find_all("img"), right? But there's a problem. In addition to the obvious "extra" images (e.g., logos), modern websites often have hidden images, blank images used for spacing and aligning elements, and other random image tags you might not be aware of. Certainly, you can't count on the only images on the page being product images.

Let's also assume that the layout of the page might change, or that, for whatever reason, you don't want to depend on the *position* of the image in the page in order to find the correct tag. This might be the case when you are trying to grab specific elements or pieces of data that are scattered randomly throughout a website. For instance, a featured product image might appear in a special layout at the top of some pages but not others.

The solution is to look for something identifying about the tag itself. In this case, you can look at the file path of the product images:

```
from urllib.request import urlopen
from bs4 import BeautifulSoup
import re

html = urlopen('http://www.pythonscraping.com/pages/page3.html')
bs = BeautifulSoup(html, 'html.parser')
images = bs.find_all('img',
    {'src':re.compile('..\/img\/gifts/img.*.jpg')})
for image in images:
    print(image['src'])
```

This prints only the relative image paths that start with *../img/gifts/img* and end in *.jpg*, the output of which is:

```
../img/gifts/img1.jpg
../img/gifts/img2.jpg
../img/gifts/img3.jpg
../img/gifts/img4.jpg
../img/gifts/img6.jpg
```

A regular expression can be inserted as any argument in a BeautifulSoup expression, allowing you a great deal of flexibility in finding target elements.

Accessing Attributes

So far, you've looked at how to access and filter tags and access content within them. However, often in web scraping you're not looking for the content of a tag; you're looking for its attributes. This becomes especially useful for tags such as a, where the URL it is pointing to is contained within the href attribute; or the img tag, where the target image is contained within the src attribute.

With tag objects, a Python list of attributes can be automatically accessed by calling this:

```
myTag.attrs
```

Keep in mind that this literally returns a Python dictionary object, which makes retrieval and manipulation of these attributes trivial. The source location for an image, for example, can be found using the following line:

```
myImgTag.attrs['src']
```

Lambda Expressions

Lambda is a fancy academic term that, in programming, simply means "a shorthand way of writing a function." In Python, we might write a function that returns the square of a number as:

```
def square(n):
    return n**2
```

We could use a lambda expression to do the same thing in one line:

```
square = lambda n: n**2
```

This assigns the variable square directly to a function that takes in a single argument n and returns n**2. But there's no rule that says functions have to be "named" or assigned to variables at all. We can simply write them as values:

```
>>> lambda r: r**2
<function <lambda> at 0x7f8f88223a60>
```

Essentially, a *lambda expression* is a function that exists alone, without being named or assigned to a variable. In Python, a lambda function cannot have more than one line of code (this is a matter of style and good taste on Python's part, rather than some fundamental rule of computer science, however).

The most common use of lambda expressions is an argument passed in to other functions. BeautifulSoup allows you to pass certain types of functions as parameters into the find_all function.

The only restriction is that these functions must take a tag object as an argument and return a boolean. Every tag object that BeautifulSoup encounters is evaluated in this function, and tags that evaluate to True are returned, while the rest are discarded.

For example, the following retrieves all tags that have exactly two attributes:

```
bs.find_all(lambda tag: len(tag.attrs) == 2)
```

Here, the function that you are passing as the argument is len(tag.attrs) == 2. Where this is True, the find_all function will return the tag. That is, it will find tags with two attributes, such as:

```
<div class="body" id="content"></div>
<span style="color:red" class="title"></span>
```

Lambda functions are so useful you can even use them to replace existing BeautifulSoup functions:

```
bs.find_all(lambda tag: tag.get_text() ==
    'Or maybe he\'s only resting?')
```

This also can be accomplished without a lambda function:

```
bs.find_all('', text='Or maybe he\'s only resting?')
```

However, if you remember the syntax for the lambda function, and how to access tag properties, you may never need to remember any other BeautifulSoup syntax again!

Because the provided lambda function can be any function that returns a True or False value, you can even combine them with regular expressions to find tags with an attribute matching a certain string pattern.

You Don't Always Need a Hammer

It can be tempting, when faced with a Gordian knot of tags, to dive right in and use multiline statements to try to extract your information. However, keep in mind that layering the techniques used in this chapter with reckless abandon can lead to code that is difficult to debug, fragile, or both. Let's look at some of the ways you can avoid altogether the need for advanced HTML parsing.

Let's say you have some target content. Maybe it's a name, statistic, or block of text. Maybe it's buried 20 tags deep in an HTML mush with no helpful tags or HTML attributes to be found. You may decide to throw caution to the wind and write something like the following line to attempt extraction:

```
bs.find_all('table')[4].find_all('tr')[2].find('td').find_all('div')[1].find('a')
```

That doesn't look so great. In addition to the aesthetics of the line, even the slightest change to the website by a site administrator might break your web scraper altogether. What if the site's web developer decides to add another table or another column of data? What if the developer adds another component (with a few div tags) to the top of the page? The preceding line is precarious and depends on the structure of the site never changing.

So what are your options?

- Look for any "landmarks" that you can use to jump right into the middle of the document, closer to the content that you actually want. Convenient CSS attributes are an obvious landmark, but you can also get creative and grab tags by their content using .find_all(text='some tag content') in a pinch.

- If there's no easy way to isolate the tag you want or any of its parents, can you find a sibling? Use the `.parent` method and then drill back down to the target tag.

- Abandon this document altogether and look for a "Print This Page" link, or perhaps a mobile version of the site that has better-formatted HTML (more on presenting yourself as a mobile device—and receiving mobile site versions—in Chapter 17).

- Don't ignore the content in the `<script>` tags or separately loaded JavaScript files. JavaScript often contains the data that you're looking for and in a nicer format! For example, I once collected nicely formatted street addresses from a website by examining the JavaScript for an embedded Google Maps application. For more information about this technique, see Chapter 11.

- Information might be available in the URL of the page itself. For example, page titles and product IDs can often be found there.

- If the information you are looking for is unique to this website for some reason, you're out of luck. If not, try to think of other sources you could get this information from. Is there another website with the same data? Is this website displaying data that it scraped or aggregated from another website?

Especially when you are faced with buried or poorly formatted data, it's important not to just start digging and write yourself into a hole that you might not be able to get out of. Take a deep breath and think of alternatives.

The techniques presented here, when used correctly, will go a long way toward writing more stable and reliable web crawlers.

## CHAPTER 6

Writing Web Crawlers

So far, you've seen single static pages with somewhat artificial canned examples. In this chapter, you'll start looking at real-world problems, with scrapers traversing multiple pages and even multiple sites.

Web crawlers are called such because they crawl across the web. At their core is an element of recursion. They must retrieve page contents for a URL, examine that page for other URLs, and retrieve *those* pages, ad infinitum.

Beware, however: just because you can crawl the web doesn't mean that you always should. The scrapers used in previous examples work great in situations where all the data you need is on a single page. With web crawlers, you must be extremely conscientious of how much bandwidth you are using and make every effort to determine whether there's a way to make the target server's load easier.

Traversing a Single Domain

Even if you haven't heard of Six Degrees of Wikipedia, you may have heard of its namesake, Six Degrees of Kevin Bacon.[1] In both games, the goal is to link two unlikely subjects (in the first case, Wikipedia articles that link to each other, and in the second case, actors appearing in the same film) by a chain containing no more than six total (including the two original subjects).

---

1 A popular parlor game created in the 1990s, *https://en.wikipedia.org/wiki/Six_Degrees_of_Kevin_Bacon*.

For example, Eric Idle appeared in *Dudley Do-Right* with Brendan Fraser, who appeared in *The Air I Breathe* with Kevin Bacon.[2] In this case, the chain from Eric Idle to Kevin Bacon is only three subjects long.

In this section, you'll begin a project that will become a Six Degrees of Wikipedia solution finder: you'll be able to take the Eric Idle page (*https://en.wikipedia.org/wiki/Eric_Idle*) and find the fewest number of link clicks that will take you to the Kevin Bacon page (*https://en.wikipedia.org/wiki/Kevin_Bacon*).

But What About Wikipedia's Server Load?

According to the Wikimedia Foundation (the parent organization behind Wikipedia), the site's web properties receive approximately 2,500 hits per *second*, with more than 99% of them to the Wikipedia domain (see the "Traffic Volume" section of the "Wikimedia in Figures" page (*https://meta.wikimedia.org/wiki/Wikimedia_in_figures_-_Wikipedia#Traffic_volume*)). Because of the sheer volume of traffic, your web scrapers are unlikely to have any noticeable impact on Wikipedia's server load. However, if you run the code samples in this book extensively or create your own projects that scrape Wikipedia, I encourage you to make a tax-deductible donation to the Wikimedia Foundation (*https://wikimediafoundation.org/wiki/Ways_to_Give*)—not just to offset your server load but also to help make education resources available for everyone else.

Also keep in mind that if you plan on doing a large project involving data from Wikipedia, you should check to make sure that data isn't already available from the Wikipedia API (*https://www.mediawiki.org/wiki/API:Main_page*). Wikipedia is often used as a website to demonstrate scrapers and crawlers because it has a simple HTML structure and is relatively stable. However, its APIs often make this same data more efficiently accessible.

You should already know how to write a Python script that retrieves an arbitrary Wikipedia page and produces a list of links on that page:

```
from urllib.request import urlopen
from bs4 import BeautifulSoup

html = urlopen('http://en.wikipedia.org/wiki/Kevin_Bacon')
bs = BeautifulSoup(html, 'html.parser')
for link in bs.find_all('a'):
    if 'href' in link.attrs:
        print(link.attrs['href'])
```

---

2 Thanks to The Oracle of Bacon (*http://oracleofbacon.org*) for satisfying my curiosity about this particular chain.

If you look at the list of links produced, you'll notice that all the articles you'd expect are there: *Apollo 13*, *Philadelphia*, *Primetime Emmy Award*, and other films that Kevin Bacon appeared in. However, there are some things that you may not want as well:

```
//foundation.wikimedia.org/wiki/Privacy_policy
//en.wikipedia.org/wiki/Wikipedia:Contact_us
```

In fact, Wikipedia is full of sidebar, footer, and header links that appear on every page, along with links to the category pages, talk pages, and other pages that do not contain different articles:

```
/wiki/Category:All_articles_with_unsourced_statements
/wiki/Talk:Kevin_Bacon
```

Recently, a friend of mine, while working on a similar Wikipedia-scraping project, mentioned he had written a large filtering function, with more than 100 lines of code, to determine whether an internal Wikipedia link was an article page. Unfortunately, he had not spent much time up-front trying to find patterns between "article links" and "other links," or he might have discovered the trick. If you examine the links that point to article pages (as opposed to other internal pages), you'll see that they all have three things in common:

- They reside within the div with the id set to bodyContent.
- The URLs do not contain colons.
- The URLs begin with */wiki/*.

You can use these rules to revise the code slightly to retrieve only the desired article links by using the regular expression ^(/wiki/)((?!:).)*$:

```
from urllib.request import urlopen
from bs4 import BeautifulSoup
import re

html = urlopen('http://en.wikipedia.org/wiki/Kevin_Bacon')
bs = BeautifulSoup(html, 'html.parser')
for link in bs.find('div', {'id':'bodyContent'}).find_all(
    'a', href=re.compile('^(/wiki/)((?!:).)*$')):
    print(link.attrs['href'])
```

Running this, you should see a list of all article URLs that the Wikipedia article on Kevin Bacon links to.

Of course, having a script that finds all article links in one, hardcoded Wikipedia article, while interesting, is fairly useless in practice. You need to be able to take this code and transform it into something more like the following:

- A single function, getLinks, that takes in a Wikipedia article URL of the form /wiki/<Article_Name> and returns a list of all linked article URLs in the same form.
- A main function that calls getLinks with a starting article, chooses a random article link from the returned list, and calls getLinks again, until you stop the program or until no article links are found on the new page.

Here is the complete code that accomplishes this:

```
from urllib.request import urlopen
from bs4 import BeautifulSoup
import datetime
import random
import re

random.seed(datetime.datetime.now())
def getLinks(articleUrl):
    html = urlopen('http://en.wikipedia.org{}'.format(articleUrl))
    bs = BeautifulSoup(html, 'html.parser')
    return bs.find('div', {'id':'bodyContent'}).find_all('a',
        href=re.compile('^(/wiki/)((?!:).)*$'))

links = getLinks('/wiki/Kevin_Bacon')
while len(links) > 0:
    newArticle = links[random.randint(0, len(links)-1)].attrs['href']
    print(newArticle)
    links = getLinks(newArticle)
```

The first thing the program does, after importing the needed libraries, is set the random-number generator seed with the current system time. This practically ensures a new and interesting random path through Wikipedia articles every time the program is run.

Pseudorandom Numbers and Random Seeds

The previous example used Python's random-number generator to select an article at random on each page in order to continue a random traversal of Wikipedia. However, random numbers should be used with caution.

Although computers are great at calculating correct answers, they're terrible at making things up. For this reason, random numbers can be a challenge. Most random-number algorithms strive to produce an evenly distributed and hard-to-predict sequence of numbers, but a "seed" number is needed to give these algorithms some-

---

thing to work with initially. The exact same seed will produce the exact same sequence of "random" numbers every time, so for this reason I've used the system clock as a starter for producing new sequences of random numbers, and thus, new sequences of random articles. This makes the program a little more exciting to run.

For the curious, the Python pseudorandom-number generator is powered by the *Mersenne Twister algorithm*. While it produces random numbers that are difficult to predict and uniformly distributed, it is slightly processor intensive. Random numbers this good don't come cheap!

Next, the program defines the `getLinks` function, which takes in an article URL of the form `/wiki/...`, prepends the Wikipedia domain name, `http://en.wikipe dia.org`, and retrieves the `BeautifulSoup` object for the HTML at that domain. It then extracts a list of article link tags, based on the parameters discussed previously, and returns them.

The main body of the program begins with setting a list of article link tags (the `links` variable) to the list of links in the initial page: *https://en.wikipedia.org/wiki/ Kevin_Bacon*. It then goes into a loop, finding a random article link tag in the page, extracting the `href` attribute from it, printing the page, and getting a new list of links from the extracted URL.

Of course, there's a bit more to solving a Six Degrees of Wikipedia problem than building a scraper that goes from page to page. You also must be able to store and analyze the resulting data. For a continuation of the solution to this problem, see Chapter 9.

Handle Your Exceptions!

Although these code examples omit most exception handling for the sake of brevity, be aware that many potential pitfalls could arise. What if Wikipedia changes the name of the `bodyContent` tag, for example? When the program attempts to extract the text from the tag, it throws an `AttributeError`.

So although these scripts might be fine to run as closely watched examples, autonomous production code requires far more exception handling than can fit into this book. Look back to Chapter 4 for more information about this.

Crawling an Entire Site

In the previous section, you took a random walk through a website, going from link to link. But what if you need to systematically catalog or search every page on a site? Crawling an entire site, especially a large one, is a memory-intensive process that is best suited to applications for which a database to store crawling results is readily available. However, you can explore the behavior of these types of applications without running them full-scale. To learn more about running these applications by using a database, see Chapter 9.

The Dark and Deep Webs

You've likely heard the terms *deep web*, *dark web*, or *hidden web* being thrown around a lot, especially in the media lately. What do they mean?

The *deep web* is any part of the web that's not part of the *surface web*.[3] The surface is part of the internet that is indexed by search engines. Estimates vary widely, but the deep web almost certainly makes up about 90% of the internet. Because Google can't do things like submit forms, find pages that haven't been linked to by a top-level domain, or investigate sites where *robots.txt* prohibits it, the surface web stays relatively small.

The *dark web*, also known as the *darknet*, is another beast entirely.[4] It is run over the existing network hardware infrastructure but uses Tor, or another client, with an application protocol that runs on top of HTTP, providing a secure channel to exchange information. Although it is possible to scrape the dark web, just as you'd scrape any other website, doing so is outside the scope of this book.

Unlike the dark web, the deep web is relatively easy to scrape. Many tools in this book will teach you how to crawl and scrape information from many places that Google-bots can't go.

When might crawling an entire website be useful, and when might it be harmful? Web scrapers that traverse an entire site are good for many things, including:

Generating a site map

A few years ago, I was faced with a problem: an important client wanted an estimate for a website redesign but did not want to provide my company with access to the internals of their current content management system and did not have a publicly available site map. I was able to use a crawler to cover the entire site, gather all internal links, and organize the pages into the actual folder structure used on the site. This allowed me to quickly find sections of the site I wasn't even aware existed and accurately count how many page designs would be required and how much content would need to be migrated.

---

3 See "Exploring a 'Deep Web' That Google Can't Grasp" (*http://nyti.ms/2pohZmu*) by Alex Wright.

4 See "Hacker Lexicon: What Is the Dark Web?" (*http://bit.ly/2psIw2M*) by Andy Greenberg.

Gathering data

Another client wanted to gather articles (stories, blog posts, news articles, etc.) in order to create a working prototype of a specialized search platform. Although these website crawls didn't need to be exhaustive, they did need to be fairly expansive (we were interested in getting data from only a few sites). I was able to create crawlers that recursively traversed each site and collected only data found on article pages.

The general approach to an exhaustive site crawl is to start with a top-level page (such as the home page) and search for a list of all internal links on that page. Every one of those links is then crawled, and additional lists of links are found on each one of them, triggering another round of crawling.

Clearly, this is a situation that can blow up quickly. If every page has 10 internal links, and a website is 5 pages deep (a fairly typical depth for a medium-size website), then the number of pages you need to crawl is 10^5, or 100,000 pages, before you can be sure that you've exhaustively covered the website. Strangely enough, although "5 pages deep and 10 internal links per page" are fairly typical dimensions for a website, very few websites have 100,000 or more pages. The reason, of course, is that the vast majority of internal links are duplicates.

To avoid crawling the same page twice, it is extremely important that all internal links discovered are formatted consistently and kept in a running set for easy lookups, while the program is running. A *set* is similar to a list, but elements do not have a specific order, and only unique elements are stored, which is ideal for our needs. Only links that are "new" should be crawled and searched for additional links:

```
from urllib.request import urlopen
from bs4 import BeautifulSoup
import re

pages = set()
def getLinks(pageUrl):
    html = urlopen('http://en.wikipedia.org{}'.format(pageUrl))
    bs = BeautifulSoup(html, 'html.parser')
    for link in bs.find_all('a', href=re.compile('^(/wiki/)')):
        if 'href' in link.attrs:
            if link.attrs['href'] not in pages:
                #We have encountered a new page
                newPage = link.attrs['href']
                print(newPage)
                pages.add(newPage)
                getLinks(newPage)
getLinks('')
```

To show you the full effect of how this web crawling business works, I've relaxed the standards of what constitutes an internal link (from previous examples). Rather than limit the scraper to article pages, it looks for all links that begin with */wiki/*, regardless of where they are on the page, and regardless of whether they contain colons. Remember: article pages do not contain colons, but file-upload pages, talk pages, and the like do contain colons in the URL.

Initially, getLinks is called with an empty URL. This is translated as "the front page of Wikipedia" as soon as the empty URL is prepended with http://en.wikipe dia.org inside the function. Then, each link on the first page is iterated through and a check is made to see whether it is in the set of pages that the script has encountered already. If not, it is added to the list, printed to the screen, and the getLinks function is called recursively on it.

A Warning About Recursion

This is a warning rarely seen in software books, but I thought you should be aware: if left running long enough, the preceding program will almost certainly crash.

Python has a default recursion limit (the number of times a program can recursively call itself) of 1,000. Because Wikipedia's network of links is extremely large, this program will eventually hit that recursion limit and stop, unless you put in a recursion counter or something to prevent that from happening.

For "flat" sites that are fewer than 1,000 links deep, this method usually works well, with a few unusual exceptions. For instance, I once encountered a bug in a dynamically generated URL that depended on the address of the current page to write the link on that page. This resulted in infinitely repeating paths like /blogs/ blogs.../blogs/blog-post.php.

For the most part, however, this recursive technique should be fine for any typical website you're likely to encounter.

Collecting Data Across an Entire Site

Web crawlers would be fairly boring if all they did was hop from one page to the other. To make them useful, you need to be able to do something on the page while you're there. Let's look at how to build a scraper that collects the title, the first paragraph of content, and the link to edit the page (if available).

As always, the first step to determine how best to do this is to look at a few pages from the site and determine a pattern. By looking at a handful of Wikipedia pages (both articles and nonarticle pages such as the privacy policy page), the following things should be clear:

- All titles (on all pages, regardless of their status as an article page, an edit history page, or any other page) have titles under h1 → span tags, and these are the only h1 tags on the page.

- As mentioned before, all body text lives under the div#bodyContent tag. However, if you want to get more specific and access just the first paragraph of text, you might be better off using div#mw-content-text → p (selecting the first paragraph tag only). This is true for all content pages except file pages (for example, *https://en.wikipedia.org/wiki/File:Orbit_of_274301_Wikipedia.svg*), which do not have sections of content text.

- Edit links occur only on article pages. If they occur, they will be found in the li#ca-edit tag, under li#ca-edit → span → a.

By modifying your basic crawling code, you can create a combination crawler/data-gathering (or at least, data-printing) program:

```
from urllib.request import urlopen
from bs4 import BeautifulSoup
import re

pages = set()
def getLinks(pageUrl):
    html = urlopen('http://en.wikipedia.org{}'.format(pageUrl))
    bs = BeautifulSoup(html, 'html.parser')
    try:
        print(bs.h1.get_text())
        print(bs.find(id ='mw-content-text').find_all('p')[0])
        print(bs.find(id='ca-edit').find('span')
            .find('a').attrs['href'])
    except AttributeError:
        print('This page is missing something! Continuing.')

    for link in bs.find_all('a', href=re.compile('^(/wiki/)')):
        if 'href' in link.attrs:
            if link.attrs['href'] not in pages:
                #We have encountered a new page
                newPage = link.attrs['href']
                print('-'*20)
                print(newPage)
                pages.add(newPage)
                getLinks(newPage)
getLinks('')
```

The for loop in this program is essentially the same as it was in the original crawling program (with the addition of printed dashes for clarity, separating the printed content).

Because you can never be entirely sure that all the data is on each page, each `print` statement is arranged in the order that it is likeliest to appear on the site. That is, the h1 title tag appears on every page (as far as I can tell, at any rate), so you attempt to get that data first. The text content appears on most pages (except for file pages), so that is the second piece of data retrieved. The Edit button appears only on pages in which both titles and text content already exist, but it does not appear on all of those pages.

Different Patterns for Different Needs

Obviously, some dangers are involved with wrapping multiple lines in an exception handler. You cannot tell which line threw the exception, for one thing. Also, if for some reason a page contains an Edit button but no title, the Edit button would never be logged. However, it suffices for many instances in which there is an order of likeliness of items appearing on the site, and inadvertently missing a few data points or keeping detailed logs is not a problem.

You might notice that in this and all the previous examples, you haven't been "collecting" data so much as "printing" it. Obviously, data in your terminal is hard to manipulate. For more on storing information and creating databases, see Chapter 9.

Handling Redirects

Redirects allow a web server to point one domain name or URL to a piece of content at a different location. There are two types of redirects:

- Server-side redirects, where the URL is changed before the page is loaded
- Client-side redirects, sometimes seen with a "You will be redirected in 10 seconds" type of message, where the page loads before redirecting to the new one

With server-side redirects, you usually don't have to worry. If you're using the urllib library with Python 3.x, it handles redirects automatically! If you're using the Requests library, make sure to set the `allow_redirects` flag to `True`:

```
r = requests.get('http://github.com', allow_redirects=True)
```

Just be aware that, occasionally, the URL of the page you're crawling might not be exactly the URL that you entered the page on.

For more information on client-side redirects, which are performed using JavaScript or HTML, see Chapter 14.

Crawling Across the Internet

Whenever I give a talk on web scraping, someone inevitably asks, "How do you build Google?" My answer is always twofold: "First, you get many billions of dollars so that you can buy the world's largest data warehouses and place them in hidden locations all around the world. Second, you build a web crawler."

When Google started in 1996, it was just two Stanford graduate students with an old server and a Python web crawler. Now that you know how to scrape the web, you're just some VC funding away from becoming the next tech multibillionaire!

In all seriousness, web crawlers are at the heart of what drives many modern web technologies, and you don't necessarily need a large data warehouse to use them. To do any cross-domain data analysis, you do need to build crawlers that can interpret and store data across the myriad of pages on the internet.

Just as in the previous example, the web crawlers you are going to build will follow links from page to page, building out a map of the web. But this time, they will not ignore external links; they will follow them.

Unknown Waters Ahead

Keep in mind that the code from the next section can go *anywhere* on the internet. If we've learned anything from Six Degrees of Wikipedia, it's that it's entirely possible to go from a site such as *http://www.sesamestreet.org/* to something less savory in just a few hops.

Kids, ask your parents before running this code. For those with sensitive constitutions or with religious restrictions that might prohibit seeing text from a prurient site, follow along by reading the code examples but be careful when running them.

Before you start writing a crawler that follows all outbound links willy-nilly, you should ask yourself a few questions:

- What data am I trying to gather? Can this be accomplished by scraping just a few predefined websites (almost always the easier option), or does my crawler need to be able to discover new websites I might not know about?

- When my crawler reaches a particular website, will it immediately follow the next outbound link to a new website, or will it stick around for a while and drill down into the current website?

- Are there any conditions under which I would not want to scrape a particular site? Am I interested in non-English content?

- How am I protecting myself against legal action if my web crawler catches the attention of a webmaster on one of the sites it runs across? (Check out Chapter 2 for more information on this subject.)

A flexible set of Python functions that can be combined to perform a variety of types of web scraping can be easily written in fewer than 60 lines of code. Here, I've omitted the library imports for brevity and broken the code up into multiple sections for the purposes of discussion. However, a full working version can be found in the GitHub repository (*https://github.com/REMitchell/python-scraping*) for this book:

```python
#Retrieves a list of all Internal links found on a page
def getInternalLinks(bs, url):
    netloc = urlparse(url).netloc
    scheme = urlparse(url).scheme
    internalLinks = set()
    for link in bs.find_all('a'):
        if not link.attrs.get('href'):
            continue
        parsed = urlparse(link.attrs['href'])
        if parsed.netloc == '':
            l = f'{scheme}://{netloc}/{link.attrs["href"].strip("/")}'
            internalLinks.add(l)
        elif parsed.netloc == internal_netloc:
            internalLinks.add(link.attrs['href'])
    return list(internalLinks)
```

The first function is `getInternalLinks`. This takes, as arguments, a BeautifulSoup object and the URL of the page. This URL is used only to identify the `netloc` (network location) and `scheme` (usually `http` or `https`) of the internal site, so it's important to note that any internal URL for the target site can be used here—it doesn't need to be the exact URL of the BeautifulSoup object passed in.

This function creates a set called `internalLinks` used to track all internal links found on the page. It checks all anchor tags for an `href` attribute that either doesn't contain a `netloc` (is a relative URL like "/careers/") or has a `netloc` that matches that of the URL passed in:

```python
#Retrieves a list of all external links found on a page
def getExternalLinks(bs, url):
    internal_netloc = urlparse(url).netloc
    externalLinks = set()
    for link in bs.find_all('a'):
        if not link.attrs.get('href'):
            continue
        parsed = urlparse(link.attrs['href'])
        if parsed.netloc != '' and parsed.netloc != internal_netloc:
            externalLinks.add(link.attrs['href'])
    return list(externalLinks)
```

The function `getExternalLinks` works similarly to `getInternalLinks`. It examines all anchor tags with an `href` attribute and looks for those that have a populated net loc that does *not* match that of the URL passed in:

```
def getRandomExternalLink(startingPage):
    bs = BeautifulSoup(urlopen(startingPage), 'html.parser')
    externalLinks = getExternalLinks(bs, startingPage)
    if not len(externalLinks):
        print('No external links, looking around the site for one')
        internalLinks = getInternalLinks(bs, startingPage)
        return getRandomExternalLink(random.choice(internalLinks))
    else:
        return random.choice(externalLinks)
```

The function `getRandomExternalLink` uses the function `getExternalLinks` to get a list of all external links on the page. If at least one link is found, it picks a random link from the list and returns it:

```
def followExternalOnly(startingSite):
    externalLink = getRandomExternalLink(startingSite)
    print(f'Random external link is: {externalLink}')
    followExternalOnly(externalLink)
```

The function `followExternalOnly` uses `getRandomExternalLink` and then recursively traverses across the internet. You can call it like this:

```
followExternalOnly('https://www.oreilly.com/')
```

This program starts at *http://oreilly.com* and randomly hops from external link to external link. Here's an example of the output it produces:

```
http://igniteshow.com/
http://feeds.feedburner.com/oreilly/news
http://hire.jobvite.com/CompanyJobs/Careers.aspx?c=q319
http://makerfaire.com/
```

External links are not always guaranteed to be found on the first page of a website. To find external links in this case, a method similar to the one used in the previous crawling example is employed to recursively drill down into a website until it finds an external link.

Figure 6-1 illustrates the operation as a flowchart.

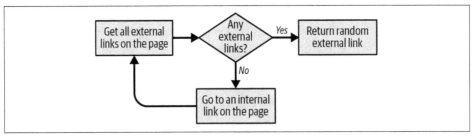

Figure 6-1. Flowchart for the script that crawls through sites on the internet

Don't Put Example Programs into Production

I keep bringing this up, but for the sake of space and readability, the example programs in this book do not always contain the necessary checks and exception handling required for production-ready code. For example, if an external link is not found anywhere on a site that this crawler encounters (unlikely, but it's bound to happen at some point if you run it long enough), this program will keep running until it hits Python's recursion limit.

One easy way to increase the robustness of this crawler would be to combine it with the connection exception-handling code in Chapter 4. This would allow the code to choose a different URL to go to if an HTTP error or server exception was encountered when retrieving the page.

Before running this code for any serious purpose, make sure that you are putting checks in place to handle potential pitfalls.

The nice thing about breaking up tasks into simple functions such as "find all external links on this page" is that the code can later be refactored to perform a different crawling task. For example, if your goal is to crawl an entire site for external links and make a note of each one, you can add the following function:

```python
# Collects a list of all external URLs found on the site
allExtLinks = []
allIntLinks = []

def getAllExternalLinks(url):
    bs = BeautifulSoup(urlopen(url), 'html.parser')
    internalLinks = getInternalLinks(bs, url)
    externalLinks = getExternalLinks(bs, url)
    for link in externalLinks:
        if link not in allExtLinks:
            allExtLinks.append(link)
            print(link)

    for link in internalLinks:
        if link not in allIntLinks:
```

```
allIntLinks.append(link)
getAllExternalLinks(link)


allIntLinks.append('https://oreilly.com')
getAllExternalLinks('https://www.oreilly.com/')
```

This code can be thought of as two loops—one gathering internal links, one gathering external links—working in conjunction with each other. The flowchart looks something like Figure 6-2.

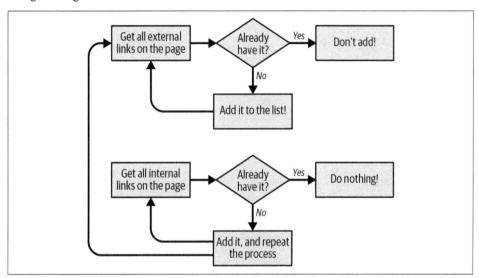

Figure 6-2. Flow diagram for the website crawler that collects all external links

Jotting down or making diagrams of what the code should do before you write the code itself is a fantastic habit to get into, and one that can save you a lot of time and frustration as your crawlers get more complicated.

## CHAPTER 7

Web Crawling Models

Writing clean, scalable code is difficult enough when you have control over your data and your inputs. Writing code for web crawlers, which may need to scrape and store a variety of data from diverse sets of websites that the programmer has no control over, often presents unique organizational challenges.

You may be asked to collect news articles or blog posts from a variety of websites, each with different templates and layouts. One website's h1 tag contains the title of the article, another's h1 tag contains the title of the website itself, and the article title is in <span id="title">.

You may need flexible control over which websites are scraped and how they're scraped, and a way to quickly add new websites or modify existing ones, as fast as possible without writing multiple lines of code.

You may be asked to scrape product prices from different websites, with the ultimate aim of comparing prices for the same product. Perhaps these prices are in different currencies, and perhaps you'll also need to combine this with external data from some other nonweb source.

Although the applications of web crawlers are nearly endless, large scalable crawlers tend to fall into one of several patterns. By learning these patterns and recognizing the situations they apply to, you can vastly improve the maintainability and robustness of your web crawlers.

This chapter focuses primarily on web crawlers that collect a limited number of "types" of data (such as restaurant reviews, news articles, company profiles) from a variety of websites and store these data types as Python objects that read and write from a database.

Planning and Defining Objects

One common trap of web scraping is defining the data that you want to collect based entirely on what's available in front of your eyes. For instance, if you want to collect product data, you may first look at a clothing store and decide that each product you scrape needs to have the following fields:

- Product name
- Price
- Description
- Sizes
- Colors
- Fabric type
- Customer rating

Looking at another website, you find that it has SKUs (stock-keeping units, used to track and order items) listed on the page. You definitely want to collect that data as well, even if it doesn't appear on the first site! You add this field:

- Item SKU

Although clothing may be a great start, you also want to make sure you can extend this crawler to other types of products. You start perusing product sections of other websites and decide you also need to collect this information:

- Hardcover/paperback
- Matte/glossy print
- Number of customer reviews
- Link to manufacturer

Clearly, this is an unsustainable approach. Simply adding attributes to your product type every time you see a new piece of information on a website will lead to far too many fields to keep track of. Not only that, but every time you scrape a new website, you'll be forced to perform a detailed analysis of the fields the website has and the fields you've accumulated so far, and potentially add new fields (modifying your Python object type and your database structure). This will result in a messy and difficult-to-read dataset that may lead to problems using it.

One of the best things you can do when deciding which data to collect is often to ignore the websites altogether. You don't start a project that's designed to be large and scalable by looking at a single website and saying, "What exists?" but by saying,

"What do I need?" and then finding ways to seek the information that you need from there.

Perhaps what you really want to do is compare product prices among multiple stores and track those product prices over time. In this case, you need enough information to uniquely identify the product, and that's it:

- Product title
- Manufacturer
- Product ID number (if available/relevant)

It's important to note that none of this information is specific to a particular store. For instance, product reviews, ratings, price, and even description are specific to the instance of that product at a particular store. That can be stored separately.

Other information (colors the product comes in, what it's made of) is specific to the product but may be sparse—it's not applicable to every product. It's important to take a step back and perform a checklist for each item you consider and ask yourself these questions:

- Will this information help with the project goals? Will it be a roadblock if I don't have it, or is it just "nice to have" but won't ultimately impact anything?
- If it *might* help in the future, but I'm unsure, how difficult will it be to go back and collect the data at a later time?
- Is this data redundant to data I've already collected?
- Does it make logical sense to store the data within this particular object? (As mentioned before, storing a description in a product doesn't make sense if that description changes from site to site for the same product.)

If you do decide that you need to collect the data, it's important to ask a few more questions to then decide how to store and handle it in code:

- Is this data sparse or dense? Will it be relevant and populated in every listing, or just a handful out of the set?
- How large is the data?
- Especially in the case of large data, will I need to regularly retrieve it every time I run my analysis, or only on occasion?
- How variable is this type of data? Will I regularly need to add new attributes, modify types (such as fabric patterns, which may be added frequently), or is it set in stone (shoe sizes)?

Let's say you plan to do some meta-analysis around product attributes and prices: for example, the number of pages a book has, or the type of fabric a piece of clothing is made of, and potentially other attributes in the future, correlated to price. You run through the questions and realize that this data is sparse (relatively few products have any one of the attributes), and that you may decide to add or remove attributes frequently. In this case, it may make sense to create a product type that looks like this:

- Product title
- Manufacturer
- Product ID number (if available/relevant)
- Attributes (optional list or dictionary)

And an attribute type that looks like this:

- Attribute name
- Attribute value

This allows you to flexibly add new product attributes over time, without requiring you to redesign your data schema or rewrite code. When deciding how to store these attributes in the database, you can write JSON to the `attribute` field, or store each attribute in a separate table with a product ID. See Chapter 9 for more information about implementing these types of database models.

You can apply the preceding questions to the other information you'll need to store as well. For keeping track of the prices found for each product, you'll likely need the following:

- Product ID
- Store ID
- Price
- Date/timestamp when price was found

But what if you have a situation in which the product's attributes actually modify the price of the product? For instance, stores might charge more for a large shirt than a small one, because the large shirt requires more labor or materials. In this case, you may consider splitting the single shirt product into separate product listings for each size (so that each shirt product can be priced independently) or creating a new item type to store information about instances of a product, containing these fields:

- Product ID
- Instance type (the size of the shirt, in this case)

And each price would then look like this:

- Product instance ID
- Store ID
- Price
- Date/Timestamp when price was found

While the subject of "products and prices" may seem overly specific, the basic questions you need to ask yourself, and the logic used when designing your Python objects, apply in almost every situation.

If you're scraping news articles, you may want basic information such as:

- Title
- Author
- Date
- Content

But say some articles contain a "revision date," or "related articles, or a "number of social media shares." Do you need these? Are they relevant to your project? How do you efficiently and flexibly store the number of social media shares when not all news sites use all forms of social media, and social media sites may grow or wane in popularity over time?

It can be tempting, when faced with a new project, to dive in and start writing Python to scrape websites immediately. The data model, left as an afterthought, often becomes strongly influenced by the availability and format of the data on the first website you scrape.

However, the data model is the underlying foundation of all the code that uses it. A poor decision in your model can easily lead to problems writing and maintaining code down the line, or difficulty in extracting and efficiently using the resulting data. Especially when dealing with a variety of websites—both known and unknown —it becomes vital to give serious thought and planning to what, exactly, you need to collect and how you need to store it.

Dealing with Different Website Layouts

One of the most impressive feats of a search engine such as Google is that it manages to extract relevant and useful data from a variety of websites, having no up-front knowledge about the website structure itself. Although we, as humans, are able to immediately identify the title and main content of a page (barring instances of extremely poor web design), it is far more difficult to get a bot to do the same thing.

Fortunately, in most cases of web crawling, you're not looking to collect data from sites you've never seen before, but from a few, or a few dozen, websites that are preselected by a human. This means that you don't need to use complicated algorithms or machine learning to detect which text on the page "looks most like a title" or which is probably the "main content." You can determine what these elements are manually.

The most obvious approach is to write a separate web crawler or page parser for each website. Each might take in a URL, string, or BeautifulSoup object, and return a Python object for the thing that was scraped.

The following is an example of a Content class (representing a piece of content on a website, such as a news article) and two scraper functions that take in a BeautifulSoup object and return an instance of Content:

```python
from bs4 import BeautifulSoup
from urllib.request import urlopen

class Content:
    def __init__(self, url, title, body):
        self.url = url
        self.title = title
        self.body = body

    def print(self):
        print(f'TITLE: {self.title}')
        print(f'URL: {self.url}')
        print(f'BODY: {self.body}')

def scrapeCNN(url):
    bs = BeautifulSoup(urlopen(url))
    title = bs.find('h1').text
    body = bs.find('div', {'class': 'article__content'}).text
    print('body: ')
    print(body)
    return Content(url, title, body)

def scrapeBrookings(url):
    bs = BeautifulSoup(urlopen(url))
    title = bs.find('h1').text
    body = bs.find('div', {'class': 'post-body'}).text
    return Content(url, title, body)

url = 'https://www.brookings.edu/research/robotic-rulemaking/'
content = scrapeBrookings(url)
content.print()

url = 'https://www.cnn.com/2023/04/03/investing/\
dogecoin-elon-musk-twitter/index.html'
content = scrapeCNN(url)
content.print()
```

As you start to add scraper functions for additional news sites, you might notice a pattern forming. Every site's parsing function does essentially the same thing:

- Selects the title element and extracts the text for the title
- Selects the main content of the article
- Selects other content items as needed
- Returns a `Content` object instantiated with the strings found previously

The only real site-dependent variables here are the CSS selectors used to obtain each piece of information. BeautifulSoup's `find` and `find_all` functions take in two arguments—a tag string and a dictionary of key/value attributes—so you can pass these arguments in as parameters that define the structure of the site itself and the location of the target data.

To make things even more convenient, rather than dealing with all of these tag arguments and key/value pairs, you can use the BeautifulSoup `select` function with a single string CSS selector for each piece of information you want to collect and put all of these selectors in a dictionary object:

```
class Content:
    """
    Common base class for all articles/pages
    """
    def __init__(self, url, title, body):
        self.url = url
        self.title = title
        self.body = body

    def print(self):
        """
        Flexible printing function controls output
        """
        print('URL: {}'.format(self.url))
        print('TITLE: {}'.format(self.title))
        print('BODY:\n{}'.format(self.body))

class Website:
    """
    Contains information about website structure
    """
    def __init__(self, name, url, titleTag, bodyTag):
        self.name = name
        self.url = url
        self.titleTag = titleTag
        self.bodyTag = bodyTag
```

Note that the `Website` class does not store information collected from the individual pages themselves, but stores instructions about *how* to collect that data. It doesn't store the title "My Page Title." It simply stores the string tag h1 that indicates where the titles can be found. This is why the class is called Website (the information here pertains to the entire website) and not Content (which contains information from just a single page).

As you write web scrapers, you may notice that you tend to do many of the same tasks over and over again. For instance: fetch the content of a page while checking for errors, get the contents of a tag, and fail gracefully if these are not found. Let's add these to a Crawler class:

```python
class Crawler:
    def getPage(url):
        try:
            html = urlopen(url)
        except Exception:
            return None
        return BeautifulSoup(html, 'html.parser')

    def safeGet(bs, selector):
        """
        Utility function used to get a content string from a Beautiful Soup
        object and a selector. Returns an empty string if no object
        is found for the given selector
        """
        selectedElems = bs.select(selector)
        if selectedElems is not None and len(selectedElems) > 0:
            return '\n'.join([elem.get_text() for elem in selectedElems])
        return ''
```

Note that the Crawler class currently does not have any state. It's simply a collection of static methods. It also seems poorly named—it doesn't do any crawling at all! You can at least make it slightly more useful by adding a getContent method to it, which takes as an argument a website object and a URL, and returns a Content object:

```python
class Crawler:

    ...

    def getContent(website, path):
        """
        Extract content from a given page URL
        """
        url = website.url+path
        bs = Crawler.getPage(url)
        if bs is not None:
            title = Crawler.safeGet(bs, website.titleTag)
            body = Crawler.safeGet(bs, website.bodyTag)
            return Content(url, title, body)
        return Content(url, '', '')
```

The following shows how these `Content`, `website`, and `Crawler` classes can be used together to scrape four different websites:

```
siteData = [
    ['O\'Reilly', 'https://www.oreilly.com', 'h1', 'div.title-description'],
    ['Reuters', 'https://www.reuters.com', 'h1', 'div.ArticleBodyWrapper'],
    ['Brookings', 'https://www.brookings.edu', 'h1', 'div.post-body'],
    ['CNN', 'https://www.cnn.com', 'h1', 'div.article__content']
]
websites = []
for name, url, title, body in siteData:
    websites.append(Website(name, url, title, body))

Crawler.getContent(
    websites[0],
    '/library/view/web-scraping-with/9781491910283'
).print()
Crawler.getContent(
    websites[1],
    '/article/us-usa-epa-pruitt-idUSKBN19W2D0'
).print()
Crawler.getContent(
    websites[2],
    '/blog/techtank/2016/03/01/idea-to-retire-old-methods-of-policy-education/'
).print()
Crawler.getContent(
    websites[3],
    '/2023/04/03/investing/dogecoin-elon-musk-twitter/index.html'
).print()
```

While this new method might not seem remarkably simpler than writing a new Python function for each new website at first glance, imagine what happens when you go from a system with 4 website sources to a system with 20 or 200 sources.

Each list of strings defining a new website is relatively easy to write. It doesn't take up much space. It can be loaded from a database or a CSV file. It can be imported from a remote source or handed off to a nonprogrammer with a little frontend experience. This programmer can fill it out and add new websites to the scraper without ever having to look at a line of code.

Of course, the downside is that you are giving up a certain amount of flexibility. In the first example, each website gets its own free-form function to select and parse HTML however necessary to get the end result. In the second example, each website needs to have a certain structure in which fields are guaranteed to exist, data must be clean coming out of the field, and each target field must have a unique and reliable CSS selector.

However, I believe that the power and relative flexibility of this approach more than makes up for its real or perceived shortcomings. The next section covers specific applications and expansions of this basic template so that you can, for example, deal with missing fields, collect different types of data, crawl through specific parts of a website, and store more-complex information about pages.

Structuring Crawlers

Creating flexible and modifiable website layout types doesn't do much good if you still have to locate each link you want to scrape by hand. Chapter 6 showed various automated methods of crawling through websites and finding new pages.

This section shows how to incorporate these methods into a well-structured and expandable website crawler that can gather links and discover data in an automated way. I present just three basic web crawler structures here; they apply to the majority of situations that you will likely encounter when crawling sites in the wild, perhaps with a few modifications here and there. If you encounter an unusual situation with your own crawling problem, I hope that you will use these structures as inspiration to create an elegant and robust crawler design.

Crawling Sites Through Search

One of the easiest ways to crawl a website is via the same method that humans use with the search bar. Although the process of searching a website for a keyword or topic and collecting a list of search results may seem like a task with a lot of variability from site to site, several key points make this surprisingly trivial:

- Most sites retrieve a list of search results for a particular topic by passing that topic as a string through a parameter in the URL. For example: `http://exam ple.com?search=myTopic`. The first part of this URL can be saved as a property of the `Website` object, and the topic can simply be appended to it.

- After searching, most sites present the resulting pages as an easily identifiable list of links, usually with a convenient surrounding tag such as `<span class="result">`, the exact format of which can also be stored as a property of the `Website` object.

- Each *result link* is either a relative URL (e.g., */articles/page.html*) or an absolute URL (e.g., *http://example.com/articles/page.html*). Whether you are expecting an absolute or relative URL, it can be stored as a property of the `Website` object.

- After you've located and normalized the URLs on the search page, you've successfully reduced the problem to the example in the previous section—extracting data from a page, given a website format.

Let's look at an implementation of this algorithm in code. The `Content` class is much the same as in previous examples. You are adding the URL property to keep track of where the content was found:

```python
class Content:
    """Common base class for all articles/pages"""

    def __init__(self, topic, url, title, body):
        self.topic = topic
        self.title = title
        self.body = body
        self.url = url

    def print(self):
        """
        Flexible printing function controls output
        """
        print('New article found for topic: {}'.format(self.topic))
        print('URL: {}'.format(self.url))
        print('TITLE: {}'.format(self.title))
        print('BODY:\n{}'.format(self.body))
```

The `Website` class has a few new properties added to it. The `searchUrl` defines where you should go to get search results if you append the topic you are looking for. The `resultListing` defines the "box" that holds information about each result, and the `resultUrl` defines the tag inside this box that will give you the exact URL for the result. The `absoluteUrl` property is a boolean that tells you whether these search results are absolute or relative URLs:

```python
class Website:
    """Contains information about website structure"""

    def __init__(self, name, url, searchUrl, resultListing,
        resultUrl, absoluteUrl, titleTag, bodyTag):
        self.name = name
        self.url = url
        self.searchUrl = searchUrl
        self.resultListing = resultListing
        self.resultUrl = resultUrl
        self.absoluteUrl=absoluteUrl
        self.titleTag = titleTag
        self.bodyTag = bodyTag
```

The `Crawler` class has also expanded. It now has a `Website` object, as well as a dictionary of URLs pointing to `Content` objects, to keep track of what it has seen before. Note that the methods `getPage` and `safeGet` have not changed and are omitted here:

```python
class Crawler:
    def __init__(self, website):
        self.site = website
        self.found = {}
```

```
def getContent(self, topic, url):
    """
    Extract content from a given page URL
    """
    bs = Crawler.getPage(url)
    if bs is not None:
        title = Crawler.safeGet(bs, self.site.titleTag)
        body = Crawler.safeGet(bs, self.site.bodyTag)
        return Content(topic, url, title, body)
    return Content(topic, url, '', '')

def search(self, topic):
    """
    Searches a given website for a given topic and records all pages found
    """
    bs = Crawler.getPage(self.site.searchUrl + topic)
    searchResults = bs.select(self.site.resultListing)
    for result in searchResults:
        url = result.select(self.site.resultUrl)[0].attrs['href']
        # Check to see whether it's a relative or an absolute URL
        url = url if self.site.absoluteUrl else self.site.url + url
        if url not in self.found:
            self.found[url] = self.getContent(topic, url)
            self.found[url].print()
```

You can call your Crawler like this:

```
siteData = [
    ['Reuters', 'http://reuters.com',
     'https://www.reuters.com/search/news?blob=',
     'div.search-result-indiv', 'h3.search-result-title a',
     False, 'h1', 'div.ArticleBodyWrapper'],
    ['Brookings', 'http://www.brookings.edu',
     'https://www.brookings.edu/search/?s=',
        'div.article-info', 'h4.title a', True, 'h1', 'div.core-block']
]
sites = []
for name, url, search, rListing, rUrl, absUrl, tt, bt in siteData:
    sites.append(Website(name, url, search, rListing, rUrl, absUrl, tt, bt))

crawlers = [Crawler(site) for site in sites]
topics = ['python', 'data%20science']

for topic in topics:
    for crawler in crawlers:
        crawler.search(topic)
```

As before, an array of data is created about each website: what the tags look like, what the URL is, and a name for tracking purposes. This data is then loaded into a list of Website objects and turned into Crawler objects.

Then it loops through each crawler in the `crawlers` list and crawls each particular site for each particular topic. Each time it successfully collects information about a page, it prints it to the console:

```
New article found for topic: python
URL: http://reuters.com/article/idUSKCN11S04G
TITLE: Python in India demonstrates huge appetite
BODY:
By 1 Min ReadA 20 feet rock python was caught on camera ...
```

Note that it loops through all topics and then loops through all websites in the inner loop. Why not do it the other way around, collecting all topics from one website and then all topics from the next website? Looping through all topics first is a way to more evenly distribute the load placed on any one web server. This is especially important if you have a list of hundreds of topics and dozens of websites. You're not making tens of thousands of requests to one website at once; you're making 10 requests, waiting a few minutes, making another 10 requests, waiting a few minutes, and so forth.

Although the number of requests is ultimately the same either way, it's generally better to distribute these requests over time as much as is reasonable. Paying attention to how your loops are structured is an easy way to do this.

Crawling Sites Through Links

Chapter 6 covered some ways of identifying internal and external links on web pages and then using those links to crawl across the site. In this section, you'll combine those same basic methods into a more flexible website crawler that can follow any link matching a specific URL pattern.

This type of crawler works well for projects when you want to gather all the data from a site—not just data from a specific search result or page listing. It also works well when the site's pages may be disorganized or widely dispersed.

These types of crawlers don't require a structured method of locating links, as in the previous section on crawling through search pages, so the attributes that describe the search page aren't required in the `Website` object. However, because the crawler isn't given specific instructions for the locations/positions of the links it's looking for, you do need some rules to tell it what sorts of pages to select. You provide a `target Pattern` (regular expression for the target URLs) and leave the boolean `absoluteUrl` variable to accomplish this:

```
class Website:
    def __init__(self, name, url, targetPattern, absoluteUrl, titleTag, bodyTag):
        self.name = name
        self.url = url
        self.targetPattern = targetPattern
        self.absoluteUrl = absoluteUrl
```

```
        self.titleTag = titleTag
        self.bodyTag = bodyTag

class Content:
    def __init__(self, url, title, body):
        self.url = url
        self.title = title
        self.body = body

    def print(self):
        print(f'URL: {self.url}')
        print(f'TITLE: {self.title}')
        print(f'BODY:\n{self.body}')
```

The Content class is the same one used in the first crawler example.

The Crawler class is written to start from the home page of each site, locate internal links, and parse the content from each internal link found:

```
class Crawler:
    def __init__(self, site):
      self.site = site
      self.visited = {}

    def getPage(url):
      try:
            html = urlopen(url)
      except Exception as e:
            print(e)
            return None
      return BeautifulSoup(html, 'html.parser')

    def safeGet(bs, selector):
      selectedElems = bs.select(selector)
      if selectedElems is not None and len(selectedElems) > 0:
            return '\n'.join([elem.get_text() for elem in selectedElems])
      return ''

    def getContent(self, url):
        """
        Extract content from a given page URL
        """
        bs = Crawler.getPage(url)
        if bs is not None:
            title = Crawler.safeGet(bs, self.site.titleTag)
            body = Crawler.safeGet(bs, self.site.bodyTag)
            return Content(url, title, body)
        return Content(url, '', '')

    def crawl(self):
        """
        Get pages from website home page
        """
```

```
        bs = Crawler.getPage(self.site.url)
        targetPages = bs.findAll('a', href=re.compile(self.site.targetPattern))
        for targetPage in targetPages:
          url = targetPage.attrs['href']
          url = url if self.site.absoluteUrl else f'{self.site.url}{targetPage}'
          if url not in self.visited:
                self.visited[url] = self.getContent(url)
                self.visited[url].print()

brookings = Website(
    'Brookings', 'https://brookings.edu', '\/(research|blog)\/',
    True, 'h1', 'div.post-body')
crawler = Crawler(brookings)
crawler.crawl()
```

As in the previous example, the `Website` object is a property of the `Crawler` object itself. This works well to store the visited pages (`visited`) in the crawler but means that a new crawler must be instantiated for each website rather than reusing the same one to crawl a list of websites.

Whether you choose to make a crawler website-agnostic or choose to make the website an attribute of the crawler is a design decision that you must weigh in the context of your own specific needs. Either approach is generally fine.

Another thing to note is that this crawler will get the pages from the home page, but it will not continue crawling after all those pages have been logged. You may want to write a crawler incorporating one of the patterns in this chapter and have it look for more targets on each page it visits. You can even follow all the URLs on each page (not just ones matching the target pattern) to look for URLs containing the target pattern.

Crawling Multiple Page Types

Unlike crawling through a predetermined set of pages, crawling through all internal links on a website can present a challenge in that you never know exactly what you're getting. Fortunately, there are a few ways to identify the page type:

By the URL
    All blog posts on a website might contain a URL (*http://example.com/blog/title-of-post*, for example).

By the presence or lack of certain fields on a site
    If a page has a date but no author name, you might categorize it as a press release. If it has a title, main image, and price but no main content, it might be a product page.

By the presence of certain tags on the page to identify the page
You can take advantage of tags even if you're not collecting the data within the tags. Your crawler might look for an element such as <div id="related-products"> to identify the page as a product page, even though the crawler is not interested in the content of the related products.

To keep track of multiple page types, you need to have multiple types of page objects in Python. This can be done in two ways.

If the pages are all similar (they all have basically the same types of content), you may want to add a pageType attribute to your existing web-page object:

```python
class Website:
    def __init__(self, name, url, titleTag, bodyTag, pageType):
        self.name = name
        self.url = url
        self.titleTag = titleTag
        self.bodyTag = bodyTag
        self.pageType = pageType
```

If you're storing these pages in an SQL-like database, this type of pattern indicates that all these pages would probably be stored in the same table and that an extra page Type column would be added.

If the pages/content you're scraping are different enough from each other (they contain different types of fields), this may warrant creating new classes for each page type. Of course, some things will be common to all web pages—they will all have a URL and likely also a name or page title. This is an ideal situation in which to use subclasses:

```python
class Product(Website):
    """Contains information for scraping a product page"""
    def __init__(self, name, url, titleTag, productNumberTag, priceTag):
        Website.__init__(self, name, url, TitleTag)
        self.productNumberTag = productNumberTag
        self.priceTag = priceTag

class Article(Website):
    """Contains information for scraping an article page"""
    def __init__(self, name, url, titleTag, bodyTag, dateTag):
        Website.__init__(self, name, url, titleTag)
        self.bodyTag = bodyTag
        self.dateTag = dateTag
```

This Product page extends the Website base class and adds the attributes prod uctNumber and price that apply only to products; the Article class adds the attributes body and date, which don't apply to products.

You can use these two classes to scrape, for example, a store website that might contain blog posts or press releases in addition to products.

Thinking About Web Crawler Models

Collecting information from the internet can be like drinking from a fire hose. There's a lot of stuff out there, and it's not always clear what you need or how you need it. The first step of any large web scraping project (and even some of the small ones) should be to answer these questions.

When collecting similar data across multiple domains or from multiple sources, your goal should almost always be to try to normalize it. Dealing with data with identical and comparable fields is much easier than dealing with data that is completely dependent on the format of its original source.

In many cases, you should build scrapers under the assumption that more sources of data will be added to them in the future, with the goal to minimize the programming overhead required to add these new sources. Even if a website doesn't appear to fit your model at first glance, there may be more subtle ways that it does conform. Being able to see these underlying patterns can save you time, money, and a lot of headaches in the long run.

The connections between pieces of data should also not be ignored. Are you looking for information that has properties such as "type," "size," or "topic" that span data sources? How do you store, retrieve, and conceptualize these attributes?

Software architecture is a broad and important topic that can take an entire career to master. Fortunately, software architecture for web scraping is a much more finite and manageable set of skills that can be relatively easily acquired. As you continue to scrape data, you will find the same basic patterns occurring over and over. Creating a well-structured web scraper doesn't require a lot of arcane knowledge, but it does require taking a moment to step back and think about your project.

## CHAPTER 8

Scrapy

Chapter 7 presented some techniques and patterns for building large, scalable, and (most important!) maintainable web crawlers. Although this is easy enough to do by hand, many libraries, frameworks, and even GUI-based tools will do this for you or at least try to make your life a little easier.

Since its release in 2008, Scrapy has quickly grown into the largest and best-maintained web scraping framework in Python. It is currently maintained by Zyte (formerly Scrapinghub).

One of the challenges of writing web crawlers is that you're often performing the same tasks again and again: find all links on a page, evaluate the difference between internal and external links, and go to new pages. These basic patterns are useful to know and to be able to write from scratch, but the Scrapy library handles many of these details for you.

Of course, Scrapy isn't a mind reader. You still need to define page templates, give it locations to start scraping from, and define URL patterns for the pages that you're looking for. But in these cases, it provides a clean framework to keep your code organized.

Installing Scrapy

Scrapy offers the tool for download (*http://scrapy.org/download/*) from its website, as well as instructions for installing Scrapy with third-party installation managers such as pip.

Because of its relatively large size and complexity, Scrapy is not usually a framework that can be installed in the traditional way with:

```
$ pip install Scrapy
```

Note that I say "usually" because, though it is theoretically possible, I usually run into one or more tricky dependency issues, version mismatches, and unsolvable bugs.

If you're determined to install Scrapy from pip, using a virtual environment is highly recommended (see "Keeping Libraries Straight with Virtual Environments" on page 45 for more on virtual environments).

The installation method I prefer is through the Anaconda package manager (*https:// docs.continuum.io/anaconda/*). Anaconda is a product from the company Continuum, designed to reduce friction when it comes to finding and installing popular Python data science packages. Many of the packages it manages, such as NumPy and NLTK, will be used in later chapters as well.

After you install Anaconda, you can install Scrapy by using this command:

```
conda install -c conda-forge scrapy
```

If you run into issues, or need up-to-date information, check out the Scrapy (*https:// doc.scrapy.org/en/latest/intro/install.html*) installation guide for more information.

Initializing a New Spider

Once you've installed the Scrapy framework, a small amount of setup needs to be done for each spider. A *spider* is a Scrapy project that, like its arachnid namesake, is designed to crawl webs. Throughout this chapter, I use "spider" to describe a Scrapy project in particular, and "crawler" to mean "any generic program that crawls the web, using Scrapy or not."

To create a new spider in the current directory, run the following from the command line:

```
$ scrapy startproject wikiSpider
```

This creates a new subdirectory in the directory the project was created in, with the title *wikiSpider*. Inside this directory is the following file structure:

- *scrapy.cfg*
- *wikiSpider*
  - *spiders*
    - *__init.py__*

— items.py

— middlewares.py

— pipelines.py

— settings.py

— __init.py__

These Python files are initialized with stub code to provide a fast means of creating a new spider project. Each section in this chapter works with this *wikiSpider* project.

Writing a Simple Scraper

To create a crawler, you will add a new file inside the child *spiders* directory at *wiki Spider/wikiSpider/spiders/article.py*. This is where all the spiders, or things that extend scrapy.Spider will go. In your newly created *article.py* file, write:

```python
from scrapy import Spider, Request

class ArticleSpider(Spider):
    name='article'

    def start_requests(self):
        urls = [
            'http://en.wikipedia.org/wiki/Python_%28programming_language%29',
            'https://en.wikipedia.org/wiki/Functional_programming',
            'https://en.wikipedia.org/wiki/Monty_Python']
        return [Request(url=url, callback=self.parse) for url in urls]

    def parse(self, response):
        url = response.url
        title = response.css('h1::text').extract_first()
        print(f'URL is: {url}')
        print(f'Title is: {title}')
```

The name of this class (`ArticleSpider`) does not reference "wiki" or "Wikipedia" at all, indicating that this class in particular is responsible for spidering through only article pages, under the broader category of *wikiSpider*, which you may later want to use to search for other page types.

For large sites with many types of content, you might have separate Scrapy items for each type (blog posts, press releases, articles, etc.), each with different fields but all running under the same Scrapy project. The name of each spider must be unique within the project.

The other key things to notice about this spider are the two functions `start_requests` and `parse`:

`start_requests`
> A Scrapy-defined entry point to the program used to generate `Request` objects that Scrapy uses to crawl the website.

`parse`
> A callback function defined by the user and passed to the `Request` object with `callback=self.parse`. Later, you'll look at more powerful things that can be done with the `parse` function, but for now it prints the title of the page.

You can run this `article` spider by navigating to the outer *wikiSpider* directory and running:

```
$ scrapy runspider wikiSpider/spiders/article.py
```

The default Scrapy output is fairly verbose. Along with debugging information, this should print out lines like:

```
2023-02-11 21:43:13 [scrapy.core.engine] DEBUG: Crawled (200) <GET https://en.wik
ipedia.org/robots.txt> (referer: None)
2023-02-11 21:43:14 [scrapy.downloadermiddlewares.redirect] DEBUG: Redirecting (3
01) to <GET https://en.wikipedia.org/wiki/Python_%28programming_language%29> from
 <GET http://en.wikipedia.org/wiki/Python_%28programming_language%29>
2023-02-11 21:43:14 [scrapy.core.engine] DEBUG: Crawled (200) <GET https://en.wik
ipedia.org/wiki/Functional_programming> (referer: None)
2023-02-11 21:43:14 [scrapy.core.engine] DEBUG: Crawled (200) <GET https://en.wik
ipedia.org/wiki/Monty_Python> (referer: None)
URL is: https://en.wikipedia.org/wiki/Functional_programming
Title is: Functional programming
2023-02-11 21:43:14 [scrapy.core.engine] DEBUG: Crawled (200) <GET https://en.wik
ipedia.org/wiki/Python_%28programming_language%29> (referer: None)
URL is: https://en.wikipedia.org/wiki/Monty_Python
Title is: Monty Python
URL is: https://en.wikipedia.org/wiki/Python_%28programming_language%29
Title is: Python (programming language)
```

The scraper goes to the three pages listed as the URLs, gathers information, and then terminates.

Spidering with Rules

The spider in the previous section isn't much of a crawler, confined to scraping only the list of URLs it's provided. It has no ability to seek new pages on its own. To turn it into a fully fledged crawler, you need to use the `CrawlSpider` class provided by Scrapy.

Code Organization Within the GitHub Repository

Unfortunately, the Scrapy framework cannot be run easily from within a Jupyter notebook, making a linear progression of code difficult to capture. For the purpose of presenting all code samples in the text, the scraper from the previous section is stored in the *article.py* file, while the following example, creating a Scrapy spider that traverses many pages, is stored in *articles.py* (note the use of the plural).

Later examples will also be stored in separate files, with new filenames given in each section. Make sure you are using the correct filename when running these examples.

This class can be found in the spiders file *articles.py* in the GitHub repository:

```python
from scrapy.linkextractors import LinkExtractor
from scrapy.spiders import CrawlSpider, Rule


class ArticleSpider(CrawlSpider):
    name = 'articles'
    allowed_domains = ['wikipedia.org']
    start_urls = ['https://en.wikipedia.org/wiki/Benevolent_dictator_for_life']
    rules = [
        Rule(
            LinkExtractor(allow=r'.*'),
            callback='parse_items',
            follow=True
        )
    ]

    def parse_items(self, response):
        url = response.url
        title = response.css('span.mw-page-title-main::text').extract_first()
        text = response.xpath('//div[@id="mw-content-text"]//text()').extract()
        lastUpdated = response.css(
            'li#footer-info-lastmod::text'
        ).extract_first()
        lastUpdated = lastUpdated.replace('This page was last edited on ', '')
        print(f'URL is: {url}')
        print(f'Title is: {title} ')
        print(f'Text is: {text}')
        print(f'Last updated: {lastUpdated}')
```

This new `ArticleSpider` extends the `CrawlSpider` class. Rather than providing a `start_requests` function, it provides a list of `start_urls` and `allowed_domains`. This tells the spider where to start crawling from and whether it should follow or ignore a link based on the domain.

A list of rules is also provided. This provides further instructions on which links to follow or ignore (in this case, you are allowing all URLs with the regular expression .*).

In addition to extracting the title and URL on each page, a couple of new items have been added. The text content of each page is extracted using an XPath selector. XPath is often used when retrieving text content including text in child tags (for example, an <a> tag inside a block of text). If you use the CSS selector to do this, all text within child tags will be ignored.

The last updated date string is also parsed from the page footer and stored in the lastUpdated variable.

You can run this example by navigating to the *wikiSpider* directory and running:

```
$ scrapy runspider wikiSpider/spiders/articles.py
```

 Warning: This Will Run Forever

While this new spider runs in the command line in the same way as the simple spider built in the previous section, it will not terminate (at least not for a very, very long time) until you halt execution by using Ctrl-C or by closing the terminal. Please be kind to Wikipedia's server load and do not run it for long.

When run, this spider traverses *wikipedia.org*, following all links under the domain *wikipedia.org*, printing titles of pages, and ignoring all external (offsite) links:

```
2023-02-11 22:13:34 [scrapy.spidermiddlewares.offsite] DEBUG: Filtered offsite
  request to 'drupal.org': <GET https://drupal.org/node/769>
2023-02-11 22:13:34 [scrapy.spidermiddlewares.offsite] DEBUG: Filtered offsite
  request to 'groups.drupal.org': <GET https://groups.drupal.org/node/5434>
2023-02-11 22:13:34 [scrapy.spidermiddlewares.offsite] DEBUG: Filtered offsite
  request to 'www.techrepublic.com': <GET https://www.techrepublic.com/article/
open-source-shouldnt-mean-anti-commercial-says-drupal-creator-dries-buytaert/>
2023-02-11 22:13:34 [scrapy.spidermiddlewares.offsite] DEBUG: Filtered offsite
  request to 'www.acquia.com': <GET https://www.acquia.com/board-member/dries-b
uytaert>
```

This is a pretty good crawler so far, but it could use a few limits. Instead of just visiting article pages on Wikipedia, it's free to roam to nonarticle pages as well, such as:

```
title is: Wikipedia:General disclaimer
```

Let's take a closer look at the line by using Scrapy's Rule and LinkExtractor:

```
rules = [Rule(LinkExtractor(allow=r'.*'), callback='parse_items',
    follow=True)]
```

This line provides a list of Scrapy `Rule` objects that define the rules that all found links are filtered through. When multiple rules are in place, each link is checked against the rules, in order. The first rule that matches is the one that is used to determine how the link is handled. If the link doesn't match any rules, it is ignored.

A `Rule` can be provided with four arguments:

`link_extractor`
The only mandatory argument, a `LinkExtractor` object.

`callback`
The function that should be used to parse the content on the page.

`cb_kwargs`
A dictionary of arguments to be passed to the callback function. This dictionary is formatted as {`arg_name1: arg_value1, arg_name2: arg_value2`} and can be a handy tool for reusing the same parsing functions for slightly different tasks.

`follow`
Indicates whether you want links found at that page to be included in a future crawl. If no callback function is provided, this defaults to `True` (after all, if you're not doing anything with the page, it makes sense that you'd at least want to use it to continue crawling through the site). If a callback function is provided, this defaults to `False`.

`LinkExtractor` is a simple class designed solely to recognize and return links in a page of HTML content based on the rules provided to it. It has a number of arguments that can be used to accept or deny a link based on CSS and XPath selectors, tags (you can look for links in more than just anchor tags!), domains, and more.

The `LinkExtractor` class can even be extended, and custom arguments can be created. See Scrapy's documentation on link extractors (*https://doc.scrapy.org/en/latest/topics/link-extractors.html*) for more information.

Despite all the flexible features of the `LinkExtractor` class, the most common arguments you'll use are these:

`allow`
Allow all links that match the provided regular expression.

`deny`
Deny all links that match the provided regular expression.

Using two separate `Rule` and `LinkExtractor` classes with a single parsing function, you can create a spider that crawls Wikipedia, identifying all article pages and flagging nonarticle pages (*articleMoreRules.py*):

```
from scrapy.linkextractors import LinkExtractor
from scrapy.spiders import CrawlSpider, Rule

class ArticleSpider(CrawlSpider):
    name = 'articles'
    allowed_domains = ['wikipedia.org']
    start_urls = ['https://en.wikipedia.org/wiki/Benevolent_dictator_for_life']
    rules = [
        Rule(
            LinkExtractor(allow='(/wiki/)((?!:).)*$'),
            callback='parse_items',
            follow=True,
            cb_kwargs={'is_article': True}
        ),
        Rule(
            LinkExtractor(allow='.*'),
            callback='parse_items',
            cb_kwargs={'is_article': False}
        )
    ]

    def parse_items(self, response, is_article):
        print(response.url)
        title = response.css('span.mw-page-title-main::text').extract_first()
        if is_article:
            url = response.url
            text = response.xpath(
                '//div[@id="mw-content-text"]//text()'
            ).extract()
            lastUpdated = response.css(
                'li#footer-info-lastmod::text'
            ).extract_first()
            lastUpdated = lastUpdated.replace(
                'This page was last edited on ',
                ''
            )
            print(f'URL is: {url}')
            print(f'Title is: {title}')
            print(f'Text is: {text}')
        else:
            print(f'This is not an article: {title}')
```

Recall that the rules are applied to each link in the order that they are presented in the list. All article pages (pages that start with *wiki/* and do not contain a colon) are passed to the parse_items function first with the default parameter is_arti cle=True. Then all the other nonarticle links are passed to the parse_items function with the argument is_article=False.

Of course, if you're looking to collect only article-type pages and ignore all others, this approach would be impractical. It would be much easier to ignore pages that don't match the article URL pattern and leave out the second rule (and the is_article variable) altogether. However, this type of approach may be useful in odd cases where information from the URL, or information collected during crawling, impacts the way the page should be parsed.

Creating Items

So far, you've looked at many ways of finding, parsing, and crawling websites with Scrapy, but Scrapy also provides useful tools to keep your collected items organized and stored in custom objects with well-defined fields.

To help organize all the information you're collecting, you need to create an Article object. Define a new item called Article inside the *items.py* file.

When you open the *items.py* file, it should look like this:

```
# -*- coding: utf-8 -*-

# Define here the models for your scraped items
#
# See documentation in:
# http://doc.scrapy.org/en/latest/topics/items.html

import scrapy

class WikispiderItem(scrapy.Item):
    # define the fields for your item here like:
    # name = scrapy.Field()
    pass
```

Replace this default Item stub with a new Article class extending scrapy.Item:

```
import scrapy

class Article(scrapy.Item):
    url = scrapy.Field()
    title = scrapy.Field()
    text = scrapy.Field()
    lastUpdated = scrapy.Field()
```

You are defining four fields that will be collected from each page: URL, title, text content, and the date the page was last edited.

If you are collecting data for multiple page types, you should define each separate type as its own class in *items.py*. If your items are large, or you start to move more parsing functionality into your item objects, you may also wish to extract each item into its own file. While the items are small, however, I like to keep them in a single file.

In the file *articleItems.py*, note the changes that were made to the `ArticleSpider` class in order to create the new `Article` item:

```python
from scrapy.linkextractors import LinkExtractor
from scrapy.spiders import CrawlSpider, Rule
from wikiSpider.items import Article

class ArticleSpider(CrawlSpider):
    name = 'articleItems'
    allowed_domains = ['wikipedia.org']
    start_urls = ['https://en.wikipedia.org/wiki/Benevolent'
        '_dictator_for_life']
    rules = [
        Rule(LinkExtractor(allow='(/wiki/)((?!:).)*$'),
            callback='parse_items', follow=True),
    ]

    def parse_items(self, response):
        article = Article()
        article['url'] = response.url
        article['title'] = response.css('h1::text').extract_first()
        article['text'] = response.xpath('//div[@id='
            '"mw-content-text"]//text()').extract()
        lastUpdated = response.css('li#footer-info-lastmod::text'
            ).extract_first()
        article['lastUpdated'] = lastUpdated.replace('This page was '
            'last edited on ', '')
        return article
```

When this file is run with

```
$ scrapy runspider wikiSpider/spiders/articleItems.py
```

it will output the usual Scrapy debugging data along with each article item as a Python dictionary:

```
2023-02-11 22:52:26 [scrapy.core.engine] DEBUG: Crawled (200) <GET https://en.wik
ipedia.org/wiki/Benevolent_dictator_for_life#bodyContent> (referer: https://en.wi
kipedia.org/wiki/Benevolent_dictator_for_life)
2023-02-11 22:52:26 [scrapy.core.engine] DEBUG: Crawled (200) <GET https://en.wik
ipedia.org/wiki/OCaml> (referer: https://en.wikipedia.org/wiki/Benevolent_dictato
r_for_life)
2023-02-11 22:52:26 [scrapy.core.engine] DEBUG: Crawled (200) <GET https://en.wik
ipedia.org/wiki/Xavier_Leroy> (referer: https://en.wikipedia.org/wiki/Benevolent_
dictator_for_life)
2023-02-11 22:52:26 [scrapy.core.scraper] DEBUG: Scraped from <200 https://en.wik
ipedia.org/wiki/Benevolent_dictator_for_life>
{'lastUpdated': ' 7 February 2023, at 01:14',
 'text': ['Title given to a small number of open-source software development '
          'leaders',
          ...
```

Using Scrapy `Items` isn't just for promoting good code organization or laying things out in a readable way. Items provide many tools for outputting and processing data, covered in the next sections.

Outputting Items

Scrapy uses the `Item` objects to determine which pieces of information it should save from the pages it visits. This information can be saved by Scrapy in a variety of ways, such as CSV, JSON, or XML files, using the following commands:

```
$ scrapy runspider articleItems.py -o articles.csv -t csv
$ scrapy runspider articleItems.py -o articles.json -t json
$ scrapy runspider articleItems.py -o articles.xml -t xml
```

Each of these runs the scraper `articleItems` and writes the output in the specified format to the provided file. This file will be created if it does not exist already.

You may have noticed that in the articles the spider created in previous examples, the text variable is a list of strings rather than a single string. Each string in this list represents text inside a single HTML element, whereas the content inside `<div id="mw-content-text">`, from which you are collecting the text data, is composed of many child elements.

Scrapy manages these more complex values well. In the CSV format, for example, it converts lists to strings and escapes all commas so that a list of text displays in a single CSV cell.

In XML, each element of this list is preserved inside child value tags:

```
<items>
<item>
    <url>https://en.wikipedia.org/wiki/Benevolent_dictator_for_life</url>
    <title>Benevolent dictator for life</title>
    <text>
        <value>For the political term, see </value>
        <value>Benevolent dictatorship</value>
        ...
    </text>
    <lastUpdated> 7 February 2023, at 01:14.</lastUpdated>
</item>
....
```

In the JSON format, lists are preserved as lists.

Of course, you can use the `Item` objects yourself and write them to a file or a database in whatever way you want, simply by adding the appropriate code to the parsing function in the crawler.

The Item Pipeline

Although Scrapy is single threaded, it is capable of making and handling many requests asynchronously. This makes it faster than the scrapers written so far in this book, although I have always been a firm believer that faster is not always better when it comes to web scraping.

The web server for the site you are trying to scrape must handle each of these requests, and it's important to be a good citizen and evaluate whether this sort of server hammering is appropriate (or even wise for your own self-interests, as many websites have the ability and the will to block what they might see as malicious scraping activity). For more information about the ethics of web scraping, as well as the importance of appropriately throttling scrapers, see Chapter 19.

With that said, using Scrapy's item pipeline can improve the speed of your web scraper even further by performing all data processing while waiting for requests to be returned, rather than waiting for data to be processed before making another request. This type of optimization can even be necessary when data processing requires a great deal of time or processor-heavy calculations.

To create an item pipeline, revisit the *settings.py* file created at the beginning of the chapter. You should see the following commented lines:

```
# Configure item pipelines
# See http://scrapy.readthedocs.org/en/latest/topics/item-pipeline.html
#ITEM_PIPELINES = {
#    'wikiSpider.pipelines.WikispiderPipeline': 300,
#}
```

Uncomment the last three lines and replace them with:

```
ITEM_PIPELINES = {
    'wikiSpider.pipelines.WikispiderPipeline': 300,
}
```

This provides a Python class, `wikiSpider.pipelines.WikispiderPipeline`, that will be used to process the data, as well as an integer that represents the order in which to run the pipeline if there are multiple processing classes. Although any integer can be used here, the numbers 0–1,000 are typically used and will be run in ascending order.

Now you need to add the pipeline class and rewrite your original spider so that the spider collects data and the pipeline does the heavy lifting of the data processing. It might be tempting to write the `parse_items` method in your original spider to return the response and let the pipeline create the `Article` object:

```
def parse_items(self, response):
    return response
```

However, the Scrapy framework does not allow this, and an Item object (such as an Article, which extends Item) must be returned. So the goal of parse_items is now to extract the raw data, doing as little processing as possible, so that it can be passed to the pipeline:

```
from scrapy.linkextractors import LinkExtractor
from scrapy.spiders import CrawlSpider, Rule
from wikiSpider.items import Article

class ArticleSpider(CrawlSpider):
    name = 'articlePipelines'
    allowed_domains = ['wikipedia.org']
    start_urls = ['https://en.wikipedia.org/wiki/Benevolent_dictator_for_life']
    rules = [
        Rule(LinkExtractor(allow='(/wiki/)((?!:).)*$'),
            callback='parse_items', follow=True),
    ]

    def parse_items(self, response):
        article = Article()
        article['url'] = response.url
        article['title'] = response.css('h1::text').extract_first()
        article['text'] = response.xpath('//div[@id='
            '"mw-content-text"]//text()').extract()
        article['lastUpdated'] = response.css('li#'
            'footer-info-lastmod::text').extract_first()
        return article
```

This file is saved as *articlePipelines.py* in the GitHub repository.

Of course, now you need to tie the *pipelines.py* file and the updated spider together by adding the pipeline. When the Scrapy project was first initialized, a file was created at *wikiSpider/wikiSpider/pipelines.py*:

```
# -*- coding: utf-8 -*-

# Define your item pipelines here
#
# Don't forget to add your pipeline to the ITEM_PIPELINES setting
# See: http://doc.scrapy.org/en/latest/topics/item-pipeline.html


class WikispiderPipeline(object):
    def process_item(self, item, spider):
        return item
```

This stub class should be replaced with your new pipeline code. In previous sections, you've been collecting two fields in a raw format, and these could use additional processing: lastUpdated (which is a badly formatted string object representing a date) and text (a messy array of string fragments).

The following should be used to replace the stub code in *wikiSpider/wikiSpider/pipelines.py*:

```
from datetime import datetime
from wikiSpider.items import Article
from string import whitespace

class WikispiderPipeline(object):
    def process_item(self, article, spider):
        dateStr = article['lastUpdated']
        article['lastUpdated'] = article['lastUpdated']
            .replace('This page was last edited on', '')
        article['lastUpdated'] = article['lastUpdated'].strip()
        article['lastUpdated'] = datetime.strptime(
            article['lastUpdated'], '%d %B %Y, at %H:%M.')
        article['text'] = [line for line in article['text']
            if line not in whitespace]
        article['text'] = ''.join(article['text'])
        return article
```

The class `WikispiderPipeline` has a method `process_item` that takes in an `Article` object, parses the `lastUpdated` string into a Python `datetime` object, and cleans and joins the text into a single string from a list of strings.

`process_item` is a mandatory method for every pipeline class. Scrapy uses this method to asynchronously pass `Items` that are collected by the spider. The parsed `Article` object that is returned here will be logged or printed by Scrapy if, for example, you are outputting items to JSON or CSV, as was done in the previous section.

You now have two choices when it comes to deciding where to do your data processing: the `parse_items` method in the spider, or the `process_items` method in the pipeline.

Multiple pipelines with different tasks can be declared in the *settings.py* file. However, Scrapy passes all items, regardless of item type, to each pipeline in order. Item-specific parsing may be better handled in the spider, before the data hits the pipeline. However, if this parsing takes a long time, you may want to consider moving it to the pipeline (where it can be processed asynchronously) and adding a check on the item type:

```
def process_item(self, item, spider):
    if isinstance(item, Article):
        # Article-specific processing here
```

Which processing to do and where to do it is an important consideration when it comes to writing Scrapy projects, especially large ones.

Logging with Scrapy

The debug information generated by Scrapy can be useful, but, as you've likely noticed, it is often too verbose. You can easily adjust the level of logging by adding a line to the *settings.py* file in your Scrapy project:

```
LOG_LEVEL = 'ERROR'
```

Scrapy uses a standard hierarchy of logging levels, as follows:

- `CRITICAL`
- `ERROR`
- `WARNING`
- `DEBUG`
- `INFO`

If logging is set to `ERROR`, only `CRITICAL` and `ERROR` logs will be displayed. If logging is set to `INFO`, all logs will be displayed, and so on.

In addition to controlling logging through the *settings.py* file, you can control where the logs go from the command line. To output logs to a separate logfile instead of the terminal, define a logfile when running from the command line:

```
$ scrapy crawl articles -s LOG_FILE=wiki.log
```

This creates a new logfile, if one does not exist, in your current directory and outputs all logs to it, leaving your terminal clear to display only the Python print statements you manually add.

More Resources

Scrapy is a powerful tool that handles many problems associated with crawling the web. It automatically gathers all URLs and compares them against predefined rules, makes sure all URLs are unique, normalizes relative URLs where needed, and recurses to go more deeply into pages.

I encourage you to check out the Scrapy documentation (*https://doc.scrapy.org/en/ latest/news.html*) as well as Scrapy's official tutorial pages (*https://docs.scrapy.org/en/ latest/intro/tutorial.html*), which provide a comprehensive discourse on the framework.

Scrapy is an extremely large, sprawling library with many features. Its features work together seamlessly but have many areas of overlap that allow users to easily develop their own particular style within it. If there's something you'd like to do with Scrapy that has not been mentioned here, there is likely a way (or several) to do it!

## CHAPTER 9

Storing Data

Although printing to the terminal is a lot of fun, it's not incredibly useful when it comes to data aggregation and analysis. To make the majority of web scrapers remotely useful, you need to be able to save the information that they scrape.

This chapter covers three main methods of data management that are sufficient for almost any imaginable application. Do you need to power the backend of a website or create your own API? You'll probably want your scrapers to write to a database. Need a fast and easy way to collect documents off the internet and put them on your hard drive? You'll probably want to create a file stream for that. Need occasional alerts, or aggregated data once a day? Send yourself an email!

Above and beyond web scraping, the ability to store and interact with large amounts of data is incredibly important for just about any modern programming application. In fact, the information in this chapter is necessary for implementing many of the examples in later sections of the book. I highly recommend that you at least skim this chapter if you're unfamiliar with automated data storage.

Media Files

You can store media files in two main ways: by reference and by downloading the file itself. Storing a file by reference is as simple as saving the text URL where the file is located on the host server but not actually downloading the file. This has several advantages:

- Scrapers run much faster and require much less bandwidth when they don't have to download files.
- You save space on your own machine by storing only the URLs.

- It is easier to write code that stores only URLs and doesn't need to deal with additional file downloads.
- You can lessen the load on the host server by avoiding large file downloads.

Here are the disadvantages:

- Embedding these URLs in your own website or application is known as *hotlinking*, and doing it is a quick way to get you in hot water on the internet.
- You do not want to use someone else's server cycles to host media for your own applications.
- The file hosted at any particular URL is subject to change. This might lead to embarrassing effects if, say, you're embedding a hotlinked image on a public blog, the blog owner finds out, and they decide to change the image to something unsavory. Less serious but still inconvenient: if you're storing the URLs with the intent to use them later, they might eventually go missing at a later date.
- Real web browsers do not just request a page's HTML and move on. They download all of the assets required by the page as well. Downloading files can make your scraper look like a human browsing the site, an advantage over merely recording links.

If you're debating whether to store a file or a URL to a file, you should ask yourself whether you're likely to view or read that file more than once or twice, or if this database of files is going to be sitting around gathering electronic dust for most of its life. If the answer is the latter, it's probably best to simply store the URL. If it's the former, read on!

The urllib library, used to retrieve the content of web pages, also contains functions to retrieve the content of files. The following program uses `urllib.request.urlretrieve` to download images from a remote URL:

```
from urllib.request import urlretrieve, urlopen
from bs4 import BeautifulSoup

html = urlopen('http://www.pythonscraping.com')
bs = BeautifulSoup(html, 'html.parser')
imageLocation = bs.find('img', {'alt': 'python-logo'})['src']
urlretrieve (imageLocation, 'logo.jpg')
```

This downloads the Python logo from *http://pythonscraping.com* and stores it as *logo.jpg* in the same directory from which the script is running.

This works well if you need to download only a single file and know what to call it and what the file extension is. But most scrapers don't download a single file and call it a day. The following downloads all internal files, linked to by any tag's src attribute, from the home page of *http://pythonscraping.com*:

```
import os
from urllib.request import urlretrieve, urlopen
from urllib.parse import urlparse
from bs4 import BeautifulSoup

downloadDir = 'downloaded'
baseUrl = 'https://pythonscraping.com/'
baseNetloc = urlparse(baseUrl).netloc

def getAbsoluteURL(source):
    if urlparse(baseUrl).netloc == '':
        return baseUrl + source
    return source

def getDownloadPath(fileUrl):
    parsed = urlparse(fileUrl)
    netloc = parsed.netloc.strip('/')
    path = parsed.path.strip('/')
    localfile = f'{downloadDir}/{netloc}/{path}'

    # Remove the filename from the path in order to
    # make the directory structure leading up to it
    localpath = '/'.join(localfile.split('/')[:-1])
    if not os.path.exists(localpath):
        os.makedirs(localpath)
    return localfile

html = urlopen(baseUrl)
bs = BeautifulSoup(html, 'html.parser')
downloadList = bs.findAll(src=True)

for download in downloadList:
    fileUrl = getAbsoluteURL(download['src'])
    if fileUrl is not None:
        try:
            urlretrieve(fileUrl, getDownloadPath(fileUrl))
            print(fileUrl)
        except Exception as e:
            print(f'Could not retrieve {fileUrl} Error: {e}')
```

Run with Caution

You know all those warnings you hear about downloading unknown files off the internet? This script downloads everything it comes across to your computer's hard drive. This includes random bash scripts, *.exe* files, and other potential malware.

Think you're safe because you'd never actually execute anything sent to your downloads folder? Especially if you run this program as an administrator, you're asking for trouble. What happens if you run across a file on a website that sends itself to *../../../../usr/bin/ python*? The next time you run a Python script from the command line, you could be deploying malware on your machine!

This program is written for illustrative purposes only; it should not be randomly deployed without more extensive filename checking, and it should be run only in an account with limited permissions. As always, backing up your files, not storing sensitive information on your hard drive, and using a little common sense go a long way.

This script uses a lambda function (introduced in Chapter 5) to select all tags on the front page that have the `src` attribute, and then cleans and normalizes the URLs to get an absolute path for each download (making sure to discard external links). Then, each file is downloaded to its own path in the local folder *downloaded* on your own machine.

Notice that Python's `os` module is used briefly to retrieve the target directory for each download and create missing directories along the path if needed. The `os` module acts as an interface between Python and the operating system, allowing it to manipulate file paths, create directories, get information about running processes and environment variables, and many other useful things.

Storing Data to CSV

CSV, or *comma-separated values*, is one of the most popular file formats in which to store spreadsheet data. It is supported by Microsoft Excel and many other applications because of its simplicity. The following is an example of a perfectly valid CSV file:

```
fruit,cost
apple,1.00
banana,0.30
pear,1.25
```

As with Python, whitespace is important here: each row is separated by a newline character, while columns within the row are separated by commas (hence the name "comma-separated"). Other forms of CSV files (sometimes called *character-separated value* files) use tabs or other characters to separate rows, but these file formats are less common and less widely supported.

If you're looking to download CSV files directly off the web and store them locally, without any parsing or modification, you don't need this section. Download them like you would any other file and save them with the CSV file format by using the methods described in the previous section.

Modifying a CSV file, or even creating one entirely from scratch, is extremely easy with Python's *csv* library:

```python
import csv

csvFile = open('test.csv', 'w+')
try:
    writer = csv.writer(csvFile)
    writer.writerow(('number', 'number plus 2', 'number times 2'))
    for i in range(10):
        writer.writerow( (i, i+2, i*2))
finally:
    csvFile.close()
```

A precautionary reminder: file creation in Python is fairly bulletproof. If *test.csv* does not already exist, Python will create the file (but not the directory) automatically. If it already exists, Python will overwrite *test.csv* with the new data.

After running, you should see a CSV file:

```
number,number plus 2,number times 2
0,2,0
1,3,2
2,4,4
...
```

One common web scraping task is to retrieve an HTML table and write it as a CSV file. Wikipedia's List of Countries with McDonald's Restaurants (*https://en.wikipedia.org/wiki/List_of_countries_with_McDonald%27s_restaurants*) provides a fairly complex HTML table with links, sorting, and other HTML garbage that needs to be discarded before it can be written to CSV. Using BeautifulSoup and the get_text() function copiously, you can do that in fewer than 20 lines:

```python
import csv
from urllib.request import urlopen
from bs4 import BeautifulSoup

html = urlopen('https://en.wikipedia.org/wiki/
        List_of_countries_with_McDonald%27s_restaurants')
bs = BeautifulSoup(html, 'html.parser')
```

```
# The main comparison table is currently the first table on the page
table = bs.find('table',{'class':'wikitable'})
rows = table.findAll('tr')
csvFile = open('countries.csv', 'wt+')
writer = csv.writer(csvFile)
try:
    for row in rows:
        csvRow = []
        for cell in row.findAll(['td', 'th']):
            csvRow.append(cell.get_text().strip())
        writer.writerow(csvRow)
finally:
    csvFile.close()
```

 There Is an Easier Way to Fetch a Single Table

This script is great to integrate into scrapers if you encounter many HTML tables that need to be converted to CSV files, or many HTML tables that need to be collected into a single CSV file. However, if you only need to do it just once, there's a better tool for that: copying and pasting. Selecting and copying all the content of an HTML table and pasting it into Excel or Google Docs will get you the CSV file you're looking for without running a script!

The result should be a well-formatted CSV file saved locally, at *countries.csv*.

MySQL

MySQL (officially pronounced "my es-kew-el," although many say, "my sequel") is the most popular open source relational database management system today. Somewhat unusually for an open source project with large competitors, its popularity has historically been neck and neck with the two other major closed source database systems: Microsoft's SQL Server and Oracle's DBMS.

Its popularity is not without cause. For most applications, it's hard to go wrong with MySQL. It's a scalable, robust, and full-featured DBMS, used by top websites: YouTube,[1] Twitter,[2] and Facebook,[3] among many others.

---

1 Joab Jackson, "YouTube Scales MySQL with Go Code" (*http://bit.ly/1LWVmc8*), *PCWorld*, December 15, 2012.

2 Jeremy Cole and Davi Arnaut, "MySQL at Twitter" (*http://bit.ly/1KHDKns*), *The Twitter Engineering Blog*, April 9, 2012.

3 "MySQL and Database Engineering: Mark Callaghan" (*http://on.fb.me/1RFMqvw*), Facebook Engineering, March 4, 2012.

Because of its ubiquity, price ("free" is a pretty great price), and out-of-box usability, it makes a fantastic database for web scraping projects, and we will use it throughout the remainder of this book.

Installing MySQL

If you're new to MySQL, installing a database might sound a little intimidating (if you're an old hat at it, feel free to skip this section). In reality, it's as simple as installing just about any other kind of software. At its core, MySQL is powered by a set of data files, stored on your server or local machine, that contain all the information stored in your database. The MySQL software layer on top of that provides a convenient way of interacting with the data via a command-line interface. For example, the following command digs through the data files and returns a list of all users in your database whose first name is "Ryan":

```
SELECT * FROM users WHERE firstname = "Ryan"
```

If you're on a Debian-based Linux distribution (or anything with `apt-get`), installing MySQL is as easy as this:

```
$ sudo apt-get install mysql-server
```

Just keep an eye on the installation process, approve the memory requirements, and enter a new password for your new root user when prompted.

For macOS and Windows, things are a little trickier. If you haven't already, you need to create an Oracle account before downloading the package.

If you're on macOS, you first need to get the installation package (*http://dev.mysql.com/downloads/mysql/*).

Select the *.dmg* package, and log in with or create your Oracle account to download the file. After the file opens, you should be guided through a fairly straightforward installation wizard (see Figure 9-1).

The default installation steps should suffice, and for the purposes of this book, I assume you have a default MySQL installation.

After MySQL is installed on macOS, you can start the MySQL server as follows:

```
$ cd /usr/local/mysql
$ sudo ./bin/mysqld_safe
```

On Windows, installing and running MySQL is slightly more complicated, but the good news is that a convenient installer (*http://dev.mysql.com/downloads/windows/installer/*) simplifies the process. Once downloaded, it will guide you through the steps you need to take (see Figure 9-2).

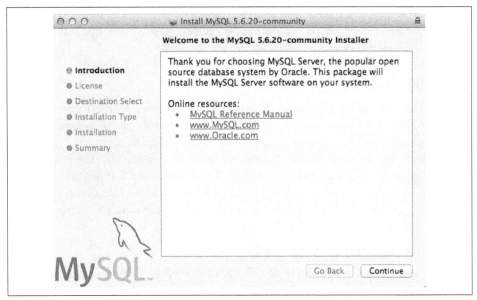

Figure 9-1. The macOS MySQL installer

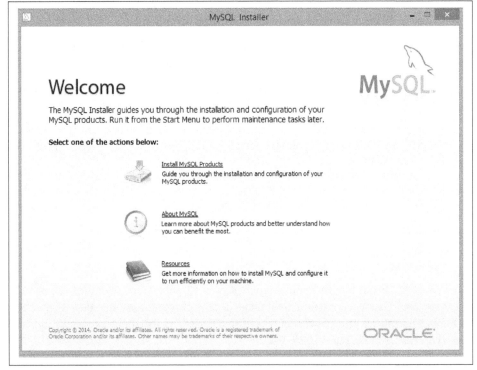

Figure 9-2. The Windows MySQL Installer

You should be able to install MySQL by using the default selections, with one exception: on the Setup Type page, I recommend you choose Server Only to avoid installing a lot of additional Microsoft software and libraries. From there, you should be able to use the default installation settings and follow the prompts to start your MySQL server.

After your MySQL server is installed and running, you will still need to be able to interact with it using the command line. On Windows, you can use the MySQL Shell (*https://dev.mysql.com/downloads/shell/*) tools. On Macs, I like to install the command-line tools with the Homebrew package manager (*https://brew.sh*):

```
$ brew install mysql
```

After installing the command-line tools, you should be able to connect to your MySQL server:

```
$ mysql -u root -p
```

This will prompt you to enter the root password that you created during installation.

Some Basic Commands

After your MySQL server is running, you have many options for interacting with the database. Plenty of software tools act as an intermediary so that you don't have to deal with MySQL commands (or at least deal with them less often). Tools such as phpMyAdmin and MySQL Workbench can make it easy to quickly view, sort, and insert data. However, it's still important to know your way around the command line.

Except for variable names, MySQL is case insensitive; for example, SELECT is the same as sELEcT. However, by convention, all MySQL keywords are in all caps when you are writing a MySQL statement. Conversely, most developers prefer to name their tables and databases in lowercase, although this standard is often ignored.

When you first log in to MySQL, there are no databases to add data to, but you can create one:

```
> CREATE DATABASE scraping;
```

Because every MySQL instance can have multiple databases, before you can start interacting with a database, you need to specify to MySQL which database you want to use:

```
> USE scraping;
```

From this point on (at least until you close the MySQL connection or switch to another database), all commands entered will be run against the new scraping database.

That all seems pretty straightforward. It must be similarly easy to create a table in the database, right? Let's try to create a table to store a collection of scraped web pages:

```
> CREATE TABLE pages;
```

This results in an error:

```
ERROR 1113 (42000): A table must have at least 1 column
```

Unlike a database, which can exist without any tables, a table in MySQL cannot exist without columns. To define columns in MySQL, you must enter them in a comma-delimited list, within parentheses, after the CREATE TABLE <tablename> statement:

```
> CREATE TABLE pages (id BIGINT(7) NOT NULL AUTO_INCREMENT,
title VARCHAR(200), content VARCHAR(10000),
created TIMESTAMP DEFAULT CURRENT_TIMESTAMP, PRIMARY KEY(id));
```

Each column definition has three parts:

- The name (id, title, created, etc.)
- The variable type (BIGINT(7), VARCHAR, TIMESTAMP)
- Optionally, any additional attributes (NOT NULL AUTO_INCREMENT)

At the end of the list of columns, you must define a table's *key*. MySQL uses keys to organize the content in the table for fast lookups. Later in this chapter, I'll describe how to use these keys to your advantage for speedier databases, but for now, using a table's id column as the key is generally the best way to go.

After the query executes, you can see what the structure of the table looks like at any time by using DESCRIBE:

```
> DESCRIBE pages;
+---------+----------------+------+-----+-------------------+----------------+
| Field   | Type           | Null | Key | Default           | Extra          |
+---------+----------------+------+-----+-------------------+----------------+
| id      | bigint(7)      | NO   | PRI | NULL              | auto_increment |
| title   | varchar(200)   | YES  |     | NULL              |                |
| content | varchar(10000) | YES  |     | NULL              |                |
| created | timestamp      | NO   |     | CURRENT_TIMESTAMP |                |
+---------+----------------+------+-----+-------------------+----------------+
4 rows in set (0.01 sec)
```

Of course, this is still an empty table. You can insert test data into the *pages* table by using the following line:

```
> INSERT INTO pages (title, content) VALUES ("Test page title",
"This is some test page content. It can be up to 10,000 characters
long.");
```

Notice that although the table has four columns (id, title, content, created), you need to define only two of them (title and content) in order to insert a row. That's because the id column is autoincremented (MySQL automatically adds a 1 each time a new row is inserted) and generally can take care of itself. In addition, the timestamp column is set to contain the current time as a default.

Of course, you *can* override these defaults:

```
> INSERT INTO pages (id, title, content, created) VALUES (3,
"Test page title",
"This is some test page content. It can be up to 10,000 characters
long.", "2014-09-21 10:25:32");
```

As long as the integer you provide for the id column doesn't already exist in the database, this override will work perfectly fine. However, it is generally bad practice to do this; it's best to let MySQL handle the id and timestamp columns unless there is a compelling reason to do it differently.

Now that you have some data in the table, you can use a wide variety of methods to select this data. Here are a few examples of SELECT statements:

```
> SELECT * FROM pages WHERE id = 2;
```

This statement tells MySQL, "Select all from pages where id equals 2." The asterisk (*) acts as a wildcard, returning all the rows where the clause (where id equals 2) is true. It returns the second row in the table, or an empty result if there is no row with an id of 2. For example, the following case-insensitive query returns all the rows where the title field contains "test" (the % symbol acts as a wildcard in MySQL strings):

```
> SELECT * FROM pages WHERE title LIKE "%test%";
```

But what if you have a table with many columns, and you want only a particular piece of data returned? Rather than selecting all, you can do something like this:

```
> SELECT id, title FROM pages WHERE content LIKE "%page content%";
```

This returns just the id and title where the content contains the phrase "page content."

DELETE statements have much the same syntax as SELECT statements:

```
> DELETE FROM pages WHERE id = 1;
```

For this reason, it is a good idea, especially when working on important databases that can't be easily restored, to write any DELETE statements as a SELECT statement first (in this case, SELECT * FROM pages WHERE id = 1), test to make sure only the rows you want to delete are returned, and then replace SELECT * with DELETE. Many programmers have horror stories of miscoding the clause on a DELETE statement, or worse, leaving it off entirely when they were in a hurry and ruining customer data. Don't let it happen to you!

Similar precautions should be taken with UPDATE statements:

```
> UPDATE pages SET title="A new title",
content="Some new content" WHERE id=2;
```

For the purposes of this book, you will be working with only simple MySQL statements, doing basic selecting, inserting, and updating. If you're interested in learning more commands and techniques with this powerful database tool, I recommend Paul DuBois's *MySQL Cookbook* (O'Reilly).

Integrating with Python

Unfortunately, Python support for MySQL is not built in. However, many open source libraries allow you to interact with a MySQL database. One of the most popular of these is PyMySQL (*https://pypi.python.org/pypi/PyMySQL*).

As of this writing, the current version of PyMySQL is 1.0.3, which can be installed using pip:

```
$ pip install PyMySQL
```

After installation, you should have access to the PyMySQL package automatically. While your local MySQL server is running, you should be able to execute the following script successfully (remember to add the root password for your database):

```
import pymysql
conn = pymysql.connect(
    host='127.0.0.1',
    unix_socket='/tmp/mysql.sock',
    user='root',
    passwd=None,
    db='mysql'
)
cur = conn.cursor()
cur.execute('USE scraping')
cur.execute('SELECT * FROM pages WHERE id=1')
print(cur.fetchone())
cur.close()
conn.close()
```

Two new types of objects are at work in this example: the connection object (conn) and the cursor object (cur).

The connection/cursor model is commonly used in database programming, although some users might find it tricky to differentiate between the two at first. The connection is responsible for, well, connecting to the database, of course, but also sending the database information, handling rollbacks (when a query or set of queries needs to be aborted and the database needs to be returned to its previous state), and creating new cursor objects.

A connection can have many cursors. A cursor keeps track of certain *state* information, such as which database it is using. If you have multiple databases and need to write information across all of them, you might have multiple cursors to handle this. A cursor also contains the results of the latest query it has executed. By calling functions on the cursor, such as `cur.fetchone()`, you can access this information.

It is important that both the cursor and the connection are closed after you are finished using them. Not doing this might result in *connection leaks*, a buildup of unclosed connections that are no longer being used, but the software isn't able to close because it's under the impression that you might still use them. This is the sort of thing that brings databases down all the time (I have both written and fixed many connection leak bugs), so remember to close your connections!

The most common thing you'll probably want to do, starting out, is to be able to store your scraping results in a database. Let's take a look at how this could be done, using a previous example: the Wikipedia scraper.

Dealing with Unicode text can be tough when web scraping. By default, MySQL does not handle Unicode. Fortunately, you can turn on this feature (just keep in mind that doing so will increase the size of your database). Because you're bound to run into a variety of colorful characters on Wikipedia, now is a good time to tell your database to expect some Unicode:

```
ALTER DATABASE scraping CHARACTER SET = utf8mb4 COLLATE = utf8mb4_unicode_ci;
ALTER TABLE pages CONVERT TO CHARACTER SET utf8mb4 COLLATE utf8mb4_unicode_ci;
ALTER TABLE pages CHANGE title title VARCHAR(200) CHARACTER SET utf8mb4 COLLATE
utf8mb4_unicode_ci;
ALTER TABLE pages CHANGE content content VARCHAR(10000) CHARACTER SET utf8mb4
COLLATE utf8mb4_unicode_ci;
```

These four lines change the default character set for the database, for the table, and for both of the two columns—from utf8mb4 (still technically Unicode, but with notoriously terrible support for most Unicode characters) to utf8mb4_unicode_ci.

You'll know that you're successful if you try inserting a few umlauts or Mandarin characters into the `title` or `content` field in the database and it succeeds with no errors.

Now that the database is prepared to accept a wide variety of all that Wikipedia can throw at it, you can run the following:

```
conn = pymysql.connect(host='127.0.0.1', unix_socket='/tmp/mysql.sock',
                       user='root', passwd=None, db='mysql', charset='utf8')
cur = conn.cursor()
cur.execute('USE scraping')
```

```
random.seed(datetime.datetime.now())

def store(title, content):
    cur.execute('INSERT INTO pages (title, content) VALUES '
        '("%s", "%s")', (title, content))
    cur.connection.commit()

def getLinks(articleUrl):
    html = urlopen('http://en.wikipedia.org'+articleUrl)
    bs = BeautifulSoup(html, 'html.parser')
    title = bs.find('h1').get_text()
    content = bs.find('div', {'id':'mw-content-text'}).find('p')
        .get_text()
    store(title, content)
    return bs.find('div', {'id':'bodyContent'}).find_all('a',
        href=re.compile('^(/wiki/)((?!:).)*$'))

links = getLinks('/wiki/Kevin_Bacon')
try:
    while len(links) > 0:
        newArticle = links[random.randint(0, len(links)-1)].attrs['href']
        print(newArticle)
        links = getLinks(newArticle)
finally:
    cur.close()
    conn.close()
```

There are a few things to note here: first, `"charset='utf8'"` is added to the database connection string. This tells the connection that it should send all information to the database as UTF-8 (and, of course, the database should already be configured to handle this).

Second, note the addition of a `store` function. This takes in two string variables, `title` and `content`, and adds them to an `INSERT` statement that is executed by the cursor and then committed by the cursor's connection. This is an excellent example of the separation of the cursor and the connection; while the cursor has stored information about the database and its own context, it needs to operate through the connection in order to send information back to the database and insert information.

Last, you'll see that a `finally` statement is added to the program's main loop, at the bottom of the code. This ensures that, regardless of how the program is interrupted or the exceptions that might be thrown during its execution (and because the web is messy, you should always assume exceptions will be thrown), the cursor and the connection will both be closed immediately before the program ends. It is a good idea to include a `try...finally` statement like this whenever you are scraping the web and have an open database connection.

Although PyMySQL is not a huge package, there are a fair number of useful functions that this book can't accommodate. You can check out their documentation (*https://pymysql.readthedocs.io/en/latest/*) at the PyMySQL site.

Database Techniques and Good Practice

Some people spend their entire careers studying, tuning, and inventing databases. I am not one of those people, and this is not that kind of book. However, as with many subjects in computer science, there are a few tricks you can learn quickly to at least make your databases sufficient, and sufficiently speedy, for most applications.

First, with few exceptions, always add id columns to your tables. All tables in MySQL must have at least one primary key (the key column that MySQL sorts on), so that MySQL knows how to order it, and it can often be difficult to choose these keys intelligently.

The debate over whether to use an artificially created id column for this key or a unique attribute such as username has raged among data scientists and software engineers for years, although I tend to lean on the side of creating id columns. This is *especially* true when you're dealing with web scraping and storing someone else's data. You have no idea what's actually unique or not unique, and I've been surprised before.

Your id column should be autoincremented and used as the primary key for all of your tables.

Second, use intelligent indexing. A dictionary (like the book, not the Python object) is a list of words indexed alphabetically. This allows quick lookups whenever you need a word, as long as you know how it's spelled. You could also imagine a dictionary that is organized alphabetically by the word's definition. This wouldn't be nearly as useful unless you were playing some strange game of *Jeopardy!* in which a definition was presented and you needed to come up with the word. But in the world of database lookups, these sorts of situations happen. For example, you might have a field in your database that you will often be querying against:

```
>SELECT * FROM dictionary WHERE definition="A small furry animal that says meow";
+------+-------+-------------------------------------+
| id   | word  | definition                          |
+------+-------+-------------------------------------+
| 200  | cat   | A small furry animal that says meow |
+------+-------+-------------------------------------+
1 row in set (0.00 sec)
```

You might very well want to add an index to this table (in addition to the index presumably already in place on the id) to the definition column to make lookups on this column faster. Keep in mind, though, that adding indexing requires more space for the new index, as well as additional processing time when inserting new rows.

Especially when you're dealing with large amounts of data, you should carefully consider the trade-offs of your indexes and how much you need to index. To make this "definitions" index a little lighter, you can tell MySQL to index only the first few characters in the column value. This command creates an index on the first 16 characters in the definition field:

```
CREATE INDEX definition ON dictionary (id, definition(16));
```

This index will make your lookups much faster when searching for words by their full definition (especially if the first 16 characters in definition values tend to be very different from each other), and not add too much in the way of extra space and up-front processing time.

On the subject of query time versus database size (one of the fundamental balancing acts in database engineering), one of the common mistakes made, especially with web scraping of large amounts of natural text data, is to store lots of repeating data. For example, say you want to measure the frequency of certain phrases that crop up across websites. These phrases might be found from a given list or automatically generated via a text-analysis algorithm. You might be tempted to store the data as something like this:

```
+--------+--------------+------+-----+---------+----------------+
| Field  | Type         | Null | Key | Default | Extra          |
+--------+--------------+------+-----+---------+----------------+
| id     | int(11)      | NO   | PRI | NULL    | auto_increment |
| url    | varchar(200) | YES  |     | NULL    |                |
| phrase | varchar(200) | YES  |     | NULL    |                |
+--------+--------------+------+-----+---------+----------------+
```

This adds a row to the database each time you find a phrase on a site and records the URL where it was found. However, by splitting the data into three separate tables, you can shrink your dataset enormously:

```
>DESCRIBE phrases
+--------+--------------+------+-----+---------+----------------+
| Field  | Type         | Null | Key | Default | Extra          |
+--------+--------------+------+-----+---------+----------------+
| id     | int(11)      | NO   | PRI | NULL    | auto_increment |
| phrase | varchar(200) | YES  |     | NULL    |                |
+--------+--------------+------+-----+---------+----------------+

>DESCRIBE urls
+-------+--------------+------+-----+---------+----------------+
| Field | Type         | Null | Key | Default | Extra          |
+-------+--------------+------+-----+---------+----------------+
| id    | int(11)      | NO   | PRI | NULL    | auto_increment |
| url   | varchar(200) | YES  |     | NULL    |                |
+-------+--------------+------+-----+---------+----------------+

>DESCRIBE foundInstances
```

```
+--------------+----------+------+-----+---------+----------------+
| Field        | Type     | Null | Key | Default | Extra          |
+--------------+----------+------+-----+---------+----------------+
| id           | int(11)  | NO   | PRI | NULL    | auto_increment |
| urlId        | int(11)  | YES  |     | NULL    |                |
| phraseId     | int(11)  | YES  |     | NULL    |                |
| occurrences  | int(11)  | YES  |     | NULL    |                |
+--------------+----------+------+-----+---------+----------------+
```

Although the table definitions are larger, you can see that the majority of the columns are just integer id fields. These take up far less space. In addition, the full text of each URL and phrase is stored exactly once.

Unless you install a third-party package or keep meticulous logs, it can be impossible to tell when a piece of data was added, updated, or removed from your database. Depending on the available space for your data, the frequency of changes, and the importance of determining when those changes happened, you might want to consider keeping several timestamps in place: created, updated, and deleted.

"Six Degrees" in MySQL

Chapter 6 introduced the Six Degrees of Wikipedia problem, in which the goal is to find the connection between any two Wikipedia articles through a series of links (i.e., find a way to get from one Wikipedia article to the next just by clicking links from one page to the next). To solve this problem, it is necessary not only to build bots that can crawl the site (which you have already done) but also store the information in an architecturally sound way to make data analysis easy later.

Autoincremented id columns, timestamps, and multiple tables: they all come into play here. To figure out how to best store this information, you need to think abstractly. A link is simply something that connects Page A to Page B. It could just as easily connect Page B to Page A, but this would be a separate link. You can uniquely identify a link by saying, "There exists a link on page A, which connects to page B. That is, INSERT INTO links (fromPageId, toPageId) VALUES (A, B); (where A and B are the unique IDs for the two pages)."

A two-table system designed to store pages and links, along with creation dates and unique IDs, can be constructed as follows:

```
CREATE DATABASE wikipedia;
USE wikipedia;

CREATE TABLE wikipedia.pages (
  id INT NOT NULL AUTO_INCREMENT,
  url VARCHAR(255) NOT NULL,
  created TIMESTAMP NOT NULL DEFAULT CURRENT_TIMESTAMP,
  PRIMARY KEY (id)
);
```

```
CREATE TABLE wikipedia.links (
  id INT NOT NULL AUTO_INCREMENT,
  fromPageId INT NULL,
  toPageId INT NULL,
  created TIMESTAMP NOT NULL DEFAULT CURRENT_TIMESTAMP,
  PRIMARY KEY (id)
);
```

Notice that, unlike with previous crawlers that print the title of the page, you're not even storing the title of the page in the pages table. Why is that? Well, recording the title of the page requires that you visit the page to retrieve it. If you want to build an efficient web crawler to fill out these tables, you want to be able to store the page, as well as links to it, even if you haven't necessarily visited the page yet.

Although this doesn't hold true for all sites, the nice thing about Wikipedia links and page titles is that one can be turned into the other through simple manipulation. For example, *http://en.wikipedia.org/wiki/Monty_Python* indicates that the title of the page is "Monty Python."

The following will store all pages on Wikipedia that have a "Bacon number" (the number of links between it and the page for Kevin Bacon, inclusive) of 6 or less:

```
from urllib.request import urlopen
from bs4 import BeautifulSoup
import re
import pymysql
from random import shuffle

conn = pymysql.connect(host='127.0.0.1', unix_socket='/tmp/mysql.sock',
                    user='root', passwd='password', db='mysql',
                        charset='utf8')
cur = conn.cursor()
cur.execute('USE wikipedia')

def insertPageIfNotExists(url):
    cur.execute('SELECT id FROM pages WHERE url = %s LIMIT 1', (url))
    page = cur.fetchone()
    if not page:
        cur.execute('INSERT INTO pages (url) VALUES (%s)', (url))
        conn.commit()
        return cur.lastrowid
    else:
        return page[0]

def loadPages():
    cur.execute('SELECT url FROM pages')
    return [row[0] for row in cur.fetchall()]

def insertLink(fromPageId, toPageId):
    cur.execute(
        'SELECT EXISTS(SELECT 1 FROM links WHERE fromPageId = %s\
```

```
  AND toPageId = %s)'
        ,(int(fromPageId),
        int(toPageId))
    )
    if not cur.fetchone()[0]:
        cur.execute('INSERT INTO links (fromPageId, toPageId) VALUES (%s, %s)',
                    (int(fromPageId), int(toPageId)))
        conn.commit()

def pageHasLinks(pageId):
    cur.execute(
        'SELECT EXISTS(SELECT 1 FROM links WHERE fromPageId = %s)'
        , (int(pageId))
    )
    return cur.fetchone()[0]


def getLinks(pageUrl, recursionLevel, pages):
    if recursionLevel > 4:
        return

    pageId = insertPageIfNotExists(pageUrl)
    html = urlopen(f'http://en.wikipedia.org{pageUrl}')
    bs = BeautifulSoup(html, 'html.parser')
    links = bs.findAll('a', href=re.compile('^(/wiki/)((?!:).)*$'))
    links = [link.attrs['href'] for link in links]

    for link in links:
        linkId = insertPageIfNotExists(link)
        insertLink(pageId, linkId)
        if not pageHasLinks(linkId):
            print(f'Getting {link}')
            pages.append(link)
            getLinks(link, recursionLevel+1, pages)
        else:
            print(f'Already fetched {link}')


getLinks('/wiki/Kevin_Bacon', 0, loadPages())
cur.close()
conn.close()
```

Three functions here use PyMySQL to interface with the database:

insertPageIfNotExists

As its name indicates, this function inserts a new page record if it does not exist already. This, along with the running list of all collected pages stored in pages, ensures that page records are not duplicated. It also serves to look up pageId numbers in order to create new links.

`insertLink`

> This creates a new link record in the database. It will not create a link if that link already exists. Even if two or more identical links *do* exist on the page, for our purposes, they are the same link, represent the same relationship, and should be counted as only one record. This also helps maintain the integrity of the database if the program is run multiple times, even over the same pages.

`loadPages`

> This loads all current pages from the database into a list, so that it can be determined whether a new page should be visited. Pages are also collected during runtime, so if this crawler is run only once, starting with an empty database, in theory `loadPage` should not be needed. In practice, however, problems may arise. The network might go down, or you might want to collect links over several periods of time, and it's important for the crawler to be able to reload itself and not lose any ground.

You should be aware of one potentially problematic subtlety of using `loadPages`, and the `pages` list it generates, to determine whether or not to visit a page: as soon as each page is loaded, all the links on that page are stored as pages, even though they have not been visited yet—just their links have been seen. If the crawler is stopped and restarted, all of these "seen but not visited" pages will never be visited, and links coming from them will not be recorded. This might be fixed by adding a boolean `visited` variable to each page record and setting it to `True` only if that page has been loaded and its own outgoing links recorded.

For our purposes, however, this solution is fine as is. If you can ensure fairly long runtimes (or just a single runtime), and it isn't a necessity to ensure a complete set of links (just a large dataset to experiment with), the addition of the `visited` variable is not necessary.

For the continuation of this problem and the final solution for getting from Kevin Bacon (*https://en.wikipedia.org/wiki/Kevin_Bacon*) to Eric Idle (*https://en.wikipedia.org/wiki/Eric_Idle*), see "Six Degrees of Wikipedia: Conclusion" on page 181 on solving directed graph problems.

Email

Just as web pages are sent over HTTP, email is sent over SMTP (Simple Mail Transfer Protocol). And just as you use a web server client to handle sending out web pages over HTTP, servers use various email clients, such as Sendmail, Postfix, or Mailman, to send and receive email.

Although sending email with Python is relatively easy, it does require that you have access to a server running SMTP. Setting up an SMTP client on your server or local machine is tricky and outside the scope of this book, but many excellent resources can help with this task, particularly if you are running Linux or macOS.

The following code examples assume that you are running an SMTP client locally. (To modify this code for a remote SMTP client, change localhost to your remote server's address.)

Sending an email with Python requires just nine lines of code:

```
import smtplib
from email.mime.text import MIMEText

msg = MIMEText('The body of the email is here')

msg['Subject'] = 'An Email Alert'
msg['From'] = 'ryan@pythonscraping.com'
msg['To'] = 'webmaster@pythonscraping.com'

s = smtplib.SMTP('localhost')
s.send_message(msg)
s.quit()
```

Python contains two important packages for sending email: *smtplib* and *email*.

Python's email module contains useful formatting functions for creating email packets to send. The MIMEText object, used here, creates an empty email formatted for transfer with the low-level MIME (Multipurpose Internet Mail Extensions) protocol, across which the higher-level SMTP connections are made. The MIMEText object, msg, contains to/from email addresses, as well as a body and a header, which Python uses to create a properly formatted email.

The smtplib package contains information for handling the connection to the server. Just like a connection to a MySQL server, this connection must be torn down every time it is created to avoid creating too many connections.

This basic email function can be extended and made more useful by enclosing it in a function:

```
import smtplib
from email.mime.text import MIMEText
from bs4 import BeautifulSoup
from urllib.request import urlopen
import time

def sendMail(subject, body):
    msg = MIMEText(body)
    msg['Subject'] = subject
    msg['From'] ='christmas_alerts@pythonscraping.com'
    msg['To'] = 'ryan@pythonscraping.com'
```

```
        s = smtplib.SMTP('localhost')
        s.send_message(msg)
        s.quit()

    bs = BeautifulSoup(urlopen('https://isitchristmas.com/'), 'html.parser')
    while(bs.find('a', {'id':'answer'}).attrs['title'] == 'NO'):
        print('It is not Christmas yet.')
        time.sleep(3600)
        bs = BeautifulSoup(urlopen('https://isitchristmas.com/'), 'html.parser')

    sendMail('It\'s Christmas!',
            'According to http://itischristmas.com, it is Christmas!')
```

This particular script checks the website *https://isitchristmas.com* (the main feature of which is a giant YES or NO, depending on the day of the year) once an hour. If it sees anything other than a NO, it will send you an email alerting you that it's Christmas.

Although this particular program might not seem much more useful than a calendar hanging on your wall, it can be slightly tweaked to do a variety of extremely useful things. It can email you alerts in response to site outages, test failures, or even the appearance of an out-of-stock product you're waiting for on Amazon—none of which your wall calendar can do.

PART II
Advanced Scraping

You've laid some web scraping groundwork; now comes the fun part. Until this point, your web scrapers have been relatively dumb. They're unable to retrieve information unless it's immediately presented to them in a nice format by the server. They take all information at face value and store it without any analysis. They get tripped up by forms, website interaction, and even JavaScript. In short, they're no good for retrieving information unless that information really wants to be retrieved.

This part of the book will help you analyze raw data to get the story beneath the data—the story that websites often hide beneath layers of JavaScript, login forms, and antiscraping measures. You'll learn how to use web scrapers to test your sites, automate processes, and access the internet on a large scale. By the end of this section, you will have the tools to gather and manipulate nearly any type of data, in any form, across any part of the internet.

Reading Documents

It is tempting to think of the internet primarily as a collection of text-based websites interspersed with newfangled web 2.0 multimedia content that can mostly be ignored for the purposes of web scraping. However, this ignores what the internet most fundamentally is: a content-agnostic vehicle for transmitting files.

Although the internet has been around in some form or another since the late 1960s, HTML didn't debut until 1992. Until then, the internet consisted mostly of email and file transmission; the concept of web pages as we know them today didn't exist. In other words, the internet is not a collection of HTML files. It is a collection of many types of documents, with HTML files often being used as a frame to showcase them. Without being able to read a variety of document types, including text, PDF, images, video, email, and more, we are missing out on a huge part of the available data.

This chapter covers dealing with documents, whether you're downloading them to a local folder or reading them and extracting data. You'll also take a look at dealing with various types of text encoding, which can make it possible to read even foreign-language HTML pages.

Document Encoding

A document's encoding tells applications—whether they are your computer's operating system or your own Python code—how to read it. This encoding can usually be deduced from its file extension, although this file extension is not mandated by its encoding. I could, for example, save *myImage.jpg* as *myImage.txt* with no problems—at least until my text editor tried to open it. Fortunately, this situation is rare, and a document's file extension is usually all you need to know to read it correctly.

On a fundamental level, all documents are encoded in 0s and 1s. On top of that, encoding algorithms define things such as "how many bits per character" or "how many bits represent the color for each pixel" (in the case of image files). On top of that, you might have a layer of compression, or some space-reducing algorithm, as is the case with PNG files.

Although dealing with non-HTML files might seem intimidating at first, rest assured that with the right library, Python will be properly equipped to deal with any format of information you want to throw at it. The only difference between a text file, a video file, and an image file is how their 0s and 1s are interpreted. This chapter covers several commonly encountered types of files: text, CSV, PDFs, and Word documents.

Notice that these are all, fundamentally, files that store text. For information about working with images, I recommend that you read through this chapter to get used to working with and storing different types of files, and then head to Chapter 16 for more information on image processing!

Text

It is somewhat unusual to have files stored as plain text online, but it is popular among bare-bones or old-school sites to have large repositories of text files. For example, the Internet Engineering Task Force (IETF) stores all of its published documents as HTML, PDF, and text files (see *https://www.ietf.org/rfc/rfc1149.txt* as an example). Most browsers will display these text files just fine, and you should be able to scrape them with no problem.

For most basic text documents, such as the practice file located at *http://www.python-scraping.com/pages/warandpeace/chapter1.txt*, you can use the following method:

```
from urllib.request import urlopen
textPage = urlopen('http://www.pythonscraping.com/'\
    'pages/warandpeace/chapter1.txt')
print(textPage.read())
```

Normally, when you retrieve a page using `urlopen`, you turn it into a `Beauti fulSoup` object in order to parse the HTML. In this case, you can read the page directly. Turning it into a BeautifulSoup object, while perfectly possible, would be counterproductive—there's no HTML to parse, so the library would be useless. Once the text file is read in as a string, you merely have to analyze it as you would any other string read into Python. The disadvantage here, of course, is that you don't have the ability to use HTML tags as context clues, pointing you in the direction of the text you actually need, versus the text you don't want. This can present a challenge when you're trying to extract certain information from text files.

Text Encoding and the Global Internet

Most of the time, a file extension is all you need to know how to read a file correctly. Strangely enough though, this rule doesn't apply to the most basic of all documents: the *.txt* file.

Reading in text by using the previously described methods will work just fine 9 times out of 10. However, dealing with text on the internet can be a tricky business. Next, we'll cover the basics of English and foreign-language encoding, from ASCII to Unicode to ISO, and how to deal with them.

A history of text encoding

ASCII was first developed in the 1960s, when bits were expensive and there was no reason to encode anything besides the Latin alphabet and a few punctuation characters. For this reason, only 7 bits were used to encode a total of 128 capital letters, lowercase letters, and punctuation. Even with all that creativity, they were still left with 33 non-printing characters, some of which were used, replaced, and/or became obsolete as technologies changed over the years. Plenty of space for everyone, right?

As any programmer knows, 7 is a strange number. It's not a nice power of 2, but it's temptingly close. Computer scientists in the 1960s fought over whether an extra bit should be added for the convenience of having a nice round number versus the practicality of files requiring less storage space. In the end, 7 bits won. However, in modern computing, each 7-bit sequence is padded with an extra 0 at the beginning,[1] leaving us with the worst of both worlds—14% larger files, and the lack of flexibility of only 128 characters.

In the early 1990s, people realized that more languages than just English existed, and that it would be really nice if computers could display them. A nonprofit named The Unicode Consortium attempted to bring about a universal text encoder by establishing encodings for every character that needs to be used in any text document, in any language. The goal was to include everything from the Latin alphabet this book is written in, to Cyrillic (кириллица), Chinese pictograms (象形), math and logic symbols (Σ, $\geq$), and even emoticons and miscellaneous symbols, such as the biohazard sign (☣) and peace symbol (☮).

The resulting encoder, as you might already know, was dubbed *UTF-8*, which stands for, confusingly, "Universal Character Set—Transformation Format 8 bit." The *8 bit* here refers not to the size of every character but to the smallest size that a character requires to be displayed.

---

1 This "padding" bit will come back to haunt us with the ISO standards a little later.

The actual size of a UTF-8 character is flexible. It can range from 1 byte to 4 bytes, depending on where it is placed in the list of possible characters (more popular characters are encoded with fewer bytes; more obscure ones require more bytes).

How is this flexible encoding achieved? The use of 7 bits with an eventual useless leading 0 looked like a design flaw in ASCII at first but proved to be a huge advantage for UTF-8. Because ASCII was so popular, Unicode decided to take advantage of this leading 0 bit by declaring all bytes starting with a 0 to indicate that only one byte is used in the character, and making the two encoding schemes for ASCII and UTF-8 identical. Therefore, the following characters are valid in both UTF-8 and ASCII:

```
01000001 - A
01000010 - B
01000011 - C
```

And the following characters are valid only in UTF-8 and will be rendered as non-printable if the document is interpreted as an ASCII document:

```
11000011 10000000 - À
11000011 10011111 - ß
11000011 10100111 - ç
```

In addition to UTF-8, other UTF standards exist, such as UTF-16, UTF-24, and UTF-32, although documents encoded in these formats are rarely encountered except in unusual circumstances, which are outside the scope of this book.

While this original "design flaw" of ASCII had a major advantage for UTF-8, the disadvantage has not entirely gone away. The first 8 bits of information in each character can still encode only 128 characters, not a full 256. In a UTF-8 character requiring multiple bytes, additional leading bits are spent, not on character encoding but on check bits used to prevent corruption. Of the 32 (8 x 4) bits in 4-byte characters, only 21 bits are used for character encoding, for a total of 2,097,152 possible characters, of which, 1,114,112 are currently allocated.

The problem with all universal language-encoding standards, of course, is that any document written in a single foreign language may be much larger than it has to be. Although your language might consist only of 100 or so characters, you will need 16 bits for each character rather than just 8 bits, as is the case for the English-specific ASCII. This makes foreign-language text documents in UTF-8 about twice the size of English-language text documents, at least for foreign languages that don't use the Latin character set.

ISO solves this problem by creating specific encodings for each language. Like Unicode, it has the same encodings that ASCII does, but it uses the padding 0 bit at the beginning of every character to allow it to create 128 special characters for all languages that require them. This works best for European languages that also rely heavily on the Latin alphabet (which remain in positions 0–127 in the encoding), but require additional special characters. This allows ISO-8859-1 (designed for the Latin alphabet) to have symbols such as fractions (e.g., ½) or the copyright sign (©).

Other ISO character sets, such as ISO-8859-9 (Turkish), ISO-8859-2 (German, among other languages), and ISO-8859-15 (French, among other languages) can also be found on the internet with some regularity.

Although the popularity of ISO-encoded documents has been declining in recent years, about 9% of websites on the internet are still encoded with some flavor of ISO,[2] making it essential to know about and check for encodings before scraping a site.

Encodings in action

In the previous section, you used the default settings for urlopen to read text documents you might encounter on the internet. This works great for most English text. However, the second you encounter Russian, Arabic, or even a word like "résumé," you might run into problems.

Take the following code, for example:

```
from urllib.request import urlopen
textPage = urlopen('http://www.pythonscraping.com/'\
    'pages/warandpeace/chapter1-ru.txt')
print(textPage.read())
```

This reads in the first chapter of the original *War and Peace* (written in Russian and French) and prints it to the screen. This screen text reads, in part:

```
b"\xd0\xa7\xd0\x90\xd0\xa1\xd0\xa2\xd0\xac \xd0\x9f\xd0\x95\xd0\xa0\xd0\x92\xd0\
x90\xd0\xaf\n\nI\n\n\xe2\x80\x94 Eh bien, mon prince.
```

In addition, visiting this page in most browsers results in gibberish (see Figure 10-1).

---

2 According to W3Techs (*https://w3techs.com/technologies/history_overview/character_encoding*), which uses web crawlers to gather these sorts of statistics.

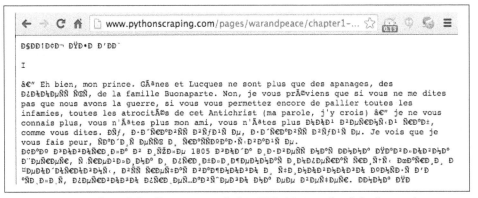

Figure 10-1. French and Cyrillic text encoded in ISO-8859-1, the default text document encoding in many browsers

Even for native Russian speakers, that might be a bit difficult to make sense of. The problem is that Python is attempting to read the document as an ASCII document, whereas the browser is attempting to read it as an ISO-8859-1 encoded document. Neither one, of course, realizes it's a UTF-8 document.

You can explicitly define the string to be UTF-8, which correctly formats the output into Cyrillic characters:

```
from urllib.request import urlopen

textPage = urlopen('http://www.pythonscraping.com/'\
    'pages/warandpeace/chapter1-ru.txt')
print(str(textPage.read(), 'utf-8'))
```

Using this concept with BeautifulSoup looks like this:

```
html = urlopen('http://en.wikipedia.org/wiki/Python_(programming_language)')
bs = BeautifulSoup(html, 'html.parser')
content = bs.find('div', {'id':'mw-content-text'}).get_text()
content = bytes(content, 'UTF-8')
content = content.decode('UTF-8')
```

Python encodes all characters into UTF-8 by default. You might be tempted to leave this alone and use UTF-8 encoding for every web scraper you write. After all, UTF-8 will also handle ASCII characters as well as foreign languages smoothly. However, it's important to remember the 9% of websites out there that use some version of ISO encoding as well, so you can never avoid this problem entirely.

Unfortunately, in the case of text documents, it's impossible to concretely determine what encoding a document has. Some libraries can examine the document and make a best guess (using a little logic to realize that "Ñ€°ÑÑ°Ð°Ð.Ñ" is probably not a word), but many times they're wrong.

Fortunately, in the case of HTML pages, the encoding is usually contained in a tag found in the <head> section of the site. Most sites, particularly English-language sites, have this tag:

```
<meta charset="utf-8" />
```

Whereas the ECMA International's website (*http://www.ecma-international.org*) has this tag:[3]

```
<META HTTP-EQUIV="Content-Type" CONTENT="text/html; charset=iso-8859-1">
```

If you plan on doing a lot of web scraping, particularly of international sites, it might be wise to look for this meta tag and use the encoding it recommends when reading the contents of the page.

CSV

When web scraping, you are likely to encounter either a CSV file or a coworker who likes data formatted in this way. Fortunately, Python has a fantastic library (*https://docs.python.org/3.4/library/csv.html*) for both reading and writing CSV files. Although this library is capable of handling many variations of CSV, this section focuses primarily on the standard format. If you have a special case you need to handle, consult the documentation!

Reading CSV Files

Python's *csv* library is geared primarily toward working with local files, on the assumption that the CSV data you need is stored on your machine. Unfortunately, this isn't always the case, especially when you're web scraping. There are several ways to work around this:

- Download the file locally by hand and point Python at the local file location.
- Write a Python script to download the file, read it, and (optionally) delete it after retrieval.
- Retrieve the file as a string from the web, and wrap the string in a StringIO object so that it behaves like a file.

Although the first two options are workable, taking up hard drive space with files when you could easily keep them in memory is bad practice. It's much better to read the file in as a string and wrap it in an object that allows Python to treat it as a file, without ever saving the file. The following script retrieves a CSV file from the internet

---

3 ECMA was one of the original contributors to the ISO standard, so it's no surprise its website is encoded with a flavor of ISO.

(in this case, a list of Monty Python albums at *http://pythonscraping.com/files/Monty-PythonAlbums.csv*) and prints it, row by row, to the terminal:

```
from urllib.request import urlopen
from io import StringIO
import csv

data = urlopen('http://pythonscraping.com/files/MontyPythonAlbums.csv')
            .read().decode('ascii', 'ignore')
dataFile = StringIO(data)
csvReader = csv.reader(dataFile)

for row in csvReader:
    print(row)
```

The output looks like this:

```
['Name', 'Year']
["Monty Python's Flying Circus", '1970']
['Another Monty Python Record', '1971']
["Monty Python's Previous Record", '1972']
...
```

As you can see from the code sample, the reader object returned by `csv.reader` is iterable and composed of Python list objects. Because of this, each row in the `csvReader` object is accessible in the following way:

```
for row in csvReader:
    print('The album "'+row[0]+'" was released in '+str(row[1]))
```

Here is the output:

```
The album "Name" was released in Year
The album "Monty Python's Flying Circus" was released in 1970
The album "Another Monty Python Record" was released in 1971
The album "Monty Python's Previous Record" was released in 1972
...
```

Notice the first line: `The album "Name" was released in Year`. Although this might be an easy-to-ignore result when writing example code, you don't want this getting into your data in the real world. A lesser programmer might simply skip the first row in the `csvReader` object, or write in a special case to handle it. Fortunately, an alternative to the `csv.reader` function takes care of all of this for you automatically. Enter `DictReader`:

```
from urllib.request import urlopen
from io import StringIO
import csv

data = urlopen('http://pythonscraping.com/files/MontyPythonAlbums.csv')
            .read().decode('ascii', 'ignore')
dataFile = StringIO(data)
dictReader = csv.DictReader(dataFile)
```

```
print(dictReader.fieldnames)

for row in dictReader:
    print(row)
```

csv.DictReader returns the values of each row in the CSV file as dictionary objects rather than list objects, with field names stored in the variable dictReader.field names and as keys in each dictionary object:

```
['Name', 'Year']
{'Name': 'Monty Python's Flying Circus', 'Year': '1970'}
{'Name': 'Another Monty Python Record', 'Year': '1971'}
{'Name': 'Monty Python's Previous Record', 'Year': '1972'}
```

The downside, of course, is that it takes slightly longer to create, process, and print these DictReader objects as opposed to csvReader, but the convenience and usability are often worth the additional overhead. Also keep in mind that, when it comes to web scraping, the overhead required for requesting and retrieving website data from an external server will almost always be the unavoidable limiting factor in any program you write, so worrying about which technique might shave microseconds off your total runtime is often a moot point!

PDF

As a Linux user, I know the pain of being sent a *.docx* file that my non-Microsoft software mangles, and struggling trying to find the codecs to interpret some new Apple media format. In some ways, Adobe was revolutionary in creating its Portable Document Format in 1993. PDFs allowed users on different platforms to view image and text documents in exactly the same way, regardless of the platform they were viewing it on.

Although storing PDFs on the web is somewhat passé (why store content in a static, slow-loading format when you could write it up as HTML?), PDFs remain ubiquitous, particularly when dealing with official forms and filings.

In 2009, a Briton named Nick Innes made the news when he requested public student test result information from the Buckinghamshire City Council, which was available under the United Kingdom's version of the Freedom of Information Act. After some repeated requests and denials, he finally received the information he was looking for—in the form of 184 PDF documents.

Although Innes persisted and eventually received a more properly formatted database, had he been an expert web scraper, he likely could have saved himself a lot of time in the courts and used the PDF documents directly, with one of Python's many PDF-parsing modules.

Unfortunately, because the PDF is a relatively simple and open source document format, the space is crowded when it comes to PDF-parsing libraries. These projects are commonly built, abandoned, revived, and built again as the years go by. The most popular, full-featured, and easy-to-use library is currently pypdf (*https://pypi.org/project/pypdf/*).

Pypdf is a free, open source library that allows users to extract text and images from PDFs. It will also allow you to perform operations on PDF files and generate them directly from Python if you want to make them rather than just read them.

You can install as usual using pip:

```
$ pip install pypdf
```

The documentation is located at *https://pypdf.readthedocs.io/en/latest/index.html*.

Here is a basic implementation that allows you to read arbitrary PDFs to a string, given a local file object:

```
from urllib.request import urlretrieve
from pypdf import PdfReader

urlretrieve(
    'http://pythonscraping.com/pages/warandpeace/chapter1.pdf',
    'chapter1.pdf'
)
reader = PdfReader('chapter1.pdf')

for page in reader.pages:
    print(page.extract_text())
```

This gives the familiar plain-text output:

```
CHAPTER I

"Well, Prince, so Genoa and Lucca are now just family estates of
the Buonapartes. But I warn you, if you don't tell me that this
means war, if you still try to defend the infamies and horrors
perpetrated by that Antichrist- I really believe he is Antichrist- I will
```

Note that the PDF file argument must be an actual file object. You must download the file first locally before you can pass it to the `Pdfreader` class. However, if you're processing large numbers of PDF files and don't want to keep the original files around, you can always overwrite the previous file by sending the same filename to `urlretrieve` after you've extracted the text.

The output from pypdf might not be perfect, especially for PDFs with images, oddly formatted text, or text arranged in tables or charts. However, for most text-only PDFs, the output should be no different than if the PDF were a text file.

Microsoft Word and .docx

At the risk of offending my friends at Microsoft: I do not like Microsoft Word. Not because it's necessarily a bad piece of software, but because of the way its users misuse it. It has a particular talent for turning what should be simple text documents or PDFs into large, slow, difficult-to-open beasts that often lose all formatting from machine to machine, and are, for whatever reason, editable when the content is often meant to be static.

Word files are designed for content creation, not content sharing. Nevertheless, they are ubiquitous on certain sites, containing important documents, information, and even charts and multimedia; in short, everything that can and should be created with HTML.

Before about 2008, Microsoft Office products used the proprietary *.doc* file format. This binary-file format was difficult to read and poorly supported by other word processors. In an effort to get with the times and adopt a standard that was used by many other pieces of software, Microsoft decided to use the Open Office XML-based standard, which made the files compatible with open source and other software.

Unfortunately, Python's support for this file format, used by Google Docs, Open Office, and Microsoft Office, still isn't great. There is the python-docx library (*http://python-docx.readthedocs.org/en/latest/*), but this only gives users the ability to create documents and read only basic file data such as the size and title of the file, not the actual contents. To read the contents of a Microsoft Office file, you'll need to roll your own solution.

The first step is to read the XML from the file:

```
from zipfile import ZipFile
from urllib.request import urlopen
from io import BytesIO

wordFile = urlopen('http://pythonscraping.com/pages/AWordDocument.docx').read()
wordFile = BytesIO(wordFile)
document = ZipFile(wordFile)
xml_content = document.read('word/document.xml')
print(xml_content.decode('utf-8'))
```

This reads a remote Word document as a binary file object (`BytesIO` is analogous to `StringIO`, used earlier in this chapter), unzips it using Python's core zipfile library (all *.docx* files are zipped to save space), and then reads the unzipped file, which is XML.

The Word document at *http://pythonscraping.com/pages/AWordDocument.docx* is shown in Figure 10-2.

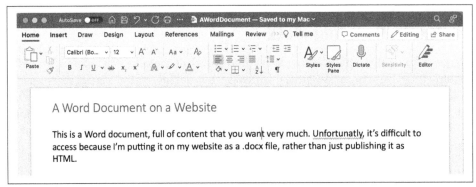

Figure 10-2. This is a Word document that's full of content you might want very much, but it's difficult to access because I'm putting it on my website as a .docx file instead of publishing it as HTML. The word "unfortunatly" is misspelled.

The output of the Python script reading my simple Word document is the following:

```
<w:document xmlns:wpc="http://schemas.microsoft.com/office/word/2010/
wordprocessingCanvas" xmlns:cx="http://schemas.microsoft.com/office/d
rawing/2014/chartex" xmlns:cx1="http://schemas.microsoft.com/office/d
rawing/2015/9/8/chartex" xmlns:cx2="http://schemas.microsoft.com/offi
ce/drawing/2015/10/21/chartex" xmlns:cx3="http://schemas.microsoft.co
m/office/drawing/2016/5/9/chartex" xmlns:cx4="http://schemas.microsof

...More schema data here...

<w:body><w:p w14:paraId="19A18025" w14:textId="54C8E458" w:rsidR="007
45992" w:rsidRDefault="00BF6C9C" w:rsidP="00BF6C9C"><w:pPr><w:pStyle
w:val="Heading1"/></w:pPr><w:r><w:t>A Word Document on a Website</w:t
></w:r></w:p><w:p w14:paraId="501E7A3A" w14:textId="77777777" w:rsidR
="00BF6C9C" w:rsidRDefault="00BF6C9C" w:rsidP="00BF6C9C"/><w:p w14:pa
raId="13929BE7" w14:textId="20FEDCDB" w:rsidR="00BF6C9C" w:rsidRPr="0
0BF6C9C" w:rsidRDefault="00BF6C9C" w:rsidP="00BF6C9C"><w:r><w:t xml:s
pace="preserve">This is a Word document, full of content that you wan
t very much. </w:t></w:r><w:proofErr w:type="spellStart"/><w:r><w:t>U
nfortuna</w:t></w:r><w:r w:rsidR="00BC14C7"><w:t>t</w:t></w:r><w:r><w
:t>ly</w:t></w:r><w:proofErr w:type="spellEnd"/><w:r><w:t xml:space="
preserve">, it's difficult to access because I'm putting it on my web
site as a .docx file, rather than just publishing it as HTML. </w:t><
/w:r></w:p><w:sectPr w:rsidR="00BF6C9C" w:rsidRPr="00BF6C9C"><w:pgSz
w:w="12240" w:h="15840"/><w:pgMar w:top="1440" w:right="1440" w:botto
m="1440" w:left="1440" w:header="720" w:footer="720" w:gutter="0"/><w
:cols w:space="720"/><w:docGrid w:linePitch="360"/></w:sectPr></w:bod
y></w:document>
```

There's clearly a lot of metadata here, but the actual text content you want is buried. Fortunately, all of the text in the document, including the title at the top, is contained in w:t tags, which makes it easy to grab:

```
from zipfile import ZipFile
from urllib.request import urlopen
from io import BytesIO
from bs4 import BeautifulSoup

wordFile = urlopen('http://pythonscraping.com/pages/AWordDocument.docx').read()
wordFile = BytesIO(wordFile)
document = ZipFile(wordFile)
xml_content = document.read('word/document.xml')

wordObj = BeautifulSoup(xml_content.decode('utf-8'), 'xml')
textStrings = wordObj.find_all('w:t')

for textElem in textStrings:
    print(textElem.text)
```

Note that instead of the *html.parser* parser that you normally use with `Beauti` `fulSoup`, you're passing it the *xml* parser. This is because colons are nonstandard in HTML tag names like `w:t`, and *html.parser* does not recognize them.

The output isn't perfect but it's getting there, and printing each `w:t` tag on a new line makes it easy to see how Word is splitting up the text:

```
A Word Document on a Website
This is a Word document, full of content that you want very much.
Unfortuna
t
ly
, it's difficult to access because I'm putting it on my website as
a .docx file, rather than just publishing it as HTML.
```

Notice that the word "unfortunatly" is split up across multiple lines. In the original XML, it is surrounded with the tag `<w:proofErr w:type="spellStart"/>`. This is how Word highlights the misspelling with a red squiggly underline.

The title of the document is preceded by the style descriptor tag `<w:pstyle` `w:val="Title">`. Although this doesn't make it extremely easy for us to identify titles (or other styled text) as such, using BeautifulSoup's navigation features can be useful:

```
textStrings = wordObj.find_all('w:t')

for textElem in textStrings:
    style = textElem.parent.parent.find('w:pStyle')
    if style is not None and style['w:val'] == 'Title':
        print('Title is: {}'.format(textElem.text))
    else:
        print(textElem.text)
```

This function easily can be expanded to print tags around a variety of text styles or label them in some other way.

Working with Dirty Data

So far in this book, I've ignored the problem of badly formatted data by using generally well-formatted data sources, dropping data entirely if it deviated from what was expected. But, in web scraping, you often can't be too picky about where you get your data, or what it looks like.

Because of errant punctuation, inconsistent capitalization, line breaks, and misspellings, dirty data can be a big problem on the web. This chapter covers a few tools and techniques to help you prevent the problem at the source by changing the way you write code and cleaning the data after it's in the database.

This is the chapter where web scraping intersects with its close relative, data science. While the job title of "data scientist" might conjure mental images of cutting-edge programming techniques and advanced mathematics, the truth is that a lot of it is grunt work. Someone has to clean and normalize these millions of records before they can be used to build a machine learning model, and that person is the data scientist.

Extract, Transform, Load

Extract, Transform, Load (ETL) is a concept used frequently in programming, particularly in industry. Many companies concern themselves with the business of moving data from one place to another place, transforming the data as they go. Data is extracted from a source, transformed through some business process, and loaded into another source.

Most of this book is involved with the "E" of ETL. That is, it focuses on extracting data from sources around the web. Chapter 9, "Storing Data" covers the "L"—loading that data into databases.

This chapter, along with Chapter 12, "Reading and Writing Natural Languages", focuses on the "T," or the transformation of data.

Mentally breaking your data applications into the three stages, Extract, Transform, and Load, can help you organize your processes and tools to create clean software structures.

Cleaning Text

Python is a programming language that lends itself very well to text processing. It's easy to write clean, functional, modular code to do even complex text processing projects. With the following code, we can scrape text from the Wikipedia article on Python at *http://en.wikipedia.org/wiki/Python_(programming_language)*:

```
from urllib.request import urlopen
from bs4 import BeautifulSoup

url = 'http://en.wikipedia.org/wiki/Python_(programming_language)'
html = urlopen(url)
bs = BeautifulSoup(html, 'html.parser')
content = bs.find('div', {'id':'mw-content-text'}).find_all('p')
content = [p.get_text() for p in content]
```

This content begins:

```
Python is a high-level, general-purpose programming language. Its
design philosophy emphasizes code readability with the use of
significant indentation via the off-side rule.[33]
```

We will perform several actions on this text:

- Remove citations, of the form "[123]"
- Remove newline characters
- Split the text into sentences
- Remove any parenthesized text containing an aside in the middle of a sentence
- Remove descriptions of illustrations not included in the text
- Make text lowercase
- Remove all punctuation

It's important to note that these functions must be applied in a particular order. For instance, removing punctuation (including square brackets) would make it difficult to identify and remove citations later on. Removing punctuation and making all text lowercase would also make it impossible to split the text into sentences.

The functions for removing newline characters and making the text lowercase are fairly straightforward:

```
def replace_newlines(text):
    return text.replace('\n', ' ')

def make_lowercase(text):
    return text.lower()
```

Here the newlines are replaced with a space character (" ") rather than removed altogether to avoid text like this:

```
It uses dynamic name resolution (late binding), which binds method
and variable names during program execution.
Its design offers some support for functional programming
in the Lisp tradition.
```

being turned into text like this:

```
It uses dynamic name resolution (late binding), which binds method
and variable names during program execution. Its design offers some
support for functional programming in the Lisp tradition.
```

Inserting the space ensures that all sentences still get a space between them.

With this in mind, we can write the function for splitting sentences:

```
def split_sentences(text):
    return [s.strip() for s in text.split('. ')]
```

Rather than splitting simply on the period, we split on the period and a space. This prevents decimals, for instance in the ubiquitous "Python 2.5," or code examples like:

```
if (c = 1) { ...}
```

from being split erroneously into sentences. In addition, we want to make sure that any double-spaced or otherwise odd sentences are cleaned by stripping each leading or trailing whitespace using the strip function before returning.

However, split_sentences can't be called right away. Many sentences contain citations immediately after them:

```
capable of exception handling and interfacing with the Amoeba
operating system.[13] Its implementation began in December 1989.[44]
```

The function for removing citations can be written like this:

```
import re

CITATION_REGEX = re.compile('\[[0-9]*\]')
def strip_citations(text):
    return re.sub(CITATION_REGEX, '', text)
```

The variable name `CITATION_REGEX` is written in uppercase, indicating that it's a constant, and pre-compiled outside of the function itself. The function could also be written as:

```
def strip_citations(text):
    return re.sub(r'\[[0-9]*\]', '', text)
```

However, this forces Python to recompile this regular expression every time the function is run (which could be thousands or millions of times, depending on the project), rather than having it pre-compiled and ready to go. While the speed of the program is not necessarily a significant bottleneck in web scraping, pre-compiling regular expressions outside of functions is easy to do and allows you to document the code through an appropriate variable name for the regular expression.

Removing parenthesized text, such as:

```
all versions of Python (including 2.7[56]) had security issues
```

and:

```
dynamic name resolution (late binding), which binds method
```

is a similar pattern to removing the citations. A good first approach might be:

```
PARENS_REGEX = re.compile('\(.*\)')
def remove_parentheses(text):
    return re.sub(PARENS_REGEX, '', text)
```

Indeed, this does remove parenthesized text in the examples above, but it also removes anything in parentheses from sections like:

```
This has the advantage of avoiding a classic C error of mistaking
an assignment operator = for an equality operator == in conditions:
if (c = 1) { ...} is syntactically valid
```

In addition, it presents a danger if there are unmatched parentheses in the text. An opening parenthesis may cause large sections of text to be removed the next time any sort of closing parenthesis is found.

To solve this, we can examine the types of characters generally seen in parenthesized text, look only for them, and limit the length of that parenthesized text:

```
PARENS_REGEX = re.compile('\([a-z A-Z \+\.,\-]{0,100}\)')
def remove_parentheses(text):
    return re.sub(PARENS_REGEX, '', text)
```

Occasionally, descriptions of illustrations not extracted in the text might be present. For example:

```
Hello world program:
```

which precedes a block of code not extracted in text.

These descriptions are generally short, start with a newline, contain only letters, and end with a colon. We can remove them with a regular expression:

```
DESCRIPTION_REGEX = re.compile('\n[a-z A-Z]*:')
def remove_descriptions(text):
    return re.sub(DESCRIPTION_REGEX, '', text)
```

At this point, we can remove the punctuation. Because so many of the previous steps depend on punctuation to be present in order to identify what text to keep and what to remove, stripping the punctuation is generally one of the last steps of any text cleaning task.

Python's string module (*https://docs.python.org/3/library/string.html*) contains many handy sets of characters, one of which is `string.punctuation`. This is a set of all the ASCII punctuation:

```
>>> import string
>>> string.punctuation
'!"#$%&\'()*+,-./:;<=>?@[\\]^_`{|}~'
```

We can take this string containing all ASCII punctuation and turn it into a regular expression using `re.escape` (which escapes any reserved regular expression symbols) and joining everything with a | character:

```
puncts = [re.escape(c) for c in string.punctuation]
PUNCTUATION_REGEX = re.compile('|'.join(puncts))

def remove_punctuation(text):
    return re.sub(PUNCTUATION_REGEX, '', text)
```

It's common, with all this string manipulation, for unicode characters to become misrepresented in the string. Especially common is the unicode "nonbreaking space" which is represented by a   in HTML and can be found frequently in text on the web. This can be seen in our Wikipedia text printed out as \xa0:

```
python\xa020 was released...
```

Regardless of which strange characters you encounter, you can fix them with Python's `unicodedata` package. Normalizing unicode characters will be the final step in cleaning the text:

```
def normalize(text):
    return unicodedata.normalize('NFKD', text)
```

At this point, you have a set of short, well-organized functions that perform a variety of text cleaning operations. Because we might want to add, remove, or change the order that the functions are called in, we can add these functions to a list and call them in a general way on our text:

```
text_operations = [
    strip_citations,
    remove_parentheses,
```

```
        remove_descriptions,
        replace_newlines,
        split_sentences,
        make_lowercase,
        remove_punctuation,
        normalize
    ]

    cleaned = content
    for op in text_operations:
        if type(cleaned) == list:
            cleaned = [op(c) for c in cleaned]
        else:
            cleaned = op(cleaned)

    print(cleaned)
```

Although Python is not generally thought of as a functional language like JavaScript or—as a more extreme example—Haskell, it's useful to remember that functions can be passed around as variables in situations like this!

Working with Normalized Text

Once you've cleaned the text, what do you do with it? One common technique is to break it up into smaller pieces of text that can be more easily quantified and analyzed. Computational linguists call these *n-grams*, where n represents the number of words in each piece of text. In this example, we'll be working specifically with 2-grams, or 2 word pieces of text.

N-grams typically do not span sentences. So we can use the text obtained in the previous section, split into sentences, and create 2-grams with each sentence in the list.

A Python function for breaking text into n-grams can be written as:

```
def getNgrams(text, n):
    text = text.split(' ')
    return [text[i:i+n] for i in range(len(text)-n+1)]

getNgrams('web scraping with python', 2)
```

The output of this function on the text "web scraping with python" is:

```
[['web', 'scraping'], ['scraping', 'with'], ['with', 'python']]
```

One problem with this function is that it returns many duplicate 2-grams. Every 2-gram it encounters gets added to the list, with no record of its frequency. Not only is it interesting to record the frequency of these 2-grams, rather than just their existence, but it can be useful in charting the effects of changes to the cleaning and data normalization algorithms. If data is normalized successfully, the total number of unique n-grams will be reduced, while the total count of n-grams found (i.e., the number of unique or nonunique items identified as n-grams) will not be reduced. In other words, there will be fewer "buckets" for the same number of n-grams.

You can do this by modifying the code that collects the n-grams to add them to a Counter object, rather than a list. Here, the cleaned variable is our list of cleaned sentences obtained in the previous section:

```
from collections import Counter

def getNgrams(text, n):
    text = text.split(' ')
    return [' '.join(text[i:i+n]) for i in range(len(text)-n+1)]

def countNGramsFromSentences(sentences, n):
    counts = Counter()
    for sentence in sentences:
        counts.update(getNgrams(sentence, n))
    return counts
```

There are many other ways to create counts of n-grams, such as adding them to a dictionary object in which the value of the list points at a count for the number of times it was seen. That has a disadvantage in that it requires a bit more management and makes sorting tricky.

However, using a Counter object also has a disadvantage: it cannot store lists, because lists are unhashable. Converting these to tuples (which are hashable) would work well and make sense in this context, as would joining the lists to strings. In this case, I've chosen to convert them to strings by using a ' '.join(text[i:i+n]) inside the list comprehension for each n-gram.

We can call the countNGramsFromSentences function with our cleaned text from the previous section and use the most_common function to get a list of 2-grams sorted by the most common ones first:

```
counts = countNGramsFromSentences(cleaned, 2)
print(counts.most_common())
```

Here are the results:

```
[('in the', 19), ('of the', 19), ('such as', 18), ('as a', 14),
('in python', 12), ('python is', 9), ('of python', 9),
('the python', 9)...
```

As of this writing, there are 2,814 unique 2-grams, with the most popular ones containing word combinations that are very common in any English text, such as "such as." Depending on your project, you may want to remove n-grams like this that do not have much relevance to the page's actual subject matter. Doing this is a topic for Chapter 12.

Beyond this, it's usually good to stop and consider how much computing power you want to expend normalizing data. There are a number of situations in which different spellings of words are equivalent, but to resolve this equivalency, you need to run a check on every single word to see whether it matches any of your preprogrammed equivalencies.

For example, "Python 1st" and "Python first" both appear in the list of 2-grams. However, to make a blanket rule that says, "All first, second, third, etc., will be resolved to 1st, 2nd, 3rd, etc. (or vice versa)" would result in an additional 10 or so checks per word.

Similarly, the inconsistent use of hyphens ("co-ordinated" versus "coordinated"), misspellings, and other natural language incongruities will affect the groupings of n-grams and might muddy the results of the output if the incongruities are common enough.

One solution, in the case of hyphenated words, might be to remove hyphens entirely and treat the word as a single string, which would require only a single operation. However, this would also mean that hyphenated phrases (an all-too-common occurrence) will be treated as a single word. Going the other route and treating hyphens as spaces might be a better option. Just be prepared for the occasional "co ordinated" and "ordinated attack" to slip in!

Cleaning Data with Pandas

This section is not about the endearing bears native to China, but the Python data analysis package: *pandas*. If you've done any work with data science and machine learning, you've likely encountered it before, as it is ubiquitous in the field.

Pandas was created as a solo project for work in 2008 by programmer Wes McKinney. In 2009, he made the project public and it quickly took off. The package filled a particular niche in data wrangling. It functioned much like a spreadsheet in some ways, with pretty printing and easy reshaping pivot functions. It also harnessed the power and flexibility of the underlying Python code and data science libraries that it was built on.

Some might recommend the Anaconda package management system (*https://www.anaconda.com*) when installing data science libraries like numpy, pandas, and scikit-learn. Although there is excellent support for these packages with Anaconda, pandas is also straightforward to install with pip:

```
pip install pandas
```

The package is, by convention, imported as `pd` rather than the full name `pandas`:

```
import pandas as pd
```

Don't Import Individual Methods and Classes from Pandas

The pandas ecosystem is large, complex, and often overlaps the namespace of built-in Python functions and packages. For this reason, pandas functions should almost always be referenced starting from pd rather than importing them directly, such as:

```
from pandas import array
from pandas.DataFrame import min
```

In these cases, the above imports might cause confusion with the built-in Python array module and min function.

One accepted exception may be for the DataFrame class, imported as:

```
from pandas import DataFrame
```

In this case, DataFrame is not found in the Python standard library and is easily-recognized as a pandas class. However, this is the one exception you are likely to see, and many still prefer to reference the DataFrame class as pd.DataFrame. Because the library is so-often referenced in code, this is one reason why the convention is to import pandas as pd rather than the full name!

The object you will be working with most often in the pandas library is the DataFrame. These are similar to spreadsheets or tables, and can be constructed in a variety of ways. For example:

```
df = pd.DataFrame([['a', 1], ['b', 2], ['c', 3]])
df.head()
```

The head method produces a pretty-printed DataFrame of the data and its columns and headers, as shown in Figure 11-1.

```
Pandas

[1]: import pandas as pd

[2]: df = pd.DataFrame([['a', 1], ['b', 2], ['c', 3]])
     df.head()

[2]:    0  1

     0  a  1

     1  b  2

     2  c  3
```

Figure 11-1. A simple pandas DataFrame

DataFrames are required to always have an index and column names. If those are not provided, as in this case, where only a simple matrix of data is supplied, they will be automatically generated. The DataFrame's index (0, 1, 2) can be seen in bold to the left, and the column names (0, 1) are at the top in bold.

Rather than working with raw Python lists and dictionaries, DataFrames provide an enormous variety convenient helper functions to sort, clean, manipulate, arrange, and display your data. If you are working with larger data sets, they also provide a speed and memory advantage over lists and dictionaries.

Cleaning

In the following examples, you'll use data scraped from Wikipedia's List of Countries with McDonald's Restaurants (*https://en.wikipedia.org/wiki/List_of_coun tries_with_McDonald%27s_restaurants*). We can use the pd.read_csv function to read data directly from a CSV file to a dataframe:

```
df = pd.read_csv('countries.csv')
df.head(10)
```

Optionally, an integer can be passed to the head method to print out a number of rows other than the default of 5. This gives a nice view of the CSV data scraped from earlier, as shown in Figure 11-2.

```
[3]: df = pd.read_csv('countries.csv')
     df.head(10)
```

#	Country/territory	Date of first store	First outlet location	Max. no. ofoperatingoutlets	Source and date of source	People per outlet	Notes
1	United States	May 15, 1940Franchise: April 15, 1955	San Bernardino, CaliforniaDes Plaines, Illinoi...	13,515[10][failed verification][11]	(source: McDonald's United States March 29, 2023)	25,132	See McDonald's USA
2	Canada (details)	June 3, 1967	Richmond, British Columbia	1,400[10]	(source: McDonald's Canada 5 February 2022)	27,551	This is the first McDonald's outside of the Un...
3	Puerto Rico(territory of United States)	December 6, 1967	San Juan	108	(source: McDonald's 2013)	29,583	First McDonald's in Latin America and in the C...
4	United States Virgin Islands(territory of Unit	September 5, 1970	St. Croix	6	(source: McDonald's 2013)	17,878	NaN

Figure 11-2. Displaying a list of countries with lds

The column names here are somewhat wordy and not well-formatted. We can rename them using the `rename` method:

```
df.rename(columns={
    '#': 'Order',
    'Country/territory': 'Country',
    'Date of first store': 'Date',
    'First outlet location': 'Location',
    'Max. no. ofoperatingoutlets': 'Outlets'
}, inplace=True)
```

Here, we pass in a dictionary to the `columns` keyword argument, where the keys are the original column names and the value is the new column name. The boolean argument `inplace` means that the columns are renamed in-place in the original DataFrame, rather than a new DataFrame being returned.

Next, we can isolate only the columns that we want to work with by passing in a list of those column names to a sort of slicing syntax using [ ] brackets:

```
df = df[['Order', 'Country', 'Date', 'Location', 'Outlets']]
```

Now that we have the relabeled DataFrame columns we want, we can look at the data. There are a few things we will want to fix up. First, the dates in the "Date of first store" or "Date" column are usually well-formatted, but they also contain extra text or even other dates. As a simple strategy, we may decide to keep the first thing that matches the "date" format and discard the rest.

Functions can be applied to an entire column in a DataFrame by first selecting that column using the same "slicing" syntax used above. A single selected column a pandas `Series` instance. The `Series` class has an `apply` method which applies a single function to each value in the Series:

```
import re

date_regex = re.compile('[A-Z][a-z]+ [0-9]{1,2}, [0-9]{4}')
df['Date'] = df['Date'].apply(lambda d: date_regex.findall(d)[0])
```

Here, I am using a lambda operator to apply a function that gets all `date_regex` matches and returns the first one as the date.

After cleaning, these dates can be converted to actual pandas datetime values using the `to_datetime` function:

```
df['Date'] = pd.to_datetime(df['Date'])
```

Often, there is a delicate balance between the fast and efficient production of "clean" data, and the preservation of completely accurate and nuanced data. For instance, our date cleaning reduced the following text in the United Kingdom row: *"England: November 13, 1974[21] Wales: December 3, 1984 Scotland: November 23, 1987[22] Northern Ireland: October 12, 1991"* into the single date: *"1974-11-13"*.

Technically, this is correct. If the country of the United Kingdom as a whole is considered, then 1974-11-13 is the first date a McDonald's appeared in it. However, it is simply happenstance that the dates were written in the cell in chronological order, and that we decided to take the first one, and also that the earliest date was the right one to choose. One might imagine many other circumstances where we might not be so lucky.

In some cases, you may do a survey of the data and decide that your chosen cleaning method is good enough. Perhaps it is correct in most of the cases you look at. Perhaps it's incorrect in one direction half the time, incorrect in the other direction the other half of the time, and things balance out for your purposes over large datasets. Or you may decide you need another method to clean or capture the data more accurately.

The "Outlets" column of the dataset presents similar challenges. This column contains text such as "*13,515[10][failed verification][11]*" and "*(excl. seasonal restaurants) 43 (including seasonal and mobile restaurants)*" which are not the clean integers that we might like for further analysis. Again, we can use a simple approach to get the first integer available in the dataset:

```
int_regex = re.compile('[0-9,]+')

def str_to_int(s):
    s = int_regex.findall(s)[0]
    s = s.replace(',','')
    return int(s)

df['Outlets'] = df['Outlets'].apply(str_to_int)
```

Although this could also be written as a lambda function, you may consider breaking the logic out into a separate function if several steps are required. This also has the advantage of allowing you to easily print out any exceptions found during exploratory data processing, for further consideration:

```
def str_to_int(s):
    try:
        s = int_regex.findall(s)[0]
        s = s.replace(',','')
    except:
        print(f'Whoops: {s}')
    return int(s)
```

Finally, the DataFrame is cleaned and ready for further analysis, as shown in Figure 11-3.

```
[96]:  df.head(10)
```

[96]:

	Order	Country	Date	Location	Outlets
0	1	United States	1940-05-15	San Bernardino, CaliforniaDes Plaines, Illinoi...	13515
1	2	Canada (details)	1967-06-03	Richmond, British Columbia	1400
2	3	Puerto Rico(territory of United States)	1967-12-06	San Juan	108
3	4	United States Virgin Islands(territory of Unit...	1970-09-05	St. Croix	6
4	5	Costa Rica	1970-12-08	San José, 4th street, between 1st and Central ...	70
5	6	Australia	1971-05-30	Yagoona, New South Wales[12]	1000
6	7	Guam(territory of United States)	1971-06-10	Dededo	6
7	8	Japan	1971-07-21	Tokyo	2900
8	9	Netherlands	1971-08-21	Zaandam	263

Figure 11-3. DataFrame with clean column headers, formatted dates, and integer data

Indexing, Sorting, and Filtering

Remember from earlier that all DataFrames have an index, whether you explicitly provide one or not. The McDonald's data itself has a convenient index: the "Order" column, which signifies the chronological order in which the countries received their first McDonald's restaurant. We can set the index using the set_index method:

```
df.set_index(['Order'], inplace=True)
df.head()
```

This discards the old index and moves the "Order" column into the index. Again, the inplace keyword argument means that this is done in-place on the original Data-Frame, rather than have a copy of the DataFrame returned.

The sort_values method can be used to sort data by one or many columns. The inplace keyword can be used in this method as well. However, because sorting is usually done for exploratory analysis and a permanent sort is not desired, it may be more useful to return the DataFrame for printing:

```
df.sort_values(by=['Outlets', 'Date'], ascending=False)
```

This shows that the countries with the most McDonald's are the United States, followed by China, and then Japan. France, I'm sure it will be pleased to know, comes in fourth place, with the greatest number of McDonald's of any European country!

Filtering DataFrames is easy with the `query` method. It takes, as an argument, a query string:

```
df.query('Outlets < 100')
```

This returns a DataFrame containing only records where the number of Outlets is less than 100. Most of the usual Python comparison operators work for DataFrame filtering using the query method, however this query language is not Python syntax. For instance, this will raise an Exception:

```
df.query('Date is not None')
```

If you want to test for the presence or absence of any empty values, the correct pandas way to do it is using the `isnull` and `notnull` query functions:

```
df.query('Date.isnull()')
df.query('Date.notnull()')
```

As you might guess, these statements capture both `None` values as well as `NaN` objects from the underlying numpy package that pandas is built on top of.

If we want to add another logic clause, you can separate them by a single ampersand:

```
df.query('Outlets < 100 & Date < "01-06-1990"')
```

An `or` statement is represented with a single pipe:

```
df.query('Outlets < 100 | Date < "01-06-1990"')
```

Note that the entire date (`"1990-01-01"`) is not required here, but will also work with just the year `"1990"`. Pandas is fairly forgiving about interpreting strings as dates, although you should always double-check that the data coming back is what you expect it to be.

More About Pandas

I sincerely hope that your journey with pandas does not end here. We are fortunate that Wes McKinney, the creator and Benevolent Dictator for Life (*https://en.wikipe dia.org/wiki/Benevolent_dictator_for_life*) of pandas, has also written a book about it: *Python for Data Analysis*.

If you plan to do more with data science, or simply want a good tool to clean and analyze data occasionally in Python, I recommend that you check it out.

Reading and Writing Natural Languages

So far, the data you have worked with in this book has been in the form of numbers or countable values. In most cases, you've simply stored the data without conducting any analysis after the fact. This chapter attempts to tackle the tricky subject of the English language.[1]

How does Google know what you're looking for when you type "cute kitten" into its image search? Because of the text that surrounds the cute kitten images. How does YouTube know to bring up a certain Monty Python sketch when you type "dead parrot" into its search bar? Because of the title and description text that accompanies each uploaded video.

In fact, even typing in terms such as "deceased bird monty python" immediately brings up the same "Dead Parrot" sketch, even though the page itself contains no mention of the words "deceased" or "bird." Google knows that a "hot dog" is a food and that a "boiling puppy" is an entirely different thing. How? It's all statistics!

Although you might not think that text analysis has anything to do with your project, understanding the concepts behind it can be extremely useful for all sorts of machine learning, as well as the more general ability to model real-world problems in probabilistic and algorithmic terms.

---

1 Although many of the techniques described in this chapter can be applied to all or most languages, it's OK for now to focus on natural language processing in English only. Tools such as Python's Natural Language Toolkit, for example, focus on English. Some 53% of the internet is still in English (with Spanish following at a mere 5.4%, according to W3Techs (*http://w3techs.com/technologies/overview/content_language/all*)). But who knows? The hold English has on the majority of the internet will almost certainly change in the future, and further updates may be necessary in the next few years.

For instance, the Shazam music service can identify audio as containing a certain song recording, even if that audio contains ambient noise or distortion. Google is working on automatically captioning images based on nothing but the image itself.[2] By comparing known images of, say, hot dogs to other images of hot dogs, the search engine can gradually learn what a hot dog looks like and observe these patterns in additional images it is shown.

Summarizing Data

In Chapter 11, you looked at breaking up text content into n-grams, or sets of phrases that are *n* words in length. At a basic level, this can be used to determine which sets of words and phrases tend to be most commonly used in a section of text. In addition, it can be used to create natural-sounding data summaries by going back to the original text and extracting sentences around some of these most popular phrases.

One piece of sample text you'll be using to do this is the inauguration speech of the ninth president of the United States, William Henry Harrison. Harrison's presidency set two records in the history of the office: one for the longest inauguration speech, and another for the shortest time in office, 32 days.

You'll use the full text of this speech (*http://pythonscraping.com/files/inaugurationS peech.txt*) as the source for many of the code samples in this chapter.

A slightly modified set of functions from the cleaning code in Chapter 11 can be used to transform this text into a list of sentences ready for splitting into n-grams:

```
import re
import string

def replace_newlines(text):
    return text.replace('\n', ' ')

def make_lowercase(text):
    return text.lower()

def split_sentences(text):
    return [s.strip() for s in text.split('. ')]

puncts = [re.escape(c) for c in string.punctuation]
PUNCTUATION_REGEX = re.compile('|'.join(puncts))
def remove_punctuation(text):
    return re.sub(PUNCTUATION_REGEX, '', text)
```

---

2 Oriol Vinyals et al, "A Picture Is Worth a Thousand (Coherent) Words: Building a Natural Description of Images" (*http://bit.ly/1HEJ8kX*), *Google Research blog*, November 17, 2014.

Then we fetch the text and call these functions in a particular order:

```
content = str(
    urlopen('http://pythonscraping.com/files/inaugurationSpeech.txt').read(),
    'utf-8'
)

text_operations = [
    replace_newlines,
    split_sentences,
    make_lowercase,
    remove_punctuation
]

cleaned = content
for op in text_operations:
    if type(cleaned) == list:
        cleaned = [op(c) for c in cleaned]
    else:
        cleaned = op(cleaned)

print(cleaned)
```

Next we use the cleaned text to get a `Counter` object of all 2-grams and find the most popular ones:

```
def getNgrams(text, n):
    text = text.split(' ')
    return [' '.join(text[i:i+n]) for i in range(len(text)-n+1)]

def countNGramsFromSentences(sentences, n):
    counts = Counter()
    for sentence in sentences:
        counts.update(getNgrams(sentence, n))
    return counts

counts = countNGramsFromSentences(cleaned, 2)
print(counts.most_common())
```

This example illustrates the convenience and power of the Python standard library collections. No, it wouldn't be particularly difficult to write a function that creates a dictionary counter, sorts it by values, and returns the most popular keys for those top values. However, knowing about the built-in collections and being able to pick the right one for the task at hand can save you many lines of code!

The output produces, in part:

```
[('of the', 213), ('in the', 65), ('to the', 61), ('by the', 41),
('the constitution', 34), ('of our', 29), ('to be', 26),
('the people', 24), ('from the', 24), ('that the', 23)...
```

Of these 2-grams, "the constitution" seems like a reasonably popular subject in the speech, but "of the," "in the," and "to the" don't seem especially noteworthy. How can you automatically and accurately get rid of unwanted words?

Fortunately, there are people out there who carefully study the differences between "interesting" words and "uninteresting" words, and their work can help us do just that. Mark Davies, a linguistics professor at Brigham Young University, maintains the Corpus of Contemporary American English (*http://corpus.byu.edu/coca/*), a collection of over 450 million words from the last decade or so of popular American publications.

The list of 5,000 most frequently found words is available for free, and fortunately, this is more than enough to act as a basic filter to weed out the most common 2-grams. Just the first one hundred words vastly improves the results, with the addition of isCommon and filterCommon functions:

```
COMMON_WORDS = ['the', 'be', 'and', 'of', 'a', 'in', 'to', 'have',
'it', 'i', 'that', 'for', 'you', 'he', 'with', 'on', 'do', 'say',
'this', 'they', 'is', 'an', 'at', 'but', 'we', 'his', 'from', 'that',
'not', 'by', 'she', 'or', 'as', 'what', 'go', 'their', 'can',
'who', 'get', 'if', 'would', 'her', 'all', 'my', 'make', 'about',
'know', 'will', 'as', 'up', 'one', 'time', 'has', 'been', 'there',
'year', 'so', 'think', 'when', 'which', 'them', 'some', 'me',
'people', 'take', 'out', 'into', 'just', 'see', 'him', 'your',
'come', 'could', 'now', 'than', 'like', 'other', 'how', 'then',
'its', 'our', 'two', 'more', 'these', 'want', 'way', 'look', 'first',
'also', 'new', 'because', 'day', 'more', 'use', 'no', 'man', 'find',
'here', 'thing', 'give', 'many', 'well']

def isCommon(ngram):
  return any([w in COMMON_WORDS for w in ngram.split(' ')])

def filterCommon(counts):
  return Counter({key: val for key, val in counts.items() if not isCommon(key)})

filterCommon(counts).most_common()
```

This produces the following 2-grams that were found more than twice in the text body:

```
('united states', 10),
('executive department', 4),
('general government', 4),
('called upon', 3),
('chief magistrate', 3),
('legislative body', 3),
('same causes', 3),
('government should', 3),
('whole country', 3)
```

Appropriately enough, the first two items in the list are "United States" and "executive department," which you would expect for a presidential inauguration speech.

It's important to note that you are using a list of common words from relatively modern times to filter the results, which might not be appropriate given that the text was written in 1841. However, because you're using only the first one hundred or so words on the list—which you can assume are more stable over time than, say, the last one hundred words—and you appear to be getting satisfactory results, you can likely save yourself the effort of tracking down or creating a list of the most common words from 1841 (although such an effort might be interesting).

Now that some key topics have been extracted from the text, how does this help you write text summaries? One way is to search for the first sentence that contains each "popular" n-gram, the theory being that the first instance will yield a satisfactory overview of the body of the content. The first five most popular 2-grams yield these bullet points:

- "The Constitution of the United States is the instrument containing this grant of power to the several departments composing the Government."
- "Such a one was afforded by the executive department constituted by the Constitution."
- "The General Government has seized upon none of the reserved rights of the States."
- "Called from a retirement which I had supposed was to continue for the residue of my life to fill the chief executive office of this great and free nation, I appear before you, fellow-citizens, to take the oaths which the constitution prescribes as a necessary qualification for the performance of its duties; and in obedience to a custom coeval with our government and what I believe to be your expectations I proceed to present to you a summary of the principles which will govern me in the discharge of the duties which I shall be called upon to perform."
- "The presses in the necessary employment of the Government should never be used to 'clear the guilty or to varnish crime.'"

Sure, it might not be published in CliffsNotes anytime soon, but considering that the original document was 217 sentences in length, and the fourth sentence ("Called from a retirement...") condenses the main subject down fairly well, it's not too bad for a first pass.

With longer blocks of text, or more varied text, it may be worth looking at 3-grams or even 4-grams when retrieving the "most important" sentences of a passage. In this case, only one 3-gram is used multiple times and that is "exclusive metallic currency" —referring to the proposal of a gold standard for US currency, which was an important issue of the day. With longer passages, using 3-grams may be appropriate.

Another approach is to look for sentences that contain the most popular n-grams. These will, of course, tend to be longer sentences, so if that becomes a problem, you can look for sentences with the highest percentage of words that are popular n-grams or create a scoring metric of your own, combining several techniques.

Markov Models

You might have heard of Markov text generators. They've become popular for entertainment purposes, as in the "That can be my next tweet!" (*http://yes.thatcan.be/my/next/tweet/*) app, as well as their use for generating real-sounding spam emails to fool detection systems.

All of these text generators are based on the Markov model, which is often used to analyze large sets of random events, where one discrete event is followed by another discrete event with a certain probability.

For example, you might build a Markov model of a weather system, as illustrated in Figure 12-1.

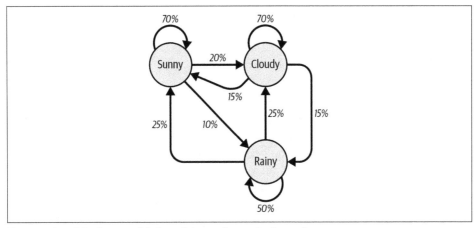

Figure 12-1. Markov model describing a theoretical weather system

In this model, each sunny day has a 70% chance of the following day also being sunny, with a 20% chance of the following day being cloudy with a mere 10% chance of rain. If the day is rainy, there is a 50% chance of rain the following day, a 25% chance of sun, and a 25% chance of clouds.

You might note several properties in this Markov model:

- All percentages leading away from any one node must add up to exactly 100%. No matter how complicated the system, there must always be a 100% chance that it can lead somewhere else in the next step.

- Although there are only three possibilities for the weather at any given time, you can use this model to generate an infinite list of weather states.

- Only the state of the current node you are on influences where you will go to next. If you're on the Sunny node, it doesn't matter if the preceding 100 days were sunny or rainy—the chances of sun the next day are exactly the same: 70%.

- It might be more difficult to reach some nodes than others. The math behind this is reasonably complicated, but it should be fairly easy to see that Rainy (with less than "100%" worth of arrows pointing toward it) is a much less likely state to reach in this system, at any given point in time, than Sunny or Cloudy.

Obviously, this is a simple system, and Markov models can grow arbitrarily large. Google's page-rank algorithm is based partly on a Markov model, with websites represented as nodes, and inbound/outbound links represented as connections between nodes. The "likelihood" of landing on a particular node represents the relative popularity of the site. That is, if our weather system represented an extremely small internet, "rainy" would have a low page rank, while "cloudy" would have a high page rank.

With all of this in mind, let's bring it back down to a more concrete example: analyzing and generating text.

Again using the inauguration speech of William Henry Harrison analyzed in the previous example, you can write the following code that generates arbitrarily long Markov chains (with the chain length set to 100) based on the structure of its text:

```
from urllib.request import urlopen
from random import randint
from collections import defaultdict

def retrieveRandomWord(wordList):
    randIndex = randint(1, sum(wordList.values()))
    for word, value in wordList.items():
        randIndex -= value
        if randIndex <= 0:
            return word

def cleanAndSplitText(text):
    # Remove newlines and quotes
    text = text.replace('\n', ' ').replace('"', '');

    # Make sure punctuation marks are treated as their own "words,"
    # so that they will be included in the Markov chain
    punctuation = [',','.',';',':']
    for symbol in punctuation:
        text = text.replace(symbol, f' {symbol} ');
    # Filter out empty words
    return [word for word in text.split(' ') if word != '']

def buildWordDict(text):
```

```
    words = cleanAndSplitText(text)
    wordDict = defaultdict(dict)
    for i in range(1, len(words)):
        wordDict[words[i-1]][words[i]] = \
        wordDict[words[i-1]].get(words[i], 0) + 1
    return wordDict

text = str(urlopen('http://pythonscraping.com/files/inaugurationSpeech.txt')
        .read(), 'utf-8')
wordDict = buildWordDict(text)

#Generate a Markov chain of length 100
length = 100
chain = ['I']
for i in range(0, length):
    newWord = retrieveRandomWord(wordDict[chain[-1]])
    chain.append(newWord)

print(' '.join(chain))
```

The output of this code changes every time it is run, but here's an example of the uncannily nonsensical text it will generate:

```
I sincerely believe in Chief Magistrate to make all necessary sacrifices and
oppression of the remedies which we may have occurred to me in the arrangement
and disbursement of the democratic claims them , consolatory to have been best
political power in fervently commending every other addition of legislation , by
the interests which violate that the Government would compare our aboriginal
neighbors the people to its accomplishment . The latter also susceptible of the
Constitution not much mischief , disputes have left to betray . The maxim which
may sometimes be an impartial and to prevent the adoption or
```

So what's going on in the code?

The function `buildWordDict` takes in the string of text, which was retrieved from the internet. It then does some cleaning and formatting, removing quotes and putting spaces around other punctuation so it is effectively treated as a separate word. After this, it builds a two-dimensional dictionary—a dictionary of dictionaries—that has the following form:

```
{word_a : {word_b : 2, word_c : 1, word_d : 1},
 word_e : {word_b : 5, word_d : 2},...}
```

In this example dictionary, word_a was found four times, two instances of which were followed by "word_b," one instance followed by word_c, and one instance followed by word_d. Then "word_e" was followed seven times: five times by word_b and twice by word_d.

If we were to draw a node model of this result, the node representing word_a would have a 50% arrow pointing toward word_b (which followed it two out of four times), a 25% arrow pointing toward word_c, and a 25% arrow pointing toward word_d.

After this dictionary is built up, it can be used as a lookup table to see where to go next, no matter which word in the text you happen to be on.[3] Using the sample dictionary of dictionaries, you might currently be on word_e, which means that you'll pass the dictionary {word_b : 5, word_d: 2} to the retrieveRandomWord function. This function in turn retrieves a random word from the dictionary, weighted by the number of times it occurs.

By starting with a random starting word (in this case, the ubiquitous "I"), you can traverse through the Markov chain easily, generating as many words as you like.

These Markov chains tend to improve in their "realism" as more text is collected, especially from sources with similar writing styles. Although this example used 2-grams to create the chain (where the previous word predicts the next word), 3-grams or higher-order n-grams can be used, where two or more words predict the next word.

Although entertaining, and a great use for megabytes of text that you might have accumulated during web scraping, applications like these can make it difficult to see the practical side of Markov chains. As mentioned earlier in this section, Markov chains model how websites link from one page to the next. Large collections of these links as pointers can form weblike graphs that are useful to store, track, and analyze. In this way, Markov chains form the foundation for both how to think about web crawling and how your web crawlers can think.

Six Degrees of Wikipedia: Conclusion

In Chapter 6, you created a scraper that collects links from one Wikipedia article to the next, starting with the article on Kevin Bacon, and in Chapter 9, stored those links in a database. Why am I bringing it up again? Because it turns out the problem of choosing a path of links that starts on one page and ends up on the target page (i.e., finding a string of pages between *https://en.wikipedia.org/wiki/Kevin_Bacon* and *https://en.wikipedia.org/wiki/Eric_Idle*) is the same as finding a Markov chain where both the first word and last word are defined.

These sorts of problems are *directed graph* problems, where A → B does not necessarily mean that B → A. The word "football" might often be followed by the word

---

3 The exception is the last word in the text, because nothing follows the last word. In our example text, the last word is a period (.), which is convenient because it has 215 other occurrences in the text and so does not represent a dead end. However, in real-world implementations of the Markov generator, the last word of the text might be something you need to account for.

"player," but you'll find that the word "player" is much less often followed by the word "football." Although Kevin Bacon's Wikipedia article links to the article on his home city, Philadelphia, the article on Philadelphia does not reciprocate by linking back to him.

In contrast, the original Six Degrees of Kevin Bacon game is an *undirected graph* problem. If Kevin Bacon starred in *Flatliners* with Julia Roberts, then Julia Roberts necessarily starred in *Flatliners* with Kevin Bacon, so the relationship goes both ways (it has no "direction"). Undirected graph problems tend to be less common in computer science than directed graph problems, and both are computationally difficult to solve.

Although much work has been done on these sorts of problems and multitudes of variations on them, one of the best and most common ways to find shortest paths in a directed graph—and thus find paths between the Wikipedia article on Kevin Bacon and all other Wikipedia articles—is through a breadth-first search.

A *breadth-first search* is performed by first searching all links that link directly to the starting page. If those links do not contain the target page (the page you are searching for), then a second level of links—pages that are linked by a page that is linked by the starting page—is searched. This process continues until either the depth limit (6 in this case) is reached or the target page is found.

A complete solution to the breadth-first search, using a table of links as described in Chapter 9, is as follows:

```
import pymysql

conn = pymysql.connect(host='127.0.0.1', unix_socket='/tmp/mysql.sock',
    user='', passwd='', db='mysql', charset='utf8')
cur = conn.cursor()
cur.execute('USE wikipedia')

def getUrl(pageId):
    cur.execute('SELECT url FROM pages WHERE id = %s', (int(pageId)))
    return cur.fetchone()[0]

def getLinks(fromPageId):
    cur.execute('SELECT toPageId FROM links WHERE fromPageId = %s',
        (int(fromPageId)))
    if cur.rowcount == 0:
        return []
    return [x[0] for x in cur.fetchall()]

def searchBreadth(targetPageId, paths=[[1]]):
    newPaths = []
    for path in paths:
        links = getLinks(path[-1])
        for link in links:
```

```
                if link == targetPageId:
                    return path + [link]
                else:
                    newPaths.append(path+[link])
        return searchBreadth(targetPageId, newPaths)

    nodes = getLinks(1)
    targetPageId = 28624
    pageIds = searchBreadth(targetPageId)
    for pageId in pageIds:
        print(getUrl(pageId))
```

getUrl is a helper function that retrieves URLs from the database given a page ID. Similarly, getLinks takes a fromPageId representing the integer ID for the current page and fetches a list of all integer IDs for pages it links to.

The main function, searchBreadth, works recursively to construct a list of all possible paths from the search page and stops when it finds a path that has reached the target page:

- It starts with a single path, [1], representing a path in which the user stays on the target page with the ID 1 (Kevin Bacon) and follows no links.

- For each path in the list of paths (in the first pass, there is only one path, so this step is brief), it gets all of the links that link out from the page represented by the last page in the path.

- For each of these outbound links, it checks whether they match the targetPageId. If there's a match, that path is returned.

- If there's no match, a new path is added to a new list of (now longer) paths, consisting of the old path plus the new outbound page link.

- If the targetPageId is not found at this level at all, a recursion occurs and searchBreadth is called with the same targetPageId and a new, longer, list of paths.

After the list of page IDs containing a path between the two pages is found, each ID is resolved to its actual URL and printed.

The output for searching for a link between the page on Kevin Bacon (page ID 1 in this database) and the page on Eric Idle (page ID 28624 in this database) is:

```
/wiki/Kevin_Bacon
/wiki/Primetime_Emmy_Award_for_Outstanding_Lead_Actor_in_a_
Miniseries_or_a_Movie
/wiki/Gary_Gilmore
/wiki/Eric_Idle
```

This translates into the relationship of links: Kevin Bacon → Primetime Emmy Award → Gary Gilmore → Eric Idle.

In addition to solving Six Degrees problems and modeling which words tend to follow which other words in sentences, directed and undirected graphs can be used to model a variety of situations encountered in web scraping. Which websites link to which other websites? Which research papers cite which other research papers? Which products tend to be shown with which other products on a retail site? What is the strength of this link? Is the link reciprocal?

Recognizing these fundamental types of relationships can be extremely helpful for making models, visualizations, and predictions based on scraped data.

Natural Language Toolkit

So far, this chapter has focused primarily on the statistical analysis of words in bodies of text. Which words are most popular? Which words are unusual? Which words are likely to come after which other words? How are they grouped together? What you are missing is understanding, to the extent that you can, what the words represent.

The *Natural Language Toolkit* (NLTK) is a suite of Python libraries designed to identify and tag parts of speech found in natural English text. Its development began in 2000, and over the past 20-plus years, dozens of developers around the world have contributed to the project. Although the functionality it provides is tremendous (entire books are devoted to NLTK), this section focuses on just a few of its uses.

Installation and Setup

The nltk module can be installed in the same way as other Python modules, either by downloading the package through the NLTK website directly or by using any number of third-party installers with the keyword "nltk." For complete installation instructions and help with troubleshooting, see the NLTK website (*http://www.nltk.org/install.html*).

After installing the module, you can browse the extensive collection of text corpora available for download and use:

```
>>> import nltk
>>> nltk.download()
```

This opens the NLTK Downloader. You can navigate it in the terminal using the commands provided its menu:

```
NLTK Downloader
---------------------------------------------------------------------
    d) Download   l) List   u) Update   c) Config   h) Help   q) Quit
---------------------------------------------------------------------
```

```
Downloader> l

Packages:

  [*] abc................ Australian Broadcasting Commission 2006
  [ ] alpino............. Alpino Dutch Treebank
  [*] averaged_perceptron_tagger Averaged Perceptron Tagger
  [ ] averaged_perceptron_tagger_ru Averaged Perceptron Tagger (Russian)
  [ ] basque_grammars..... Grammars for Basque
  [ ] bcp47.............. BCP-47 Language Tags
  [ ] biocreative_ppi..... BioCreAtIvE (Critical Assessment of Information
                          Extraction Systems in Biology)
  [ ] bllip_wsj_no_aux.... BLLIP Parser: WSJ Model
  [*] book_grammars....... Grammars from NLTK Book
  [*] brown.............. Brown Corpus
  [ ] brown_tei.......... Brown Corpus (TEI XML Version)
  [ ] cess_cat........... CESS-CAT Treebank
  [ ] cess_esp........... CESS-ESP Treebank
  [*] chat80............. Chat-80 Data Files
  [*] city_database....... City Database
  [*] cmudict............ The Carnegie Mellon Pronouncing Dictionary (0.6)
  [ ] comparative_sentences Comparative Sentence Dataset
  [ ] comtrans........... ComTrans Corpus Sample
  [*] conll2000.......... CONLL 2000 Chunking Corpus

Hit Enter to continue:
```

The last page of the corpora list contains its collections:

```
Collections:
  [P] all-corpora........ All the corpora
  [P] all-nltk........... All packages available on nltk_data gh-pages
                          branch
  [P] all................ All packages
  [*] book.............. Everything used in the NLTK Book
  [P] popular............ Popular packages
  [P] tests.............. Packages for running tests
  [ ] third-party........ Third-party data packages

([*] marks installed packages; [P] marks partially installed collections)
```

For the exercises here, we will be using the book collection. You can download it through the downloader interface, or in Python:

```
nltk.download('book')
```

Statistical Analysis with NLTK

NLTK is great for generating statistical information about word counts, word frequency, and word diversity in sections of text. If all you need is a relatively straightforward calculation (e.g., the number of unique words used in a section of text), importing `nltk` might be overkill—it's a large module. However, if you need to do relatively extensive analysis of a text, you have functions at your fingertips that will give you just about any metric you want.

Analysis with NLTK always starts with the `Text` object. `Text` objects can be created from simple Python strings in the following way:

```
from nltk import word_tokenize
from nltk import Text

tokens = word_tokenize('Here is some not very interesting text')
text = Text(tokens)
```

The input for the `word_tokenize` function can be any Python text string. Any text can be passed in, but the NLTK corpora are handy for playing around with the features and for research. You can use the NLTK collection downloaded in the previous section by importing everything from the book module:

```
from nltk.book import *
```

This loads the nine books:

```
*** Introductory Examples for the NLTK Book ***
Loading text1, ..., text9 and sent1, ..., sent9
Type the name of the text or sentence to view it.
Type: 'texts()' or 'sents()' to list the materials.
text1: Moby Dick by Herman Melville 1851
text2: Sense and Sensibility by Jane Austen 1811
text3: The Book of Genesis
text4: Inaugural Address Corpus
text5: Chat Corpus
text6: Monty Python and the Holy Grail
text7: Wall Street Journal
text8: Personals Corpus
text9: The Man Who Was Thursday by G . K . Chesterton 1908
```

You will be working with **text6**, "Monty Python and the Holy Grail" (the screenplay for the 1975 movie), in all of the following examples.

Text objects can be manipulated much like normal Python arrays, as if they were an array containing words of the text. Using this property, you can count the number of unique words in a text and compare it against the total number of words (remember that a Python **set** holds only unique values):

```
>>> len(text6)/len(set(text6))
7.833333333333333
```

The preceding shows that each word in the script was used about eight times on average. You can also put the text into a frequency distribution object to determine some of the most common words and the frequencies for various words:

```
>>> from nltk import FreqDist
>>> fdist = FreqDist(text6)
>>> fdist.most_common(10)
[(':', 1197), ('.', 816), ('!', 801), (',', 731), ("'", 421), ('[', 3
19), (']', 312), ('the', 299), ('I', 255), ('ARTHUR', 225)]
>>> fdist["Grail"]
34
```

Because this is a screenplay, some artifacts of how it is written can pop up. For instance, "ARTHUR" in all caps crops up frequently because it appears before each of King Arthur's lines in the script. In addition, a colon (:) appears before every single line, acting as a separator between the name of the character and the character's line. Using this fact, we can see that there are 1,197 lines in the movie!

What we have called 2-grams in previous chapters, NLTK refers to as *bigrams* (from time to time, you might also hear 3-grams referred to as *trigrams*, but I prefer 2-gram and 3-gram rather than bigram or trigram). You can create, search, and list 2-grams extremely easily:

```
>>> from nltk import bigrams
>>> bigrams = bigrams(text6)
>>> bigramsDist = FreqDist(bigrams)
>>> bigramsDist[('Sir', 'Robin')]
18
```

To search for the 2-grams "Sir Robin," you need to break it into the tuple ("Sir", "Robin"), to match the way the 2-grams are represented in the frequency distribution. There is also a `trigrams` module that works in the same way. For the general case, you can also import the `ngrams` module:

```
>>> from nltk import ngrams
>>> fourgrams = ngrams(text6, 4)
>>> fourgramsDist = FreqDist(fourgrams)
>>> fourgramsDist[('father', 'smelt', 'of', 'elderberries')]
1
```

Here, the `ngrams` function is called to break a text object into n-grams of any size, governed by the second parameter. In this case, you're breaking the text into 4-grams. Then, you can demonstrate that the phrase "father smelt of elderberries" occurs in the screenplay exactly once.

Frequency distributions, text objects, and n-grams also can be iterated through and operated on in a loop. The following prints out all 4-grams that begin with the word "coconut," for instance:

```
from nltk.book import *
from nltk import ngrams

fourgrams = ngrams(text6, 4)

[f for f in fourgrams if f[0] == 'coconut']
```

The NLTK library has a vast array of tools and objects designed to organize, count, sort, and measure large swaths of text. Although we've barely scratched the surface of their uses, most of these tools are well designed and operate rather intuitively for someone familiar with Python.

Lexicographical Analysis with NLTK

So far, you've compared and categorized all the words you've encountered based only on the value they represent by themselves. There is no differentiation between homonyms or the context in which the words are used.

Although some people might be tempted to dismiss homonyms as rarely problematic, you might be surprised at how frequently they crop up. Most native English speakers probably don't often register that a word is a homonym, much less consider that it might be confused for another word in a different context.

"He was objective in achieving his objective of writing an objective philosophy, primarily using verbs in the objective case" is easy for humans to parse but might make a web scraper think the same word is being used four times and cause it to simply discard all the information about the meaning behind each word.

In addition to sussing out parts of speech, being able to distinguish between a word used in one way versus another might be useful. For example, you might want to look for company names made up of common English words, or analyze someone's opinions about a company. "ACME Products is good" and "ACME Products is not bad" can have the same basic meaning, even if one sentence uses "good" and the other uses "bad."

Penn Treebank's Tags

NLTK uses a popular system of tagging parts of speech developed by the University of Pennsylvania's Penn Treebank Project (*https://catalog.ldc.upenn.edu/docs/LDC95T7/cl93.html*). Although some of the tags make sense (e.g., CC is a coordinating conjunction), others can be confusing (e.g., RP is a particle). Use the following as a reference for the tags referred to in this section:

CC	Coordinating conjunction
CD	Cardinal number
DT	Determiner
EX	Existential "there"
FW	Foreign word
IN	Preposition, subordinating conjunction
JJ	Adjective
JJR	Adjective, comparative

JJS	Adjective, superlative
LS	List item marker
MD	Modal
NN	Noun, singular or mass
NNS	Noun, plural
NNP	Proper noun, singular
NNPS	Proper noun, plural
PDT	Predeterminer
POS	Possessive ending
PRP	Personal pronoun
PRP$	Possessive pronoun
RB	Adverb
RBR	Adverb, comparative
RBS	Adverb, superlative
RP	Particle
SYM	Symbol
TO	"to"
UH	Interjection
VB	Verb, base form
VBD	Verb, past tense
VBG	Verb, gerund or present participle
VBN	Verb, past participle
VBP	Verb, non-third-person singular present
VBZ	Verb, third person singular present
WDT	wh-determiner
WP	Wh-pronoun
WP$	Possessive wh-pronoun
WRB	Wh-adverb

In addition to measuring language, NLTK can assist in finding meaning in the words based on context and its own sizable dictionaries. At a basic level, NLTK can identify parts of speech:

```
>>> from nltk.book import *
>>> from nltk import word_tokenize
>>> text = word_tokenize('Strange women lying in ponds distributing swords'\
'is no basis for a system of government.')
>>> from nltk import pos_tag
>>> pos_tag(text)
[('Strange', 'NNP'), ('women', 'NNS'), ('lying', 'VBG'), ('in', 'IN')
, ('ponds', 'NNS'), ('distributing', 'VBG'), ('swords', 'NNS'), ('is'
, 'VBZ'), ('no', 'DT'), ('basis', 'NN'), ('for', 'IN'), ('a', 'DT'),
('system', 'NN'), ('of', 'IN'), ('government', 'NN'), ('.', '.')]
```

Each word is separated into a *tuple* containing the word and a tag identifying the part of speech (see the preceding sidebar for more information about these tags). Although this might seem like a straightforward lookup, the complexity needed to perform the task correctly becomes apparent with the following example:

```
>>> text = word_tokenize('The dust was thick so he had to dust')
>>> pos_tag(text)
[('The', 'DT'), ('dust', 'NN'), ('was', 'VBD'), ('thick', 'JJ'),
('so', 'RB'), ('he', 'PRP'), ('had', 'VBD'), ('to', 'TO'), ('dust', 'VB')]
```

Notice that the word "dust" is used twice in the sentence: once as a noun, and again as a verb. NLTK identifies both usages correctly, based on their context in the sentence. NLTK identifies parts of speech by using a context-free grammar defined by the English language. *Context-free grammars* are sets of rules that define which things are allowed to follow other things in ordered lists. In this case, they define which parts of speech are allowed to follow other parts of speech. Whenever an ambiguous word such as "dust" is encountered, the rules of the context-free grammar are consulted, and an appropriate part of speech that follows the rules is selected.

Machine Learning and Machine Training

You can have NLTK generate brand-new context-free grammars when training it, for example, on a foreign language. If you tag large sections of text by hand in the language by using the appropriate Penn Treebank tags, you can feed them back into NLTK and train it to properly tag other text it might encounter. This type of training is a necessary component of any machine-learning activity that you will revisit in Chapter 16, when training scrapers to recognize CAPTCHA characters.

What's the point of knowing whether a word is a verb or a noun in a given context? It might be neat in a computer science research lab, but how does it help with web scraping?

A common problem in web scraping deals with search. You might be scraping text off a site and want to search it for instances of the word "google," but only when it's being used as a verb, not a proper noun. Or you might be looking only for instances of the company Google and don't want to rely on people's correct use of capitalization in order to find those instances. Here, the `pos_tag` function can be extremely useful:

```
from nltk import word_tokenize, sent_tokenize, pos_tag
sentences = [
    'Google is one of the best companies in the world.',
    ' I constantly google myself to see what I\'m up to.'
]
nouns = ['NN', 'NNS', 'NNP', 'NNPS']

for sentence in sentences:
```

```
for word, tag in pos_tag(word_tokenize(sentence)):
    if word.lower() == 'google' and tag in nouns:
        print(sentence)
```

This prints only sentences that contain the word "google" (or "Google") as some sort of a noun, not a verb. Of course, you could be more specific and demand that only instances of Google tagged with "NNP" (a proper noun) are printed, but even NLTK makes mistakes at times, and it can be good to leave yourself a little wiggle room, depending on the application.

Much of the ambiguity of natural language can be resolved using NLTK's `pos_tag` function. By searching text for instances of your target word or phrase *plus* its tag, you can greatly increase the accuracy and effectiveness of your scraper's searches.

Additional Resources

Processing, analyzing, and understanding natural language by machine is one of the most difficult tasks in computer science, and countless volumes and research papers have been written on the subject. I hope that the coverage here will inspire you to think beyond conventional web scraping, or at least give you some initial direction about where to begin when undertaking a project that requires natural language analysis.

Many excellent resources are available on introductory language processing and Python's Natural Language Toolkit. In particular, Steven Bird, Ewan Klein, and Edward Loper's book *Natural Language Processing with Python* (O'Reilly) presents both a comprehensive and introductory approach to the topic.

In addition, James Pustejovsky and Amber Stubbs' *Natural Language Annotations for Machine Learning* (O'Reilly) provides a slightly more advanced theoretical guide. You'll need knowledge of Python to implement the lessons; the topics covered work perfectly with Python's Natural Language Toolkit.

Crawling Through Forms and Logins

One of the first questions that comes up when you start to move beyond the basics of web scraping is: "How do I access information behind a login screen?" The web is increasingly moving toward interaction, social media, and user-generated content. Forms and logins are an integral part of these types of sites and almost impossible to avoid. Fortunately, they are also relatively easy to deal with.

Until this point, most of our interactions with web servers in our example scrapers have consisted of using HTTP GET to request information. This chapter focuses on the POST method, which pushes information to a web server for storage and analysis.

Forms basically give users a way to submit a POST request that the web server can understand and use. Just as link tags on a website help users format GET requests, HTML forms help them format POST requests. Of course, with a little bit of coding, it is possible to create these requests ourselves and submit them with a scraper.

Python Requests Library

Although it's possible to navigate web forms by using only the Python core libraries, sometimes a little syntactic sugar makes life a lot sweeter. When you start to do more than a basic GET request with urllib, looking outside the Python core libraries can be helpful.

The Requests library (*http://www.python-requests.org*) is excellent at handling complicated HTTP requests, cookies, headers, and much more. Here's what Requests creator Kenneth Reitz has to say about Python's core tools:

Python's standard urllib2 module provides most of the HTTP capabilities you need, but the API is thoroughly broken. It was built for a different time—and a different web. It requires an enormous amount of work (even method overrides) to perform the simplest of tasks.

Things shouldn't be this way. Not in Python.

As with any Python library, the Requests library can be installed with any third-party Python library manager, such as pip, or by downloading and installing the source file (*https://github.com/kennethreitz/requests/tarball/master*).

Submitting a Basic Form

Most web forms consist of a few HTML fields, a Submit button, and an action page, where the actual form processing is done. The HTML fields usually consist of text but might also contain a file upload or other nontext content.

Most popular websites block access to their login forms in their *robots.txt* file (Chapter 2 discusses the legality of scraping such forms), so to play it safe I've constructed a series of different types of forms and logins at *pythonscraping.com* that you can run your web scrapers against. *http://pythonscraping.com/pages/files/form.html* is the location of the most basic of these forms.

The entirety of the HTML code for the form is as follows:

```
<form method="post" action="processing.php">
First name: <input type="text" name="firstname"><br>
Last name: <input type="text" name="lastname"><br>
<input type="submit" value="Submit">
</form>
```

A couple of things to notice here: first, the names of the two input fields are `first name` and `lastname`. This is important. The names of these fields determine the names of the variable parameters that will be `POST`ed to the server when the form is submitted. If you want to mimic the action that the form will take when `POST`ing your own data, you need to make sure that your variable names match up.

The second thing to note is that the action of the form is at *processing.php* (the absolute path is *http://pythonscraping.com/pages/files/processing.php*). Any `POST` requests to the form should be made on *this* page, not on the page where the form itself resides. Remember: the purpose of HTML forms is only to help website visitors format proper requests to send to the page that does the real action. Unless you are doing research to format the request itself, you don't need to bother much with the page that the form can be found on.

Submitting a form with the Requests library can be done in four lines, including the import and the instruction to print the content (yes, it's that easy):

```
import requests

params = {'firstname': 'Ryan', 'lastname': 'Mitchell'}
r = requests.post(
    'http://pythonscraping.com/pages/files/processing.php',
    data=params
)
print(r.text)
```

After the form is submitted, the script should return with the page's content:

```
Hello there, Ryan Mitchell!
```

This script can be applied to many simple forms encountered on the internet. The form to sign up for the "Web Scraping with Python" newsletter, for example, looks like this:

```
<form id="eclg-form">
 <div class="input-field">
   <label>First Name</label>
   <input type="text" name="first_name" class="eclg_firstname">
 </div>
 <div class="input-field">
   <label>Last Name</label>
   <input type="text" name="last_name" class="eclg_lastname">
 </div>
 <div class="input-field">
   <label>Email</label>
   <input type="text" name="email" class="eclg_email">
 </div>
 <div class="input-field input-submit">
   <button type="button" id="eclg-submit-btn">Send </button>
   <div class="eclg_ajax_loader" style="display: none;">
<img decoding="async" src="https://pythonscraping.com/wp-content/
plugins/email-capture-lead-generation//images/ajax_loader.gif">
</div>
   </div>
 <div class="eclg-message-container"></div>
</form>
```

Although it can look daunting at first, remember that in most cases (we'll cover the exceptions later), you're looking for only two things:

- The name of the field (or fields) you want to submit with the data. In this case, first name first_name, last name last_name, and email address email.

- The action attribute of the form itself; that is, the page that the form posts data to.

In this case, the action of the form isn't obvious. Unlike a traditional HTML form, this page uses a JavaScript program that detects the form submission and submits it to the proper URL.

In cases like this, using your browser's network tools can come in handy. Simply open up the Network tab, fill out the form, hit the Submit button, and observe the values being sent over the network (Figure 13-1).

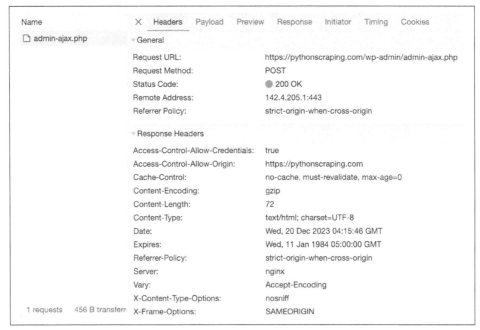

Figure 13-1. A request sent to the newsletter form at pythonscraping.com

Although you could wade through convoluted JavaScript and eventually arrive at the same answer, using the Network tab allows you to see trivially that the form contents are being submitted to *https://pythonscraping.com/wp-admin/admin-ajax.php*.

In addition, the Payload tab reveals a fourth form value sent to this endpoint: `action: eclg_add_newsletter`.

With this, we can replicate the form submission in Python:

```
import requests
params = {
    'firstname': 'Ryan',
    'lastname': 'Mitchell',
    'email': 'ryanemitchell@gmail.com',
    'action': 'eclg_add_newsletter'
}
r = requests.post('https://pythonscraping.com/wp-admin/admin-ajax.php',
```

```
                    data=params)
    print(r.text)
```

In this case, the form provides a JSON-formatted response:

```
{"status":"1","errmsg":"You have subscribed successfully!."}
```

Radio Buttons, Checkboxes, and Other Inputs

Obviously, not all web forms are a collection of text fields followed by a Submit button. Standard HTML contains a wide variety of possible form input fields: radio buttons, checkboxes, and select boxes, to name a few. HTML5 adds sliders (range input fields), email, dates, and more. With custom JavaScript fields, the possibilities are endless, with color pickers, calendars, and whatever else the developers come up with next.

Regardless of the seeming complexity of any sort of form field, you need to worry about only two things: the name of the element and its value. The element's name easily can be determined by looking at the source code and finding the name attribute. The value can sometimes be trickier, as it might be populated by JavaScript immediately before form submission. Color pickers, as an example of a fairly exotic form field, will likely have a value of something like #F03030.

If you're unsure of the format of an input field's value, you can use various tools to track the GET and POST requests your browser is sending to and from sites. The best and perhaps most obvious way to track GET requests, as mentioned before, is to look at the URL of a site. If the URL is something like:

```
http://domainname.com?thing1=foo&thing2=bar
```

you know that this corresponds to a form of this type:

```
<form method="GET" action="someProcessor.php">
<input type="someCrazyInputType" name="thing1" value="foo" />
<input type="anotherCrazyInputType" name="thing2" value="bar" />
<input type="submit" value="Submit" />
</form>
```

which corresponds to the Python parameter object:

```
{'thing1':'foo', 'thing2':'bar'}
```

Again, if you're stuck with a complicated-looking POST form, and you want to see exactly which parameters your browser is sending to the server, the easiest way is to use your browser's inspector or developer tool to view them (see Figure 13-2).

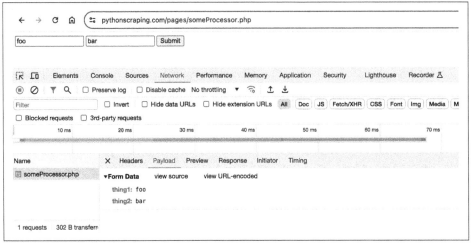

Figure 13-2. The Form Data section, highlighted in a box, shows the POST parameters "thing1" and "thing2" with their values "foo" and "bar"

Submitting Files and Images

Although file uploads are common on the internet, file uploads are not something often used in web scraping. It is possible, however, that you might want to write a test for your own site that involves a file upload. At any rate, it's a useful thing to know how to do.

There is a practice file upload form at *http://pythonscraping.com/pages/files/ form2.html*. The form on the page has the following markup:

```
<form action="processing2.php" method="post" enctype="multipart/form-data">
  Submit a jpg, png, or gif: <input type="file" name="uploadFile"><br>
  <input type="submit" value="Upload File">
</form>
```

Except for the `<input>` tag having the type attribute `file`, it looks essentially the same as the text-based forms used in the previous examples. Fortunately, the way the forms are used by the Python Requests library is also similar:

```
import requests

files = {'uploadFile': open('files/python.png', 'rb')}
r = requests.post('http://pythonscraping.com/pages/files/processing2.php',
                  files=files)
print(r.text)
```

Note that in lieu of a simple string, the value submitted to the form field (with the name uploadFile) is now a Python File object, as returned by the open function. In this example, you're submitting an image file, stored on your local machine, at the path *../files/Python-logo.png*, relative to where the Python script is being run from.

Yes, it's really that easy!

Handling Logins and Cookies

So far, we've mostly discussed forms that allow you to submit information to a site or let you view needed information on the page immediately after the form. How is this different from a login form, which lets you exist in a permanent "logged-in" state throughout your visit to the site?

Most modern websites use cookies to keep track of who is logged in and who is not. After a site authenticates your login credentials, it stores them in your browser's cookie, which usually contains a server-generated token, timeout, and tracking information. The site then uses this cookie as a sort of proof of authentication, which is shown to each page you visit during your time on the site. Before the widespread use of cookies in the mid-1990s, keeping users securely authenticated and tracking them was a huge problem for websites.

Although cookies are a great solution for web developers, they can be problematic for web scrapers. You can submit a login form all day long, but if you don't keep track of the cookie the form sends back to you afterward, the next page you visit will act as though you've never logged in at all.

I've created a simple login form at *http://pythonscraping.com/pages/cookies/login.html* (the username can be anything, but the password must be "password"). This form is processed at *http://pythonscraping.com/pages/cookies/welcome.php*, which contains a link to the main page, *http://pythonscraping.com/pages/cookies/profile.php*.

If you attempt to access the welcome page or the profile page without logging in first, you'll get an error message and instructions to log in first before continuing. On the profile page, a check is done on your browser's cookies to see whether its cookie was set on the login page.

Keeping track of cookies is easy with the >Requests library:

```
import requests

params = {'username': 'Ryan', 'password': 'password'}
r = requests.post(
    'https://pythonscraping.com/pages/cookies/welcome.php',
    params)
print(r.text)

print('Cookie is set to:')
```

```
print(r.cookies.get_dict())
print('Going to profile page...')
r = requests.get('https://pythonscraping.com/pages/cookies/profile.php',
                 cookies=r.cookies)
print(r.text)
```

Here you're sending the login parameters to the welcome page, which acts as the processor for the login form. You retrieve the cookies from the results of the last request, print the result for verification, and then send them to the profile page by setting the `cookies` argument.

This works well for simple situations, but what if you're dealing with a more complicated site that frequently modifies cookies without warning, or if you'd rather not even think about the cookies to begin with? The Requests `session` function works perfectly in this case:

```
session = requests.Session()

params = {'username': 'Ryan', 'password': 'password'}
s = session.post('https://pythonscraping.com/pages/cookies/welcome.php', params)
print('Cookie is set to:')
print(s.cookies.get_dict())
print('Going to profile page...')
s = session.get('https://pythonscraping.com/pages/cookies/profile.php')
print(s.text)
```

In this case, the session object (retrieved by calling `requests.Session()`) keeps track of session information, such as cookies, headers, and even information about protocols you might be running on top of HTTP, such as HTTPAdapters.

Requests is a fantastic library, second perhaps only to Selenium (covered in Chapter 14) in the completeness of what it handles without programmers having to think about it or write the code themselves. Although it might be tempting to sit back and let the library do all the work, it's extremely important always to be aware of what the cookies look like and what they are controlling when you are writing web scrapers. It could save many hours of painful debugging or figuring out why a website is behaving strangely!

HTTP Basic Access Authentication

Before the advent of cookies, one popular way to handle logins was with HTTP *basic access authentication*. You still see it from time to time, especially on high-security or corporate sites, and with some APIs. I've created a page at *http://pythonscraping.com/pages/auth/login.php* that has this type of authentication (Figure 13-3).

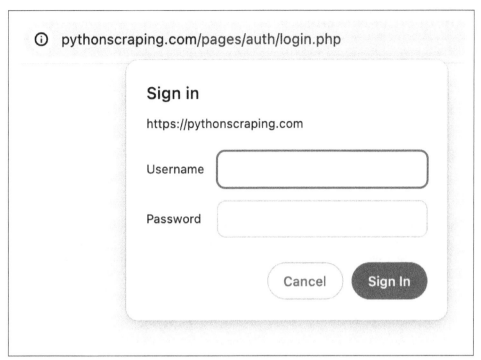

Figure 13-3. The user must provide a username and password to get to the page pro-tected by basic access authentication

As usual with these examples, you can log in with any username, but the password must be "password."

The Requests package contains an `auth` module specifically designed to handle HTTP authentication:

```
import requests
from requests.auth import AuthBase
from requests.auth import HTTPBasicAuth

auth = HTTPBasicAuth('ryan', 'password')
r = requests.post(
    url='https://pythonscraping.com/pages/auth/login.php', auth=auth)
print(r.text)
```

Although this appears to be a normal `POST` request, an `HTTPBasicAuth` object is passed as the `auth` argument in the request. The resulting text will be the page pro-tected by the username and password (or an Access Denied page, if the request failed).

Other Form Problems

Web forms are a hot point of entry for malicious bots. You don't want bots creating user accounts, taking up valuable server processing time, or submitting spam comments on a blog. For this reason, security features often are incorporated into HTML forms on modern websites that might not be immediately apparent.

 For help with CAPTCHAs, check out Chapter 16, which covers image processing and text recognition in Python.

If you encounter a mysterious error, or the server is rejecting your form submission for an unknown reason, check out Chapter 17, which covers honeypots, hidden fields, and other security measures that websites take to protect their forms.

Scraping JavaScript

Client-side scripting languages are languages that are run in the browser itself, rather than on a web server. The success of a client-side language depends on your browser's ability to interpret and execute the language correctly.

While there are hundreds of server-side programming languages, there's only one client-side programming language. This is because of the difficulty of getting every browser manufacturer to agree on a standard. This is a good thing when it comes to web scraping: the fewer languages there are to deal with, the better.

Other Client-Side Programming Languages

Some readers may take issue with the sentence: "There's only one client-side programming language." Technically, languages such as ActionScript and VBScript exist. However, these are no longer supported and, in the case of VBScript, was only ever supported by a single browser. For this reason, they are very rarely seen.

If you want to be pedantic about it, absolutely anyone can make a new client-side programming language! There are likely many of them out there! The only issue is getting widespread support by browsers to make that language effective and put it into use by others.

Some have also argued that CSS and HTML are programming languages in themselves. I agree with this in theory. Lara Schenck has an excellent and entertaining blog post on the subject: *https://notlaura.com/is-css-turing-complete/*.

However, in practice, CSS and HTML are generally treated as markup languages separate from "programming languages" and, besides, are covered extensively in this book.

JavaScript is, by far, the most common and most well-supported client-side scripting language on the web today. It can be used to collect information for user tracking, submit forms without reloading the page, embed multimedia, and even power entire online games. Even deceptively simple-looking pages often contain multiple pieces of JavaScript. You can find it embedded between script tags in the page's source code:

```
<script>
    alert("This creates a pop-up using JavaScript");
</script>
```

A Brief Introduction to JavaScript

Having at least some idea of what is going on in the code you are scraping can be immensely helpful. With that in mind, it's a good idea to familiarize yourself with JavaScript.

JavaScript is a weakly typed language, with a syntax that is often compared to C++ and Java. Although certain elements of the syntax, such as operators, loops, and arrays, might be similar, the weak typing and scriptlike nature of the language can make it a difficult beast for some programmers to deal with.

For example, the following recursively calculates values in the Fibonacci sequence up to 100 and prints them to the browser's developer console:

```
<script>
function fibonacci(a, b){
    var nextNum = a + b;
    console.log(nextNum+" is in the Fibonacci sequence");
    if(nextNum < 100){
        fibonacci(b, nextNum);
    }
}
fibonacci(1, 1);
</script>
```

Notice that all variables are identified by preceding them with `var`. This is similar to the `$` sign in PHP or the type declaration (`int`, `String`, `List`, etc.) in Java or C++. Python is unusual in that it doesn't have this sort of explicit variable declaration.

JavaScript is also good at passing functions around:

```
<script>
var fibonacci = function() {
    var a = 1; var b = 1;
    return function () {
        [b, a] = [a + b, b];
        return b;
    }
}
var fibInstance = fibonacci();
```

```
console.log(fibInstance()+" is in the Fibonacci sequence");
console.log(fibInstance()+" is in the Fibonacci sequence");
console.log(fibInstance()+" is in the Fibonacci sequence");
</script>
```

This might seem daunting at first, but it becomes simple if you think in terms of lambda expressions (covered in Chapter 5). The variable `fibonacci` is defined as a function. The value of its function returns a function that prints increasingly large values in the Fibonacci sequence. Each time it is called, it returns the Fibonacci-calculating function, which executes again and increases the values in the function.

You might also see functions like these written in the arrow syntax introduced in JavaScript ES6 (ECMAScript 6, introduced in 2015):

```
<script>
const fibonacci = () => {
    var a = 1; var b = 1;
    return () => {
        [b, a] = [a + b, b];
        return b;
    }
}
const fibInstance = fibonacci();
console.log(fibInstance()+" is in the Fibonacci sequence");
console.log(fibInstance()+" is in the Fibonacci sequence");
console.log(fibInstance()+" is in the Fibonacci sequence");
</script>
```

Here, I'm using the JavaScript keyword `const` to indicate a constant variable that will not be reassigned later. You might also see the keyword `let`, indicating a variable that may be reassigned. These were also introduced in ES6.

Passing around functions as variables is also extremely useful when it comes to handling user actions and callbacks, and it is worth getting comfortable with this style of programming when it comes to reading JavaScript.

Common JavaScript Libraries

Although the core JavaScript language is important to know, you can't get far on the modern web without using at least one of the language's many third-party libraries. You might see one or more of these commonly used libraries when looking at page source code.

Executing JavaScript by using Python can be extremely time-consuming and processor intensive, especially if you're doing it on a large scale. Knowing your way around JavaScript and being able to parse it directly (without needing to execute it to acquire the information) can be extremely useful and save you a lot of headaches.

jQuery

jQuery is an extremely common library, used by more than 70% of all websites.[1]. A site using jQuery is readily identifiable because it will contain an import to jQuery somewhere in its code:

```
<script src="http://ajax.googleapis.com/ajax/libs/jquery/1.9.1/jquery.min.js"></script>
```

If jQuery is found on a site, you must be careful when scraping it. jQuery is adept at dynamically creating HTML content that appears only after the JavaScript is executed. If you scrape the page's content by using traditional methods, you will retrieve only the preloaded page that appears before the JavaScript has created the content (this scraping problem is covered in more detail in "Ajax and Dynamic HTML" on page 208).

In addition, these pages are more likely to contain animations, interactive content, and embedded media that might make scraping challenging.

Google Analytics

Google Analytics is used by about 50% of all websites,[2] making it perhaps the most common JavaScript library and the most popular user tracking tool on the internet. Both *http://pythonscraping.com* and *http://www.oreilly.com/* use Google Analytics.

Determining whether a page is using Google Analytics is easy. It will have JavaScript at the bottom, similar to the following (taken from the O'Reilly Media site):

```
<!-- Google Analytics -->
<script type="text/javascript">

var _gaq = _gaq || [];
_gaq.push(['_setAccount', 'UA-4591498-1']);
_gaq.push(['_setDomainName', 'oreilly.com']);
_gaq.push(['_addIgnoredRef', 'oreilly.com']);
_gaq.push(['_setSiteSpeedSampleRate', 50]);
_gaq.push(['_trackPageview']);
```

---

1 See Web Technology Surveys analysis at *https://w3techs.com/technologies/details/js-jquery* W3Techs uses web crawlers to monitor trends in technology usage over time.

2 W3Techs, "Usage Statistics and Market Share of Google Analytics for Websites" (*http://w3techs.com/technologies/details/ta-googleanalytics/all/all*).

```
(function() { var ga = document.createElement('script'); ga.type =
'text/javascript'; ga.async = true; ga.src = ('https:' ==
document.location.protocol ? 'https://ssl' : 'http://www') +
'.google-analytics.com/ga.js'; var s =
document.getElementsByTagName('script')[0];
s.parentNode.insertBefore(ga, s); })();

</script>
```

This script handles Google Analytics-specific cookies used to track your visit from page to page. This can sometimes be a problem for web scrapers that are designed to execute JavaScript and handle cookies (such as those that use Selenium, discussed later in this chapter).

If a site uses Google Analytics or a similar web analytics system, and you do not want the site to know that it's being crawled or scraped, make sure to discard any cookies used for analytics or discard cookies altogether.

Google Maps

If you've spent any time on the internet, you've almost certainly seen *Google Maps* embedded in a website. Its API makes it extremely easy to embed maps with custom information on any site.

If you're scraping any sort of location data, understanding how Google Maps works makes it easy to obtain well-formatted latitude/longitude coordinates and even addresses. One of the most common ways to denote a location in Google Maps is through a *marker* (also known as a *pin*).

Markers can be inserted into any Google Map by using code such as:

```
var marker = new google.maps.Marker({
    position: new google.maps.LatLng(-25.363882,131.044922),
    map: map,
    title: 'Some marker text'
});
```

Python makes it easy to extract all instances of coordinates that occur between `google.maps.LatLng(` and `)` to obtain a list of latitude/longitude coordinates.

Using Google's Reverse Geocoding API (*https://developers.google.com/maps/documen tation/javascript/examples/geocoding-reverse*), you can resolve these coordinate pairs to addresses that are well formatted for storage and analysis.

Ajax and Dynamic HTML

Until now, the only way we've had of communicating with a web server is to send it some sort of HTTP request via the retrieval of a new page. If you've ever submitted a form or retrieved information from a server without reloading the page, you've likely used a website that uses Ajax.

Contrary to what some believe, Ajax is not a language but a group of technologies used to accomplish a certain task (much like web scraping, come to think of it). *Ajax* stands for *Asynchronous JavaScript and XML* and is used to send information to and receive it from a web server without making a separate page request.

 You should never say, "This website will be written in Ajax." It would be correct to say, "This website will use Ajax to communicate with the web server."

Like Ajax, *dynamic HTML* (DHTML) is a collection of technologies used for a common purpose. DHTML is HTML code, CSS language, or both that changes as client-side scripts change HTML elements on the page. A button might appear only after the user moves the cursor, a background color might change on a click, or an Ajax request might trigger a new block of content to load.

Note that although the word "dynamic" is generally associated with words like "moving," or "changing" the presence of interactive HTML components, moving images, or embedded media does not necessarily make a page DHTML, even though it might look dynamic. In addition, some of the most boring, static-looking pages on the internet can have DHTML processes running behind the scenes that depend on the use of JavaScript to manipulate the HTML and CSS.

If you scrape many websites, you will soon run into a situation in which the content you are viewing in your browser does not match the content you see in the source code you're retrieving from the site. You might view the output of your scraper and scratch your head, trying to figure out where everything you're seeing on the exact same page in your browser has disappeared to.

The web page might also have a loading page that appears to redirect you to another page of results, but you'll notice that the page's URL never changes when this redirect happens.

Both of these are caused by a failure of your scraper to execute the JavaScript that is making the magic happen on the page. Without the JavaScript, the HTML just sort of sits there, and the site might look very different from what it looks like in your web browser, which executes the JavaScript without problem.

There are several giveaways that a page might be using Ajax or DHTML to change or load the content, but in situations like this, there are only two solutions: scrape the content directly from the JavaScript; or use Python packages capable of executing the JavaScript itself and scrape the website as you view it in your browser.

Executing JavaScript in Python with Selenium

Selenium (*http://www.seleniumhq.org*) is a powerful web scraping tool developed originally for website testing. These days, it's also used when the accurate portrayal of websites—as they appear in a browser—is required. Selenium works by automating browsers to load the website, retrieve the required data, and even take screenshots or assert that certain actions happen on the website.

Selenium does not contain its own web browser; it requires integration with third-party browsers in order to run. If you were to run Selenium with Firefox, for example, you would see a Firefox instance open up on your screen, navigate to the website, and perform the actions you had specified in the code. Although this might be neat to watch, I prefer my scripts to run quietly in the background and often use Chrome's *headless* mode to do that.

A *headless browser* loads websites into memory and executes JavaScript on the page, but does it without any graphic rendering of the website to the user. By combining Selenium with headless Chrome, you can run an extremely powerful web scraper that handles cookies, JavaScript, headers, and everything else you need with ease, as if you were using a rendered browser.

Installing and Running Selenium

You can download the Selenium library from its website (*https://pypi.python.org/pypi/selenium*) or use a third-party installer such as pip to install it from the command line.

```
$ pip install selenium
```

Previous versions of Selenium required that you also manually download a webdriver file that would allow it to interface with your web browser. This webdriver is called such because it is a software *driver* for the web browser. Much like a software driver for a hardware device, it allows the Python Selenium package to interface with and control your browser.

Unfortunately, because new versions of browsers are released frequently, and are much more frequently updated thanks to automatic updates, this meant that Selenium drivers also had to be frequently updated. Navigating to the browser driver's website (such as *http://chromedriver.chromium.org/downloads*), downloading the new file, and replacing the old file was a frequent chore. In Selenium 4, released in October 2021, this entire process was replaced by the webdriver manager Python package.

The webdriver manager can be installed with pip:

```
$ pip install webdriver-manager
```

When called, the webdriver manager downloads the latest driver:

```
from selenium import webdriver
from selenium.webdriver.chrome.service import Service
from webdriver_manager.chrome import ChromeDriverManager

driver = webdriver.Chrome(service=Service(ChromeDriverManager().install()))
driver.get("http://www.python.org")
time.sleep(2)
driver.close()
```

Of course, if this script is being run frequently, it's inefficient to install a new driver file each time just in case the Chrome browser was updated since the last time it ran. The output of the driver manager installation is simply the path in your driver directory where the driver is located:

```
CHROMEDRIVER_PATH = ChromeDriverManager().install()
driver = webdriver.Chrome(service=Service(CHROMEDRIVER_PATH))
```

If you still enjoy downloading files by hand, you can do that by passing your own path into the Service object:

```
from selenium import webdriver
from selenium.webdriver.chrome.service import Service

CHROMEDRIVER_PATH = 'drivers/chromedriver_mac_arm64/chromedriver'
driver = webdriver.Chrome(service=Service(CHROMEDRIVER_PATH))
driver.get("http://www.python.org")
time.sleep(2)
driver.close()
```

Although plenty of pages use Ajax to load data, I've created a sample page at *http://pythonscraping.com/pages/javascript/ajaxDemo.html* to run your scrapers against. This page contains some sample text, hardcoded into the page's HTML, that is replaced by Ajax-generated content after a two-second delay. If you were to scrape this page's data by using traditional methods, you'd get only the loading page, without getting the data that you want.

The Selenium library is an API called on the object webdriver (*https://selenium-python.readthedocs.io/api.html*). Note that this is a Python object representing or acting as an interface to the webdriver application you downloaded. While the same terms "driver" and "webdriver" are often used interchangeably for both things (the Python object and the application itself) it's important to distinguish them conceptually.

The webdriver object is a bit like a browser in that it can load websites, but it can also be used like a BeautifulSoup object to find page elements, interact with elements on the page (send text, click, etc.), and do other actions to drive the web scrapers.

The following code retrieves text behind an Ajax "wall" on the test page:

```python
from selenium import webdriver
from selenium.webdriver.common.by import By
from selenium.webdriver.chrome.options import Options
import time

chrome_options = Options()
chrome_options.add_argument("--headless")
driver = webdriver.Chrome(
    service=Service(CHROMEDRIVER_PATH),
    options=chrome_options
)
driver.get('http://pythonscraping.com/pages/javascript/ajaxDemo.html')
time.sleep(3)
print(driver.find_element(By.ID, 'content').text)
driver.close()
```

This creates a new Selenium webdriver, using the Chrome library, which tells the webdriver to load a page and then pauses execution for three seconds before looking at the page to retrieve the (hopefully loaded) content.

When you instantiate a new Chrome webdriver in Python, you can pass it a variety of options through the Options object. In this case, we're using the --headless option to make the webdriver run in the background:

```python
chrome_options = Options()
chrome_options.add_argument('--headless')
```

Whether you used the driver manager package to install a driver or downloaded it yourself, you must pass this path into the Service object, as well as pass in your options, to create a new webdriver:

```python
driver = webdriver.Chrome(
    service=Service(CHROMEDRIVER_PATH),
    options=chrome_options
)
```

If everything is configured correctly, the script should take a few seconds to run and then result in the following text:

```
Here is some important text you want  to retrieve!
A button to click!
```

Selenium Selectors

In previous chapters, you've selected page elements using BeautifulSoup selectors, such as find and find_all. Selenium uses a very similar set of methods to select elements: find_element and find_elements.

There are so many ways to find and select elements from HTML, you might think that Selenium would use a wide variety of arguments and keyword arguments for these methods. However, for both find_element and find_elements there are only two arguments for both of these functions: the By object and the string selector.

The By object specifies how the selector string should be interpreted, with the following list of options:

By.ID
> Used in the example; finds elements by their HTML id attribute.

By.NAME
> Finds HTML tags by their name attribute. This is handy for HTML forms.

By.XPATH
> Uses an XPath expression to select matching elements. The XPath syntax will be covered in more detail later in this chapter.

By.LINK_TEXT
> Finds HTML <a> tags by the text they contain. For example, a link labeled "Next" can be selected using (By.LINK_TEXT, 'Next').

By.PARTIAL_LINK_TEXT
> Similar to LINK_TEXT but matches on a partial string.

By.TAG_NAME
> Finds HTML tags by their tag name.

By.CLASS_NAME
> Used to find elements by their HTML class attribute. Why is this function CLASS_NAME and not simply CLASS? Using the form object.CLASS would create problems for Selenium's Java library, where .class is a reserved method. To keep the Selenium syntax consistent between languages, CLASS_NAME is used instead.

```
By.CSS_SELECTOR
```
Finds elements by their class, id, or tag name, using the #idName, .class Name, tagName convention.

In the previous example, you used the selector driver.find_element(By.ID, 'con tent'), although the following selectors would have worked as well:

```
driver.find_element(By.CSS_SELECTOR, '#content')
driver.find_element(By.TAG_NAME, 'div')
```

Of course, if you want to select multiple elements on the page, most of these element selectors can return a Python list of elements by using elements (i.e., make it plural):

```
driver.find_elements(By.CSS_SELECTOR, '#content')
driver.find_elements(By.TAG_NAME, 'div')
```

If you still want to use BeautifulSoup to parse this content, you can, by using web-driver's page_source function, which returns the page's source, as viewed by the DOM at that current time, as a string:

```
pageSource = driver.page_source
bs = BeautifulSoup(pageSource, 'html.parser')
print(bs.find(id='content').get_text())
```

Waiting to Load

Note that although the page itself contains an HTML button, Selenium's .text function retrieves the text value of the button in the same way that it retrieves all other content on the page.

If the time.sleep pause is changed to one second instead of three, the text returned changes to the original:

```
This is some content that will appear on the page while it's loading.
 You don't care about scraping this.
```

Although this solution works, it is somewhat inefficient, and implementing it could cause problems on a large scale. Page-load times are inconsistent, depending on the server load at any particular millisecond, and natural variations occur in connection speed. Although this page load should take just over two seconds, you're giving it an entire three seconds to make sure that it loads completely. A more efficient solution would repeatedly check for the existence of a particular element on a fully loaded page and return only when that element exists.

The following program uses the presence of the button with the ID loadedButton to declare that the page has been fully loaded:

```
from selenium import webdriver
from selenium.webdriver.common.by import By
from selenium.webdriver.support.ui import WebDriverWait
```

```
from selenium.webdriver.support import expected_conditions as EC

chrome_options = Options()
chrome_options.add_argument("--headless")
driver = webdriver.Chrome(
    service=Service(CHROMEDRIVER_PATH),
    options=chrome_options)

driver.get('http://pythonscraping.com/pages/javascript/ajaxDemo.html')
try:
    element = WebDriverWait(driver, 10).until(
                    EC.presence_of_element_located((By.ID, 'loadedButton')))
finally:
    print(driver.find_element(By.ID, 'content').text)
    driver.close()
```

This script has several new imports, most notably `WebDriverWait` and `expected _conditions`, both of which are combined here to form what Selenium calls an *implicit wait*.

An implicit wait differs from an explicit wait in that it waits for a certain state in the DOM to occur before continuing, while an explicit wait defines a hardcoded time as in the previous example, which has a wait of three seconds. In an implicit wait, the triggering DOM state is defined by `expected_condition` (note that the import is cast to `EC` here, a common convention used for brevity). Expected conditions can be many things in the Selenium library, including:

- An alert box pops up.
- An element (such as a text box) is put into a *selected* state.
- The page's title changes, or text is now displayed on the page or in a specific element.
- An element is now visible to the DOM, or an element disappears from the DOM.

Most of these expected conditions require that you specify an element to watch for in the first place. Elements are specified using locators. Note that locators are not the same as selectors (see "Selenium Selectors" on page 212 for more on selectors). A *locator* is an abstract query language, using the `By` object, which can be used in a variety of ways, including to make selectors.

In the following code, a locator is used to find elements with the ID `loadedButton`:

```
EC.presence_of_element_located((By.ID, 'loadedButton'))
```

Locators also can be used to create selectors, using the `find_element` webdriver function:

```
print(driver.find_element(By.ID, 'content').text)
```

If you do not need to use a locator, don't; it will save you an import. However, this handy tool is used for a variety of applications and has a great degree of flexibility.

XPath

XPath (short for *XML Path*) is a query language used for navigating and selecting portions of an XML document. Founded by the W3C in 1999, it is occasionally used in languages such as Python, Java, and C# when dealing with XML documents.

Although BeautifulSoup does not support XPath, many of the other libraries in this book, such as Scrapy and Selenium, do. It often can be used in the same way as CSS selectors (such as `mytag#idname`), although it is designed to work with more generalized XML documents rather than HTML documents in particular.

The XPath syntax has four major concepts:

Root nodes versus nonroot nodes
> `/div` will select the div node only if it is at the root of the document.
> `//div` selects all divs anywhere in the document.

Attribute selection
> `//@href` selects any nodes with the attribute `href`.
> `//a[@href='http://google.com']` selects all links in the document that point to Google.

Selection of nodes by position
> `//a[3]` selects the third link in the document.
> `//table[last()]` selects the last table in the document.
> `//a[position() < 3]` selects the first two links in the document.

Asterisks (*) match any set of characters or nodes and can be used in a variety of situations
> `//table/tr/*` selects all children of `tr` tags in all tables (this is good for selecting cells using both `th` and `td` tags).
> `//div[@*]` selects all `div` tags that have any attributes.

XPath syntax also has many advanced features. Over the years, it has developed into a relatively complicated query language, with boolean logic, functions (such as `posi tion()`), and a variety of operators not discussed here.

If you have an HTML or XML selection problem that cannot be addressed by the functions shown here, see Microsoft's XPath Syntax page (*https://msdn.microsoft.com/ en-us/enus/library/ms256471*).

Additional Selenium WebDrivers

In the previous section, the Chrome WebDriver (ChromeDriver) was used with Selenium. In most cases, there is little reason to have a browser pop up on the screen and start scraping the web, so running this in headless mode can be convenient. However, running in nonheadless mode, and/or using different browser drivers can be good practice for a number of reasons:

- Troubleshooting. If your code is running in headless mode and fails, the failure may be difficult to diagnose without seeing the page in front of you.
- You can also pause the code execution and interact with the web page or use the inspector tools while your scraper is running in order to diagnose problems.
- Tests may depend on a specific browser in order to run. A failure in one browser but not in another may point at a browser-specific problem.

In most cases it is preferable to use the webdriver manager to get your browser drivers. For instance, you can use the webdriver manager for Firefox and Microsoft Edge:

```
from webdriver_manager.firefox import GeckoDriverManager
from webdriver_manager.microsoft import EdgeChromiumDriverManager

print(GeckoDriverManager().install())
print(EdgeChromiumDriverManager().install())
```

However, if you need a deprecated browser version or a browser not available through the webdriver manager (such as Safari) you may still need to manually download the driver files.

Many groups, both official and unofficial, are involved in the creation and maintenance of Selenium webdrivers for every major browser today. The Selenium group curates a collection of these webdrivers (*http://www.seleniumhq.org/download/*) for easy reference.

Handling Redirects

Client-side redirects are page redirects that are executed in your browser by JavaScript, rather than a redirect performed on the server, before the page content is sent. It can sometimes be tricky to tell the difference when visiting a page in your web browser. The redirect might happen so fast that you don't notice any delay in loading time and assume that a client-side redirect is actually a server-side redirect.

However, when scraping the web, the difference is obvious. A server-side redirect, depending on how it is handled, can be traversed easily by Python's urllib library without any help from Selenium (for more information on doing this, see Chapter 6).

Client-side redirects won't be handled at all unless something is executing the JavaScript.

Selenium is capable of handling these JavaScript redirects in the same way that it handles other JavaScript execution; however, the primary issue with these redirects is when to stop page execution—that is, how to tell when a page is done redirecting. A demo page at *http://pythonscraping.com/pages/javascript/redirectDemo1.html* gives an example of this type of redirect, with a two-second pause.

You can detect that redirect in a clever way by "watching" an element in the DOM when the page initially loads, and then repeatedly calling that element until Selenium throws a `StaleElementReferenceException`; the element is no longer attached to the page's DOM and the site has redirected:

```
from selenium import webdriver
from selenium.webdriver.chrome.options import Options
from selenium.common.exceptions import StaleElementReferenceException
import time

def waitForLoad(driver):
    elem = driver.find_element(By.TAG_NAME, "html")
    count = 0
    for _ in range(0, 20):
        try:
            elem == driver.find_element(By.TAG_NAME, "html")
        except StaleElementReferenceException:
            return
        time.sleep(0.5)
    print("Timing out after 10 seconds and returning")

chrome_options = Options()
chrome_options.add_argument("--headless")
driver = webdriver.Chrome(
    service=Service(CHROMEDRIVER_PATH),
    options=chrome_options
)
driver.get("http://pythonscraping.com/pages/javascript/redirectDemo1.html")
waitForLoad(driver)
print(driver.page_source)
driver.close()
```

This script checks the page every half second, with a timeout of 10 seconds, although the times used for the checking time and timeout can be easily adjusted up or down, as needed.

Alternatively, you can write a similar loop checking the current URL of the page until the URL changes or it matches a specific URL that you're looking for.

Waiting for elements to appear and disappear is a common task in Selenium, and you can also use the same WebDriverWait function used in the previous button loading example. Here you're providing it a timeout of 15 seconds and an XPath selector that looks for the page body content to accomplish the same task:

```
from selenium.webdriver.common.by import By
from selenium.webdriver.support.ui import WebDriverWait
from selenium.webdriver.chrome.options import Options
from selenium.webdriver.support import expected_conditions as EC
from selenium.common.exceptions import TimeoutException

chrome_options = Options()
chrome_options.add_argument("--headless")
driver = webdriver.Chrome(
    executable_path='drivers/chromedriver',
    options=chrome_options)
driver.get('http://pythonscraping.com/pages/javascript/redirectDemo1.html')
try:
    txt = 'This is the page you are looking for!'
    bodyElement = WebDriverWait(driver, 15).until(
        EC.presence_of_element_located((
            By.XPATH,
            f'//body[contains(text(), "{txt}")]'
        ))
    )
    print(bodyElement.text)
except TimeoutException:
    print('Did not find the element')
```

A Final Note on JavaScript

Most sites today on the internet use JavaScript.[3] Fortunately for us, in many cases this use of JavaScript will not affect how you scrape the page. The JavaScript may be limited to powering a site's tracking tools, controlling a small section of the site, or manipulating a drop-down menu, for example. In cases where it does impact how you scrape the site, the JavaScript can be executed with tools like Selenium to produce the simple HTML page you've been learning to scrape in the first part of this book.

Remember: just because a site uses JavaScript does not mean that all the traditional web scraping tools go out the window. The purpose of JavaScript is ultimately to produce HTML and CSS code that can be rendered by the browser, or to communicate

---

3 W3Techs, "Usage Statistics of JavaScript as Client-Side Programming Language on Websites" (*http://w3techs.com/technologies/details/cp-javascript/all/all*).

with the server dynamically, through HTTP requests and responses. Once Selenium is used, the HTML and CSS on the page can be read and parsed as you would with any other website code, and HTTP requests and responses can be sent and handled by your code via the techniques in earlier chapters, even without using Selenium.

In addition, JavaScript can even be a benefit to web scrapers, because its use as a "browser-side content management system" may expose useful APIs to the outside world, letting you obtain the data more directly. For more information on this, see Chapter 15.

If you are still having difficulty with a particularly hairy JavaScript situation, you can find information on Selenium and interacting directly with dynamic websites, including drag-and-drop interfaces, in Chapter 17.

Crawling Through APIs

JavaScript has traditionally been the bane of web crawlers everywhere. At one point in the ancient history of the internet, you could be guaranteed that a request for an HTML page made to the web server would represent the same HTML website you would see in a browser.

As JavaScript and Ajax content generation and loading become more ubiquitous, that situation is becoming less common. In Chapter 14, you looked at one way of solving this: using Selenium to automate a browser and fetch the data. This is an easy thing to do. It works almost all of the time.

The problem is that, when you have a "hammer" as powerful and effective as Selenium, every web scraping problem starts to look a lot like a nail.

In this chapter, you'll look at cutting through the JavaScript entirely (no need to execute it or even load it!) and getting straight to the source of the data: the APIs that generate it.

A Brief Introduction to APIs

Although countless books, talks, and guides have been written about the intricacies of REST, GraphQL, JSON, and XML APIs, at their core they are based on a simple concept. An *API*, or Application Programming Interface, defines a standardized syntax that allows one piece of software to communicate with another piece of software, even though they might be written in different languages or otherwise structured differently.

This section focuses on web APIs (in particular, APIs that allow a web server to communicate to a browser) and uses the term *API* to refer specifically to that type. But you may want to keep in mind that, in other contexts, *API* is also a generic term that can be used to, say, allow a Java program to communicate with a Python program running on the same machine. An API does not always have to be "across the internet" and does not necessarily involve any web technologies.

Web APIs are most often used by developers who are using a well-advertised and documented public service. For example, the US National Weather Service provides a weather API (*https://www.weather.gov/documentation/services-web-api*) that gives current weather data and forecasts for any location. Google has dozens of APIs in its Developers section (*https://console.developers.google.com*) for language translations, analytics, and geolocation.

The documentation for these APIs typically describes routes or *endpoints*, as URLs that you can request, with variable parameters, either in the path of the URL or as GET parameters.

For example, the following provides `pathparam` as a parameter in the route path:

```
http://example.com/the-api-route/pathparam
```

And this provides `pathparam` as the value for the parameter `param1`:

```
http://example.com/the-api-route?param1=pathparam
```

Both methods of passing variable data to the API are frequently used, although, like many topics in computer science, philosophic debate has raged on when and where variables should be passed through the path or through the parameters.

The response from the API is usually returned in a JSON or XML format. JSON is far more popular in modern times than XML, but you may still see some XML responses. Many APIs allow you to change the response type, using another parameter to define which type of response you would like.

Here's an example of a JSON-formatted API response:

```
{"user":{"id": 123, "name": "Ryan Mitchell", "city": "Boston"}}
```

Here's an example of an XML-formatted API response:

```
<user><id>123</id><name>Ryan Mitchell</name><city>Boston</city></user>
```

ip-api.com provides an easy-to-use and simple API that translates IP addresses to actual physical addresses. You can try a simple API request by entering the following in your browser:[1]

---

1 This API resolves IP addresses to geographic locations and is one you'll be using later in the chapter as well.

```
http://ip-api.com/json/50.78.253.58
```

This should produce a response like the following:

```
{"as": "AS7922 Comcast Cable Communications, LLC","city": "Boston",
"country": "United States","countryCode": "US",
"isp": "Comcast Cable Communications","lat": 42.3584,"lon": -71.0598,
"org": "Boston Park Plaza Hotel","query": "50.78.253.58",
"region": "MA","regionName": "Massachusetts","status": "success",
"timezone": "America/New_York","zip": "02116"}
```

Notice that the request contains the parameter json in the path. You can request an
XML or CSV response by changing this parameter accordingly:

```
http://ip-api.com/xml/50.78.253.58
http://ip-api.com/csv/50.78.253.58
```

HTTP Methods and APIs

In the previous section, you looked at APIs making a GET request to the server for
information. There are four main ways (or *methods*) to request information from a
web server via HTTP:

- GET
- POST
- PUT
- DELETE

Technically, more than these four exist (such as HEAD, OPTIONS, and CONNECT), but
they are rarely used in APIs, and it is unlikely that you will ever see them. The vast
majority of APIs limit themselves to these four methods or even a subset of these four
methods. It is common to see APIs that use only GET, or use only GET and POST.

GET is what you use when you visit a website through the address bar in your
browser. GET is the method you are using when you make a call to *http://ip-api.com/
json/50.78.253.58*. You can think of GET as saying, "Hey, web server, please retrieve/get
me this information."

A GET request, by definition, makes no changes to the information in the server's
database. Nothing is stored; nothing is modified. Information is only read.

POST is what you use when you fill out a form or submit information, presumably to a
backend script on the server. Every time you log in to a website, you are making
a POST request with your username and (hopefully) encrypted password. If you are
making a POST request with an API, you are saying, "Please store this information in
your database."

PUT is less commonly used when interacting with websites but is used from time to time in APIs. A PUT request is used to update an object or information. An API might require a POST request to create a new user, for example, but it might need a PUT request if you want to update that user's email address.[2]

DELETE is used, as you might imagine, to delete an object. For instance, if you send a DELETE request to *http://example.com/user/23*, it will delete the user with the ID 23. DELETE methods are not often encountered in public APIs, which are primarily created to disseminate information or allow users to create or post information, rather than allow users to remove that information from their databases.

Unlike GET requests, POST, PUT, and DELETE requests allow you to send information in the body of a request, in addition to the URL or route from which you are requesting data.

Just like the response that you receive from the web server, this data in the body is typically formatted as JSON or, less commonly, as XML, and the format of this data is defined by the syntax of the API. For example, if you are using an API that creates comments on blog posts, you might make a PUT request to:

```
http://example.com/comments?post=123
```

with the following request body:

```
{"title": "Great post about APIs!", "body": "Very informative. Really helped me
out with a tricky technical challenge I was facing. Thanks for taking the time
to write such a detailed blog post about PUT requests!", "author": {"name":"Ryan
Mitchell", "website": "http://pythonscraping.com", "company": "O'Reilly Media"}}
```

Note that the ID of the blog post (123) is passed as a parameter in the URL, where the content for the new comment you are making is passed in the body of the request. Parameters and data may be passed in both the parameter and the body. Which parameters are required and where they are passed is determined, again, by the syntax of the API.

More About API Responses

As you saw in the ip-api.com example at the beginning of the chapter, an important feature of APIs is that they have well-formatted responses. The most common types of response formatting are *eXtensible Markup Language* (XML) and *JavaScript Object Notation* (JSON).

---

[2] In reality, many APIs use POST requests in lieu of PUT requests when updating information. Whether a new entity is created or an old one is merely updated is often left to how the API request itself is structured. However, it's still good to know the difference, and you will often encounter PUT requests in commonly used APIs.

In recent years, JSON has become vastly more popular than XML for a couple of major reasons. First, JSON files are generally smaller than well-designed XML files. Compare, for example, the following XML data, which clocks in at 98 characters:

```
<user><firstname>Ryan</firstname><lastname>Mitchell</lastname><username>Kludgist
</username></user>
```

And now look at the same data in JSON:

```
{"user":{"firstname":"Ryan","lastname":"Mitchell","username":"Kludgist"}}
```

This is only 73 characters, or a whopping 36% smaller than the equivalent XML.

Of course, one could argue that the XML could be formatted like this:

```
<user firstname="ryan" lastname="mitchell" username="Kludgist"></user>
```

But this is considered bad practice because it doesn't support deep nesting of data. Regardless, it still requires 71 characters, about the same length as the equivalent JSON.

Another reason JSON is quickly becoming more popular than XML is due to a shift in web technologies. In the past, it was more common for a server-side script such as PHP or .NET to be on the receiving end of an API. Nowadays, it is likely that a framework, such as Angular or Backbone, will be sending and receiving API calls. Server-side technologies are somewhat agnostic as to the form in which their data comes. But JavaScript libraries like Backbone find JSON easier to handle.

Although APIs are typically thought of as having either an XML response or a JSON response, anything is possible. The response type of the API is limited only by the imagination of the programmer who created it. CSV is another typical response output (as seen in the ip-api.com example). Some APIs may even be designed to generate files. A request may be made to a server to generate an image with some particular text overlaid on it or to request a particular XLSX or PDF file.

Some APIs return no response at all. For example, if you are making a request to a server to create a new blog post comment, it may return only an HTTP response code 200, meaning "I posted the comment; everything is great!" Others may return a minimal response like this:

```
{"success": true}
```

If an error occurs, you may get a response like this:

```
{"error": {"message": "Something super bad happened"}}
```

Or if the API is not particularly well configured, you may get a nonparsable stack trace or some plain English text. When making a request to an API, it's usually wise to first check that the response you get is actually JSON (or XML, or CSV, or whatever format you're expecting back).

Parsing JSON

In this chapter, you've looked at various types of APIs and how they function, and you've looked at sample JSON responses from these APIs. Now let's look at how to parse and use this information.

At the beginning of the chapter you saw the example of the ip-api.com API, which resolves IP addresses to physical addresses:

```
http://ip-api.com/json/50.78.253.58
```

You can take the output of this request and use Python's JSON-parsing functions to decode it:

```
import json
from urllib.request import urlopen

def getCountry(ipAddress):
    response = urlopen('http://ip-api.com/json/'+ipAddress).read()
        .decode('utf-8')
    responseJson = json.loads(response)
    return responseJson.get('countryCode')

print(getCountry('50.78.253.58'))
```

This prints the country code for the IP address 50.78.253.58.

The JSON parsing library used is part of Python's core library. Just type in `import json` at the top, and you're all set! Unlike many languages that might parse JSON into a special JSON object or JSON node, Python uses a more flexible approach and turns JSON objects into dictionaries, JSON arrays into lists, JSON strings into strings, and so forth. In this way, it is extremely easy to access and manipulate values stored in JSON.

The following gives a quick demonstration of how Python's JSON library handles the values that might be encountered in a JSON string:

```
import json

jsonString = '{"arrayOfNums":[{"number":0},{"number":1},{"number":2}],
               "arrayOfFruits":[{"fruit":"apple"},{"fruit":"banana"},
                                {"fruit":"pear"}]}'
jsonObj = json.loads(jsonString)

print(jsonObj.get('arrayOfNums'))
print(jsonObj.get('arrayOfNums')[1])
print(jsonObj.get('arrayOfNums')[1].get('number') +
      jsonObj.get('arrayOfNums')[2].get('number'))
print(jsonObj.get('arrayOfFruits')[2].get('fruit'))
```

Here is the output:

```
[{'number': 0}, {'number': 1}, {'number': 2}]
{'number': 1}
3
pear
```

Line 1 is a list of dictionary objects, line 2 is a dictionary object, line 3 is an integer (the sum of the integers accessed in the dictionaries), and line 4 is a string.

Undocumented APIs

So far in this chapter, we've discussed only APIs that are documented. Their developers intend them to be used by the public, publish information about them, and assume that the APIs will be used by other developers. But the vast majority of APIs don't have any published documentation at all.

But why would you create an API without any public documentation? As mentioned in the beginning of this chapter, it all has to do with JavaScript.

Traditionally, the web servers for dynamic websites had several tasks whenever a user requested a page:

- Handle GET requests from users requesting a page of a website
- Retrieve the data from the database that appears on that page
- Format the data into the HTML template for the page
- Send that formatted HTML to the user

As JavaScript frameworks became more ubiquitous, many of the HTML creation tasks handled by the server moved into the browser. The server might send a hardcoded HTML template to the user's browser, but separate Ajax requests would be made to load the content and place it in the correct slots in that HTML template. All this would happen on the browser/client side.

This was initially a problem for web scrapers. They were accustomed to making a request for an HTML page and getting back exactly that—an HTML page with all of the content already in place. Instead, they now got an HTML template without any content.

Selenium was used to solve this problem. Now the programmer's web scraper could become the browser, request the HTML template, execute any JavaScript, allow all the data to load in its place, and only *then* scrape the page for data. Because the HTML was all loaded, it was essentially reduced to a previously solved problem—the problem of parsing and formatting existing HTML.

However, because the entire content management system (that used to reside only in the web server) had essentially moved to the browser client, even the simplest websites could balloon into several megabytes of content and a dozen HTTP requests.

In addition, when Selenium is used, all of the "extras" that the user doesn't necessarily care about are loaded: calls to tracking programs, loading sidebar ads, calls to tracking programs for the sidebar ads. Images, CSS, third-party font data—all of it needs to be loaded. This may seem great when you're using a browser to browse the web, but if you're writing a web scraper that needs to move fast, collect specific data, and place the lowest possible load on the web server, you can be loading a hundred times more data than you need.

But there's a silver lining to all of this JavaScript, Ajax, and web modernization: because servers are no longer formatting the data into HTML, they often act as thin wrappers around the database itself. This thin wrapper simply extracts data from the database and returns it to the page via an API.

Of course, these APIs aren't meant to be used by anyone or anything besides the web page itself, and so developers leave them undocumented and assume (or hope) that no one will notice them. But they do exist.

The American retail giant target.com, for example, loads all of its search results via JSON. You can search for a product on their site by visiting *https://www.target.com/s?searchTerm=web%20scraping%20with%20python*.

If you scrape this page using urllib or the Requests library, you won't find any search results. These are loaded separately via an API call to the URL:

```
https://redsky.target.com/redsky_aggregations/v1/web/plp_search_v2
```

Because Target's API requires a key for each request, and those API keys time out, I recommend that you try this out yourself and see the JSON results.

You could, of course, use Selenium to load all the search results and parse the resulting HTML. However, you would be making about 260 requests and transferring megabytes of data with each search. Using the API directly, you make only one request and transfer approximately only the 10 kb of nicely formatted data that you need.

Finding Undocumented APIs

You've used the Chrome inspector in previous chapters to examine the contents of an HTML page, but now you'll use it for a slightly different purpose: to examine the requests and responses of the calls that are used to construct that page.

To do this, open the Chrome inspector window and click the Network tab, shown in Figure 15-1.

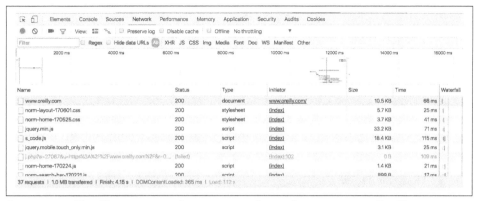

Figure 15-1. The Chrome network inspector tool provides a view into all calls your browser is making and receiving

Note that you need to open this window before the page loads. It does not track network calls while it's closed.

While the page is loading, you'll see a line appear in real time whenever your browser makes a call back to the web server for additional information to render the page. This may include an API call.

Finding undocumented APIs can take a little detective work (to take the detective work out of this, see "Documenting Undocumented APIs" on page 230), especially with larger sites with lots of network calls. Generally, though, you'll know it when you see it.

API calls tend to have several features that are useful for locating them in the list of network calls:

- They often have JSON or XML in them. You can filter the list of requests by using the search/filter field.

- With GET requests, the URL will contain the parameter values passed to them. This will be useful if, for example, you're looking for an API call that returns the results of a search or is loading data for a specific page. Simply filter the results with the search term you used, page ID, or other identifying information.

- They will usually be of the type XHR.

APIs may not always be obvious, especially in large sites with lots of features that may make hundreds of calls while loading a single page. However, spotting the metaphorical needle in the haystack becomes much easier with a little practice.

Documenting Undocumented APIs

After you've found an API call being made, it's often useful to document it to some extent, especially if your scrapers will rely heavily on the call. You may want to load several pages on the website, filtering for the target API call in the inspector console Network tab. By doing this, you can see how the call changes from page to page and identify the fields that it accepts and returns.

Every API call can be identified and documented by paying attention to the following fields:

- HTTP method used
- Inputs
  - Path parameters
  - Headers (including cookies)
  - Body content (for PUT and POST calls)
- Outputs
  - Response headers (including cookies set)
  - Response body type
  - Response body fields

Combining APIs with Other Data Sources

Although the raison d'être of many modern web applications is to take existing data and format it in a more appealing way, I would argue that this isn't an interesting thing to do in most instances. If you're using an API as your only data source, the best you can do is merely copy someone else's database that already exists and which is, essentially, already published. What can be far more interesting is to take two or more data sources and combine them in a novel way or use an API as a tool to look at scraped data from a new perspective.

Let's look at one example of how data from APIs can be used in conjunction with web scraping to see which parts of the world contribute the most to Wikipedia.

If you've spent much time on Wikipedia, you've likely come across an article's revision history page, which displays a list of recent edits. If users are logged in to Wikipedia when they make the edit, their username is displayed. If they are not logged in, their IP address is recorded, as shown in Figure 15-2.

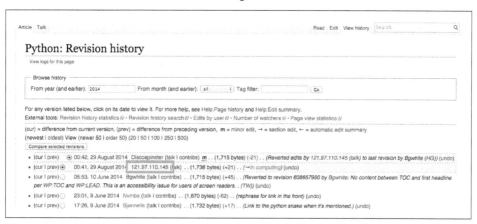

Figure 15-2. The IP address of an anonymous editor on the revision history page for Wikipedia's Python entry

The IP address provided on the history page is 121.97.110.145. By using the ip-api.com API, that IP address is from Quezon, Philippines, as of this writing (IP addresses can occasionally shift geographically).

This information isn't all that interesting on its own, but what if you could gather many points of geographic data about Wikipedia edits and where they occur? A few years ago, I did just that and used Google's GeoChart library (*https://develop ers.google.com/chart/interactive/docs/gallery/geochart*) to create an interesting chart (*http://www.pythonscraping.com/pages/wikipedia.html*) that shows the origins of edits to the English-language Wikipedia, as well as the Wikipedias written in other languages (Figure 15-3).

Figure 15-3. Visualization of Wikipedia edits created using Google's GeoChart library

Creating a basic script that crawls Wikipedia, looks for revision history pages, and then looks for IP addresses on those revision history pages isn't difficult. Using modified code from Chapter 6, the following script does just that:

```
def getLinks(articleUrl):
    html = urlopen(f'http://en.wikipedia.org{articleUrl}')
    bs = BeautifulSoup(html, 'html.parser')
    return bs.find('div', {'id':'bodyContent'}).findAll('a',
        href=re.compile('^(/wiki/)((?!:).)*$'))

def getHistoryIPs(pageUrl):
    #Format of revision history pages is:
    #http://en.wikipedia.org/w/index.php?title=Title_in_URL&action=history
    pageUrl = pageUrl.replace('/wiki/', '')
    historyUrl = f'http://en.wikipedia.org/w/index.php?title={pageUrl}\
&action=history'
    print(f'history url is: {historyUrl}')
    bs = BeautifulSoup(urlopen(historyUrl), 'html.parser')
    #finds only the links with class "mw-anonuserlink" which has IP addresses
    #instead of usernames
    ipAddresses = bs.findAll('a', {'class':'mw-anonuserlink'})
    return set([ip.get_text() for ip in ipAddresses])

links = getLinks('/wiki/Python_(programming_language)')

while(len(links) > 0):
    for link in links:
        print('-'*20)
        historyIPs = getHistoryIPs(link.attrs['href'])
        for historyIP in historyIPs:
```

```
                print(historyIP)

        newLink = links[random.randint(0, len(links)-1)].attrs['href']
        links = getLinks(newLink)
```

This program uses two main functions: getLinks (which was also used in Chapter 6), and the new getHistoryIPs, which searches for the contents of all links with the class mw-anonuserlink (indicating an anonymous user with an IP address, rather than a username) and returns it as a set.

This code also uses a somewhat arbitrary (yet effective for the purposes of this example) search pattern to look for articles from which to retrieve revision histories. It starts by retrieving the histories of all Wikipedia articles linked to by the starting page (in this case, the article on the Python programming language). Afterward, it randomly selects a new starting page and retrieves all revision history pages of articles linked to by that page. It will continue until it hits a page with no links.

Now that you have code that retrieves IP addresses as a string, you can combine this with the getCountry function from the previous section to resolve these IP addresses to countries. You'll modify getCountry slightly to account for invalid or malformed IP addresses that result in a 404 Not Found error:

```
def getCountry(ipAddress):
    try:
        response = urlopen(f'https://ipwho.is/{ipAddress}').read().decode('utf-8')
    except HTTPError:
        return None
    responseJson = json.loads(response)
    return responseJson.get('country_code')

links = getLinks('/wiki/Python_(programming_language)')

while(len(links) > 0):
    for link in links:
        print('-'*20)
        historyIPs = getHistoryIPs(link.attrs["href"])
        for historyIP in historyIPs:
            print(f'{historyIP} is from {getCountry(historyIP)}')

    newLink = links[random.randint(0, len(links)-1)].attrs['href']
    links = getLinks(newLink)
```

Here's the sample output:

```
--------------------
history url is: http://en.wikipedia.org/w/index.php?title=Programming_paradigm&a
ction=history
2405:201:2009:80b0:41bc:366f:a49c:52f2 is from IN
115.186.189.53 is from PK
103.252.145.68 is from IN
2405:201:400b:7058:b128:89fd:5248:f249 is from IN
```

```
172.115.220.47 is from US
2806:1016:d:54b6:8950:4501:c00b:507a is from MX
36.255.87.160 is from IN
2603:6011:1100:a1d0:31bd:8a11:a0c8:e4c3 is from US
2806:108e:d:bd2c:a577:db4f:2867:2b5c is from MX
2409:4042:e8f:8d39:b50c:f4ca:91b8:eb9d is from IN
107.190.108.84 is from CA
--------------------
history url is: http://en.wikipedia.org/w/index.php?title=Multi-paradigm_program
ming_language&action=history
98.197.198.46 is from US
75.139.254.117 is from US
```

More About APIs

This chapter has shown a few ways that modern APIs are commonly used to access data on the web, and how those APIs can be used to build faster and more powerful web scrapers. If you're looking to build APIs instead of just using them, or if you want to learn more about the theory of their construction and syntax, I recommend *RESTful Web APIs* by Leonard Richardson, Mike Amundsen, and Sam Ruby (O'Reilly). This book provides a strong overview of the theory and practice of using APIs on the web. In addition, Mike Amundsen has a fascinating video series, *Designing APIs for the Web* (*http://oreil.ly/1GOXNhE*) (O'Reilly), that teaches you how to create your own APIs—a useful thing to know if you decide to make your scraped data available to the public in a convenient format.

While some might bemoan the ubiquity of JavaScript and dynamic websites, making traditional "grab and parse the HTML page" practices outdated, I, for one, welcome our new robot overlords. As dynamic websites rely less on HTML pages for human consumption and more on strictly formatted JSON files for HTML consumption, this provides a boon for everyone trying to get clean, well-formatted data.

The web is no longer a collection of HTML pages with occasional multimedia and CSS adornments. It's a collection of hundreds of file types and data formats, whizzing hundreds at a time to form the pages that you consume through your browser. The real trick is often to look beyond the page in front of you and grab the data at its source.

Image Processing and Text Recognition

From Google's self-driving cars to vending machines that recognize counterfeit currency, machine vision is a huge field with far-reaching goals and implications. This chapter focuses on one small aspect of the field: text recognition—specifically, how to recognize and use text-based images found online by using a variety of Python libraries.

Using an image in lieu of text is a common technique when you don't want text to be found and read by bots. This is often seen on contact forms when an email address is partially or completely rendered as an image. Depending on how skillfully it is done, it might not even be noticeable to human viewers, but bots have a difficult time reading these images, and the technique is enough to stop most spammers from acquiring your email address.

CAPTCHAs, of course, take advantage of the fact that users can read security images but most bots can't. Some CAPTCHAs are more difficult than others, an issue we'll tackle later in this book.

But CAPTCHAs aren't the only place on the web where scrapers need image-to-text translation assistance. Even to, many documents are scanned from hard copies and put on the web, making these documents inaccessible as far as much of the internet is concerned, although they are "hiding in plain sight." Without image-to-text capabilities, the only way to make these documents accessible is for a human to type them up by hand—and nobody has time for that.

Translating images into text is called *optical character recognition*, or *OCR*. A few major libraries can perform OCR, and many other libraries support them or are built on top of them. This system of libraries can get fairly complicated, so I recommend you read the next section before attempting any of the exercises in this chapter.

All example images used throughout this chapter can be found in the GitHub repository folder *Chapter16_ImageProcessingFiles*. For the sake of brevity, all in-text code samples will refer to this directory simply as *files*.

Overview of Libraries

Python is a fantastic language for image processing and reading, image-based machine-learning, and even image creation. Although many libraries can be used for image processing, I'll focus on two: Pillow and Tesseract.

These two libraries make for a powerful complementary duo when it comes to processing and doing OCR on images from around the web. *Pillow* performs the first pass, cleaning and filtering images, and *Tesseract* attempts to match the shapes found in those images to its library of known text.

This chapter covers their installation and basic usage, along with several examples of this library duo working together. I'll also cover some advanced Tesseract training, so that you can train Tesseract to OCR additional fonts and languages (or even CAPTCHAs) that you might encounter on the web.

Pillow

Although Pillow might not be the most fully featured image-processing library, it has all the features you are likely to need and then some—unless you plan to rewrite Photoshop in Python, in which case you're reading the wrong book! Pillow also has the advantage of being one of the better-documented third-party libraries and is extremely easy to use out of the box.

Forked off the Python Imaging Library (PIL) for Python 2.x, Pillow adds support for Python 3.x. Like its predecessor, Pillow allows you to easily import and manipulate images with a variety of filters, masks, and even pixel-specific transformations:

```
from PIL import Image, ImageFilter

kitten = Image.open('kitten.jpg')
blurryKitten = kitten.filter(ImageFilter.GaussianBlur)
blurryKitten.save('kitten_blurred.jpg')
blurryKitten.show()
```

In the preceding example, the image *kitten.jpg* will open in your default image viewer with a blur added to it and will also be saved in its blurrier state as *kitten_blurred.jpg* in the same directory.

You will use Pillow to perform preprocessing on images to make them more machine readable, but as mentioned before, you can do many other things with the library aside from these simple filter applications. For more information, check out the Pillow documentation (*http://pillow.readthedocs.org*).

Tesseract

Tesseract is an OCR library. Sponsored by Google (a company obviously well-known for its OCR and machine-learning technologies), Tesseract is widely regarded to be the best, most accurate, open source OCR system available.

In addition to being accurate, it is also extremely flexible. It can be trained to recognize any number of fonts (as long as those fonts are relatively consistent within themselves, as you will see soon). It also can be expanded to recognize any Unicode character.

This chapter uses both the command-line program *Tesseract* along with its third-party Python wrapper *pytesseract*. Both will be explicitly named as one of these two, so know that when you see Tesseract, I'm referring to the command-line software, and when you see pytesseract, I'm specifically referring to its third-party Python wrapper.

Installing Tesseract

For Windows users, there is a convenient executable installer (*https://code.google.com/p/tesseract-ocr/downloads/list*). As of this writing, the current version is 3.02, although newer versions should be fine as well.

Linux users can install Tesseract with `apt-get`:

```
$ sudo apt-get tesseract-ocr
```

Installing Tesseract on a Mac is slightly more complicated, although it can be done easily with many third-party installers, such as Homebrew (*http://brew.sh*), which was used in Chapter 9 to install MySQL. For example, you can install Homebrew and use it to install Tesseract in two lines:

```
$ /bin/bash -c "$(curl -fsSL https://raw.githubusercontent.com/Homebrew/install/\
HEAD/install.sh)"
$ brew install tesseract
```

Tesseract also can be installed from the source, on the project's download page (*https://code.google.com/p/tesseract-ocr/downloads/list*).

To convert images to text, Tesseract uses machine learning models that have been trained on large datasets in various languages (or sets of characters). To view the available models that come with your installation, use the command:

```
$ tesseract --list-langs
```

This will print the directory where the models are stored (*/usr/local/share* on Linux, and */opt/homebrew/share/tessdata/* on a Mac installed with HomeBrew) and the models that are available.

After Tesseract is installed, you're ready to install the Python wrapper library, pytesseract, which uses your existing Tesseract installation to read image files and output strings and objects that can be used in Python scripts.

As usual, you can install pytesseract via pip:

```
$ pip install pytesseract
```

Pytesseract can be used in conjunction with PIL to read text from images:

```
from PIL import Image
import pytesseract

print(pytesseract.image_to_string(Image.open('files/test.png')))
```

If pytesseract does not recognize that you have Tesseract installed, you can get the location of your Tesseract installation using the command:

```
$ which tesseract
```

and, in Python, point pytesseract to the location by including this line:

```
pytesseract.pytesseract.tesseract_cmd = '/path/to/tesseract'
```

Pytesseract has several useful features in addition to returning the OCR results of an image as in the code sample above. It can estimate box files (pixel locations for the boundaries of each character):

```
print(pytesseract.image_to_boxes(Image.open('files/test.png')))
```

It can also return a complete output of all data, such as confidence scores, page and line numbers, box data, as well as other information:

```
print(pytesseract.image_to_data(Image.open('files/test.png')))
```

The default output for these last two files is as space- or tab-delimited string files, but you can also get output as dictionaries or (if decoding in UTF-8 isn't sufficient) byte strings:

```
from PIL import Image
import pytesseract
from pytesseract import Output

print(pytesseract.image_to_data(Image.open('files/test.png'),
    output_type=Output.DICT))
print(pytesseract.image_to_string(Image.open('files/test.png'),
    output_type=Output.BYTES))
```

This chapter uses a combination of the pytesseract library, as well as command-line Tesseract and triggering Tesseract from Python via the `subprocess` library. Although the pytesseract library is useful and convenient, there are some Tesseract functions it cannot do, so it's good to be familiar with all methods.

NumPy

While NumPy is not required for straightforward OCR, you will need it if you want to train Tesseract to recognize additional character sets or fonts introduced later in this chapter. You will also be using it for simple math tasks (such as weighted averages) in some of the code samples later in this chapter.

NumPy is a powerful library used for linear algebra and other large-scale math applications. NumPy works well with Tesseract because of its ability to mathematically represent and manipulate images as large arrays of pixels.

NumPy can be installed using any third-party Python installer such as pip, or by downloading the package (*https://pypi.python.org/pypi/numpy*) and installing with `$ python setup.py install`.

Even if you don't plan on running any of the code samples that use it, I highly recommend installing it or adding it to your Python arsenal. It serves to round out Python's built-in math library and has many useful features, particularly for operations with lists of numbers.

By convention, NumPy is imported as `np` and can be used as follows:

```
import numpy as np

numbers = [100, 102, 98, 97, 103]
print(np.std(numbers))
print(np.mean(numbers))
```

This example prints the standard deviation and mean of the set of numbers provided to it.

Processing Well-Formatted Text

With any luck, most of the text that you'll need to process will be relatively clean and well formatted. Well-formatted text generally meets several requirements, although the line between what is "messy" and what is "well formatted" can be subjective.

In general, well-formatted text:

- Is written in one standard font (excluding handwriting fonts, cursive fonts, or excessively decorative fonts)
- If copied or photographed, has extremely crisp lines, with no copying artifacts or dark spots
- Is well aligned, without slanted letters
- Does not run off the image, nor is there cut-off text or margins on the edges of the image

Some of these things can be fixed in preprocessing. For instance, images can be converted to grayscale, brightness and contrast can be adjusted, and the image can be cropped and rotated as needed. However, some fundamental limitations might require more extensive training. See "Reading CAPTCHAs and Training Tesseract" on page 248.

Figure 16-1 is an ideal example of well-formatted text.

> This is some text, written in Arial, that will be read by
> Tesseract. Here are some symbols: !@#$%^&*()

Figure 16-1. Sample text saved as a .tiff file, to be read by Tesseract

In the *files* directory, you can run Tesseract from the command line to read this file and write the results to a text file:

```
$ tesseract text.png textoutput
$ cat textoutput.txt
```

The output contains the contents of the newly created *textoutput.txt* file:

```
This is some text, written in Arial, that will be read by
Tesseract. Here are some symbols: !|@#$%&*()
```

You can see that the results are mostly accurate, although it added an extra pipe character between the ! and the @. On the whole, though, this lets you read the text fairly comfortably.

After blurring the image text, creating some JPG compression artifacts, and adding a slight background gradient, the Tesseract's results get much worse (see Figure 16-2).

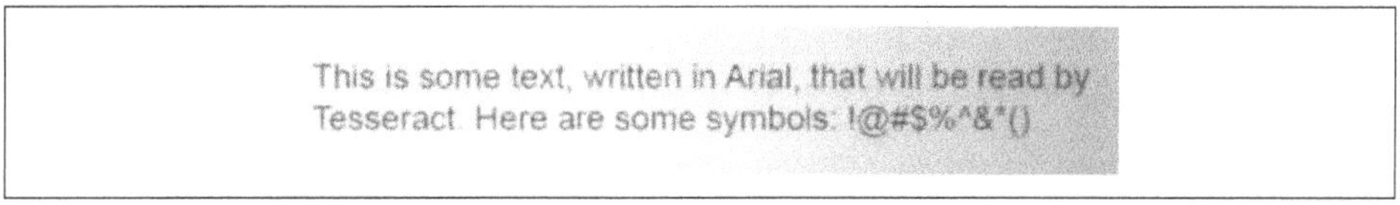

Figure 16-2. Unfortunately, many of the documents you will encounter on the internet will look more like this than the previous example

Rather than write the results to a file, you can also pass a dash character (-) where the filename would normally be, and Tesseract will echo the results to the terminal:

```
$ tesseract text_bad.png -
```

Tesseract is not able to deal with this image nearly as well mainly because of the background gradient and produces the following output:

```
This is some text, written In Arlal, that"
Tesseract. Here are some symbols: _
```

Notice that the text is cut off as soon as the background gradient makes the text more difficult to distinguish, and that the last character from each line is wrong, as Tesseract tries futilely to make sense of it. In addition, the JPG artifacts and blurring make it difficult for Tesseract to distinguish between a lowercase *i* and an uppercase *I* and the number *1*.

This is where using a Python script to clean your images first comes in handy. Using the Pillow library, you can create a threshold filter to get rid of the gray in the background, bring out the text, and make the image clearer for Tesseract to read.

In addition, instead of using Tesseract from the command line, you can use the pytesseract library to run the Tesseract commands and read the resulting file:

```python
from PIL import Image
import pytesseract

def cleanFile(filePath, newFilePath):
    image = Image.open(filePath)

    #Set a threshold value for the image, and save
    image = image.point(lambda x: 0 if x < 143 else 255)
    image.save(newFilePath)
    return image

image = cleanFile('files/textBad.png', 'files/textCleaned.png')

#call tesseract to do OCR on the newly created image
print(pytesseract.image_to_string(image))
```

The resulting image, automatically created as *text_cleaned.png*, is shown in Figure 16-3.

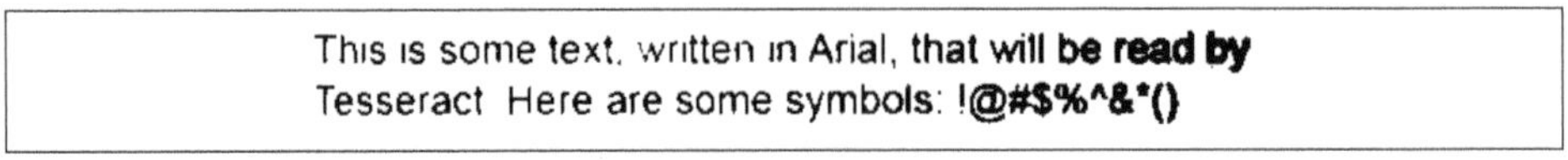

> This is some text, written in Arial, that will **be read by**
> Tesseract Here are some symbols: !@#$%^&*()

Figure 16-3. This image was created by passing the previous "messy" version of the image through a threshold filter

Apart from some barely legible or missing punctuation, the text is readable, at least to us. Tesseract gives it its best shot:

```
This is some text, written In Anal, that will be read by
Tesseract Here are some symbols: !@#$%"&'()
```

The periods and commas, being extremely small, are the first victims of this image wrangling and nearly disappear, both from our view and Tesseract's. There's also the unfortunate misinterpretation of "Arial" as "Anal," the result of Tesseract interpreting the *r* and the *i* as the single character *n*.

Still, it's an improvement over the previous version, in which nearly half of the text was cut off.

Tesseract's greatest weakness seems to be backgrounds with varying brightness. Tesseract's algorithms attempt to adjust the contrast of the image automatically before reading the text, but you can probably get better results doing this yourself with a tool like the Pillow library.

Images you should definitely fix before submitting to Tesseract are those that are tilted, have large areas of nontext, or have other problems.

Adjusting Images Automatically

In the previous example, the value 143 was chosen experimentally as the "ideal" threshold to adjust all image pixels to black or white, in order for Tesseract to read the image. But what if you have many images, all with slightly different grayscale problems, and aren't reasonably able to go and adjust all of them by hand?

One way to find the best solution (or at least, a pretty good one) is to run Tesseract against a range of images adjusted to different values and algorithmically choose the one with the best result, as measured by some combination of the number of characters and/or strings Tesseract is able to read, and the "confidence" with which it reads those characters.

Which algorithm you use, exactly, may vary slightly from application to application, but this is one example of iterating through image-processing thresholds to find the "best" setting:

```
import pytesseract
from pytesseract import Output
from PIL import Image
```

```
import numpy as np

def cleanFile(filePath, threshold):
    image = Image.open(filePath)
    #Set a threshold value for the image, and save
    image = image.point(lambda x: 0 if x < threshold else 255)
    return image

def getConfidence(image):
    data = pytesseract.image_to_data(image, output_type=Output.DICT)
    text = data['text']
    confidences = []
    numChars = []

    for i in range(len(text)):
        if data['conf'][i] > -1:
            confidences.append(data['conf'][i])
            numChars.append(len(text[i]))

    return np.average(confidences, weights=numChars), sum(numChars)

filePath = 'files/textBad.png'

start = 80
step = 5
end = 200

for threshold in range(start, end, step):
    image = cleanFile(filePath, threshold)
    scores = getConfidence(image)
    print("threshold: " + str(threshold) + ", confidence: "
        + str(scores[0]) + " numChars " + str(scores[1]))
```

This script has two functions:

cleanFile

Takes in an original "bad" file and a threshold variable to run the PIL threshold tool with. It processes the file and returns the PIL image object.

getConfidence

Takes in the cleaned PIL image object and runs it through Tesseract. It calculates the average confidence of each recognized string (weighted by the number of characters in that string), as well as the number of recognized characters.

By varying the threshold value and getting the confidence and number of recognized characters at each value, you get the output:

```
threshold: 80, confidence: 61.8333333333 numChars 18
threshold: 85, confidence: 64.9130434783 numChars 23
threshold: 90, confidence: 62.2564102564 numChars 39
threshold: 95, confidence: 64.5135135135 numChars 37
threshold: 100, confidence: 60.7878787879 numChars 66
```

```
threshold: 105, confidence: 61.9078947368 numChars 76
threshold: 110, confidence: 64.6329113924 numChars 79
threshold: 115, confidence: 69.7397260274 numChars 73
threshold: 120, confidence: 72.9078947368 numChars 76
threshold: 125, confidence: 73.582278481 numChars 79
threshold: 130, confidence: 75.6708860759 numChars 79
threshold: 135, confidence: 76.8292682927 numChars 82
threshold: 140, confidence: 72.1686746988 numChars 83
threshold: 145, confidence: 75.5662650602 numChars 83
threshold: 150, confidence: 77.5443037975 numChars 79
threshold: 155, confidence: 79.1066666667 numChars 75
threshold: 160, confidence: 78.4666666667 numChars 75
threshold: 165, confidence: 80.1428571429 numChars 70
threshold: 170, confidence: 78.4285714286 numChars 70
threshold: 175, confidence: 76.3731343284 numChars 67
threshold: 180, confidence: 76.7575757576 numChars 66
threshold: 185, confidence: 79.4920634921 numChars 63
threshold: 190, confidence: 76.0793650794 numChars 63
threshold: 195, confidence: 70.6153846154 numChars 65
```

There is a clear trend among both the average confidence in the result, as well as the number of characters recognized. Both tend to peak around a threshold of 145, which is close to the manually found "ideal" result of 143.

Thresholds of both 140 and 145 give the maximum number of recognized characters (83), but a threshold of 145 gives the highest confidence for those found characters, so you may want to go with that result and return the text that was recognized at that threshold as the "best guess" for what text the image contains.

Of course, simply finding the "most" characters does not necessarily mean that all of those characters are real. At some thresholds, Tesseract could split single characters into multiple ones, or interpret random noise in the image as a text character that doesn't actually exist. In this case, you may want to rely more heavily on the average confidence of each score.

For example, if you find results that read (in part):

```
threshold: 145, confidence: 75.5662650602 numChars 83
threshold: 150, confidence: 97.1234567890 numChars 82
```

it would probably be a no-brainer to go with the result that gives you over a 20% increase in confidence, with only a one-character loss, and assume that the result with a threshold of 145 was simply incorrect, or perhaps split a character or found something that wasn't there.

This is the part where some up-front experimentation to perfect your threshold selection algorithm may come in handy. For instance, you may want to select the score for which the *product* of the confidence and the number of characters is maximized (in this case, 145 still wins with a product of 6272, and in our imaginary example, the threshold 150 would win with a product of 7964) or some other metric.

Note that this type of selection algorithm also works with arbitrary PIL tool values besides just `threshold`. You also can use it to select two or more values by varying the values of each and similarly selecting the best resulting score.

Obviously, this type of selection algorithm is computationally intensive. You're running both PIL and Tesseract many times on every single image, whereas if you know the "ideal" threshold values ahead of time, you have to run them only once.

Keep in mind that, as you start to work with the images you're processing, you may start to notice patterns in the "ideal" values found. Instead of trying every threshold from 80 to 200, you may realistically need to try only thresholds from 130 to 180.

You may even take another approach and choose thresholds that are, say, 20 apart on the first pass, and then use a greedy algorithm to hone in on the best result by decreasing your step size for thresholds between the "best" solutions found in the previous iteration. This may also work best when you're dealing with multiple variables.

Scraping Text from Images on Websites

Using Tesseract to read text from an image on your hard drive might not seem all that exciting, but it can be a powerful tool when used with a web scraper. Images can inadvertently obfuscate text on websites (as with the JPG copy of a menu on a local restaurant site), but they can also purposefully hide the text, as I'll show in the next example.

Although Amazon's *robots.txt* file allows scraping of the site's product pages, book previews typically don't get picked up by passing bots. That's because the book previews are loaded via user-triggered Ajax scripts, and the images are carefully hidden in layers of divs and an iframe. Of course, even if you could get to the images, there's the not-so-small matter of reading them as text.

The following script accomplishes just this feat: it navigates to the large-print edition of Tolstoy's *The Death of Ivan Ilyich*, opens the reader, collects image URLs, and then systematically downloads, reads, and prints the text from each one.

Picking a Test Subject

When it comes to processing fonts it hasn't been trained on, Tesseract fares much better with large-format editions of books, especially if the images are small. The next section covers how to train Tesseract on different fonts, which can help it read much smaller font sizes, including previews for non-large-print book editions!

Note that this code depends on a live Amazon listing as well as several architectural features of the Amazon website to run correctly. If this listing goes down or is replaced, please fill free to substitute the URL of another book with a Preview feature (I find that large print, sans serif fonts work well).

Because this is relatively complex code that draws on multiple concepts from previous chapters, I've added comments throughout to make it a little easier to understand what's going on:

```python
# Retrieve and image URL and read the image as text
def image_to_text(image):
    urlretrieve(image, 'page.jpg')
    imageList.append(image)
    print(pytesseract.image_to_string(Image.open('page.jpg')))

# Create new Selenium driver
driver = webdriver.Chrome(service=Service(CHROMEDRIVER_PATH))

driver.get(
    'https://www.amazon.com/Death-Ivan-Ilyich-Nikolayevich-Tolstoy/\
dp/1427027277')

# Click on the book preview button
driver.find_element(By.ID, 'litb-canvas-click-wrapper').click()
try:
    # Wait for iframe to load
    WebDriverWait(driver, 600).until(
        EC.presence_of_element_located((By.ID, 'litb-read-frame'))
    )
except TimeoutException:
    print('Did not find the iframe')

# Switch to iframe
frame = driver.find_element(By.ID, 'litb-read-frame')
driver.switch_to.frame(frame)

try:
    Wait for preview reader to load
    WebDriverWait(driver, 600).until(
        EC.presence_of_element_located((By.ID, 'kr-renderer'))
    )
except TimeoutException:
    print('Did not find the images')

# Collect all images inside divs with the "data-page" attribute
images = driver.find_elements(By.XPATH, '//div[@data-page]/img')
for image in images:
    image_url = image.get_attribute('src')
    image_to_text(image_url)

driver.quit()
```

Although this script can, in theory, be run with any type of Selenium webdriver, I've found that it currently works most reliably with Chrome.

As you have experienced with the Tesseract reader before, this prints many long passages of the book mostly legibly, as seen in the preview of the first chapter:

```
Chapter I

During an interval in the Melvinski trial in the large
building of the Law Courts the members and public
prosecutor met in Ivan Egorovich Shebek's private
room, where the conversation turned on the celebrated
Krasovski case. Fedor Vasilievich warmly maintained
that it was not subject to their jurisdiction, Ivan
Egorovich maintained the contrary, while Peter
Ivanovich, not having entered into the discussion at
the start, took no part in it but looked through the
Gazette which had just been handed in.

"Gentlemen," he said, "Ivan Ilych has died!"
```

The large print and sans serif font makes for a flawless transcription of the images. In cases where errors in the transcription might occur, they can be fixed by making guesses based on a dictionary word list (perhaps with additions based on relevant proper nouns like "Melvinski").

Occasionally, an error may span an entire word, such as on page three of the text:

```
it is he who is dead and not 1.
```

In this case the word "I" is replaced by the character "1." A Markov chain analysis might be useful here, in addition to a word dictionary. If any part of the text contains an extremely uncommon phrase ("and not 1"), it might be assumed that the text was actually the more common phrase ("and not I").

Of course, it helps that these character substitutions follow predictable patterns: "vi" becomes "w," and "I" becomes "1." If these substitutions occur frequently in your text, you might create a list of them that can be used to "try" new words and phrases, selecting the solution that makes the most sense. An approach might be to substitute frequently confused characters, and use a solution that matches a word in a dictionary, or is a recognized (or most common) n-gram.

If you do take this approach, be sure to read Chapter 12 for more information about working with text and natural language processing.

Although the text in this example is a common sans serif font and Tesseract should be able to recognize it with relative ease, sometimes a little retraining helps improve the accuracy as well. The next section discusses another approach to solving the problem of mangled text with a little up-front time investment.

By providing Tesseract with a large collection of text images with known values, Tesseract can be "taught" to recognize the same font in the future with far greater precision and accuracy, even despite occasional background and positioning problems in the text.

Reading CAPTCHAs and Training Tesseract

Although the word *CAPTCHA* is familiar to most, far fewer people know what it stands for: *Completely Automated Public Turing Test to Tell Computers and Humans Apart*. Its unwieldy acronym hints at its rather unwieldy role in obstructing otherwise perfectly usable web interfaces, as both humans and nonhuman robots often struggle to solve CAPTCHA tests.

The Turing test was first described by Alan Turing in his 1950 paper, "Computing Machinery and Intelligence." In the paper, he described a theoretical scenario in which a human being could communicate with both humans and artificial intelligence programs through a computer terminal. If the human was unable to distinguish the humans from the AI programs during a casual conversation, the AI programs would be considered to have passed the Turing test. The artificial intelligence, Turing reasoned, would be genuinely "thinking" for all intents and purposes.

Seventy years after the theoretical inception of Turing tests, today CAPTCHAs are primarily used to infuriate humans rather than machines. In 2017, Google shut down its iconic reCAPTCHA due in large part to its tendency to block legitimate website users.[1] (See Figure 16-4 for an example.) Many other companies followed suit, replacing the traditional text-based CAPTCHAs with alternative bot blockers.

Figure 16-4. Text from Google reCAPTCHA, prior to 2017

Although CAPTCHAs have declined somewhat in popularity, they are still commonly used, especially on smaller sites. They are also useful as a source of sample "difficult" text for a computer to read. Perhaps your goal is not solving CAPTCHAs but reading badly scanned PDFs or handwritten notes. The principles are the same.

With that in mind, I've created a form that robots are "blocked" from submitting because it requires solving a CAPTCHA: *https://pythonscraping.com/humans-only/*. In

---

1 See Rhett Jones, "Google Has Finally Killed the CAPTCHA," Gizmodo, March 11, 2017, *https://gizmodo.com/google-has-finally-killed-the-captcha-1793190374*.

this section, you will train the Tesseract library on its specific font and text variations in order to solve this CAPTCHA with high reliability.

In case you are a robot and have trouble reading this image, "U8DG" is the solution to the CAPTCHA in Figure 16-5. Tesseract, being a robot, certainly has trouble solving it.

Figure 16-5. The bot-proof captcha at https://pythonscraping.com/humans-only/

```
$ tesseract U8DG.png -

u& DS
```

In this case, Tesseract returns five characters (including a space) and gets only one of the characters, the uppercase D, correctly.

The issue isn't that Tesseract is bad at reading text, or that this CAPTCHA is too difficult for a computer to comprehend—it's that this particular handwriting font is dissimilar to the regular English-language fonts that Tesseract has been trained on "out of the box." Fortunately, it is possible to train it to recognize additional fonts, characters, and languages.

Training Tesseract

Whether you're training for CAPTCHAs or any other text, there are a few factors to consider that greatly impact Tesseract's performance and the approach you might take for training it:

- Do characters overlap in the image, or can you draw a neat rectangle around each character without parts of any other character infringing on this rectangle?
- Are there multiple variations of the font or style of writing or is only a single font used?
- Are there any background images, lines, or other distracting garbage in the image?

- Is there high contrast with clear boundaries between the characters and the background?
- Is the font a fairly standard serif or sans serif font, or is it an unusual font with random elements and perhaps a "handwriting" style?

If there is some overlap of the characters in some of the text samples, you might consider using only text samples where no overlap occurs. If overlap occurs in every text sample, consider preprocessing to separate characters before training.

Scraping and preparing images

Preprocessing helps remove any background junk and improves the color, contrast, and separation of characters in images.

How Many Images Do You Need?

How many images should you obtain? I recommend about 10 examples per character, or more if there is high variation or randomness in your text. Tesseract does occasionally discard files as being unreadable, for having overlapping boxes, or for other arcane reasons, so you may want some buffer room on top of that. If you find that your OCR results aren't quite as good as you'd like, or Tesseract is stumbling over certain characters, it's a good debugging step to create additional training data and try again.

In addition, if there are multiple variations of fonts in the same text sample or if there are other variations involved (randomly tilted or obfuscated text), you may need more training data.

If the font is fairly standard and there are no other severe complicating factors, make sure you've tried Tesseract without additional training first! The performance without training may be acceptable for your needs, and training can be a very time-consuming process.

Training requires giving Tesseract at least a few examples of each character you want it to be able to recognize. The following downloads 100 sample CAPTCHA images, each containing four characters, for a total of 400 character samples:

```
from bs4 import BeautifulSoup
from urllib.request import urlopen, urlretrieve
import os

if not os.path.exists('captchas'):
    os.mkdir('captchas')

for i in range(0, 100):
    bs = BeautifulSoup(urlopen('https://pythonscraping.com/humans-only/'))
```

```
imgUrl = bs.find('img', {'class': 'wpcf7-captchac'})['src']
urlretrieve(imgUrl, f'captchas/{imgUrl.split("/")[-1]}')
```

After reviewing the downloaded training images, it's time to decide what sort of pre-processing, if any, needs to be done. The images in this CAPTCHA have gray text on a black background. You can write a `cleanImage` function that transforms this into black text on a white background and adds a white border to make sure each character has separation from the edge of the image:

```
def cleanImage(imagePath):
    image = Image.open(imagePath)
    image = image.point(lambda x: 255 if x<143 else 0)
    image = ImageOps.expand(image,border=20,fill='white')
    image.save(imagePath)

for filename in os.listdir('captchas'):
    if '.png' in filename:
        cleanImage(f'captchas/{filename}')
```

Creating box files with the Tesseract trainer project

Next, you need to use these cleaned images to create *box files*. A box file contains each character in the image on its own line, followed by the bounding box coordinates for that character. For example, a CAPTCHA image with the characters "AK6F" might have the corresponding box file:

```
A 32 34 54 58
K 66 32 91 56
6 101 34 117 57
F 135 32 156 57
```

I've created a project at *https://github.com/REMitchell/tesseract-trainer* that contains, among other things, a web app that assists in creating these box files. To create box files using this project, follow these steps:

1. Rename each CAPTCHA image to its solution. For example, the image containing "AK6F" would be renamed to "AK6F.png."

2. In the Tesseract trainer project, open the file *createBoxes.html* in the web browser of your choice.

3. Click the "Add a new file" link and select the multiple image files that you renamed in step 1.

4. The web app will automatically generate boxes based on the image's name. Drag these boxes around their corresponding character, as shown in Figure 16-6.

5. When you are happy with the placement of the boxes, click "Download .box" to download the box file, and the next image should appear.

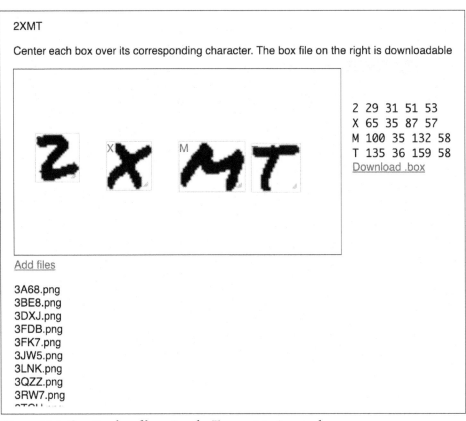

Figure 16-6. *Creating box files using the Tesseract trainer tool*

As an optional step, I recommend putting on a good podcast or TV show, because it's going to be a couple of hours of boring work. Exactly how long depends on how many boxes you need to draw.

The next step after creating your box files is to show off all your hard work to Tesseract and let it get training. The end goal of this process is to create a *traineddata* file that you can add to your Tesseract language directory.

In the Tesseract trainer project at *https://github.com/REMitchell/tesseract-trainer*, I've included a file called trainer.py. This script expects a *data* directory in the project root with the directories *cleaned* and *box* under it:

- *data*
  - *cleaned*
    - CAPTCHA images with any preprocessing and cleaning done, with the filenames matching the box files
  - *box*
    - Box files, as downloaded from the web app

After creating your folders of *.box* files and image files, copy this data into a backup folder before doing any further manipulation on it. Although running training scripts over the data is unlikely to delete anything, it's better safe than sorry when hours worth of work put into *.box* file creation are involved.

Training Tesseract from box files

Performing the data analysis and creating the training files required for Tesseract involves many steps involves many steps. The *trainer.py* file does all of them for you.

The initial settings and steps that this program takes can be seen in the __init__ and runAll methods of the class:

```
CLEANED_DIR = 'cleaned'
BOX_DIR = 'box'
EXP_DIR = 'exp'
class TesseractTrainer():
    def __init__(self, languageName, fontName, directory='data'):
        self.languageName = languageName
        self.fontName = fontName
        self.directory = directory

    def runAll(self):
        os.chdir(self.directory)
        self.createDirectories()
        self.createFontProperties()
        prefixes = self.renameFiles()
        self.createTrainingFiles(prefixes)
        self.extractUnicode()
        self.runShapeClustering()
        self.runMfTraining()
        self.runCnTraining()
        self.createTessData()
```

At the bottom of *trainer.py* a new TesseractTrainer instance is created and the runAll method is called:

```
trainer = TesseractTrainer('captcha', 'captchaFont')
trainer.runAll()
```

The three attributes passed into the `TesseractTrainer` object are:

`languageName`
> The three-letter language code that Tesseract uses to keep track of languages. For specific training scenarios, I prefer to create a new language rather than combine it or use it to replace Tesseract's pre-trained English data.

`fontName`
> The name for your chosen font. This can be anything, but it must be a single word without spaces. In practice, this is just for internal purposes during training, and you're unlikely to see it or need to reference it.

`directory`
> The directory name containing the directories of your cleaned images and box files. By default, this is data. If you have multiple projects, you can pass in a unique data directory name for each project to keep everything organized.

Let's look at some of the individual methods used.

`createDirectories` does some initial housekeeping and creates subdirectories such as the *exp* directory, which will later store the trained files.

`createFontProperties` creates a required file, *font_properties*, that lets Tesseract know about the new font you are creating:

```
captchaFont 0 0 0 0 0
```

This file consists of the name of the font, followed by 1s and 0s indicating whether italic, bold, or other versions of the font should be considered. Training fonts with these properties is an interesting exercise but unfortunately outside the scope of this book.

`renameFiles` renames all your *.box* files and their corresponding image files with the names required by Tesseract (the file numbers here are sequential digits to keep multiple files separate):

- *<languageName>.<fontName>.exp<fileNumber>.box*
- *<languageName>.<fontName>.exp<fileNumber>.tiff*

`extractUnicode` looks at all of the created *.box* files and determines the total set of characters available to be trained. The resulting Unicode file will tell you how many different characters you've found and could be a good way to quickly see if you're missing anything.

The next three functions, runShapeClustering, runMfTraining, and runCtTraining, create the files shapetable, pfftable, and normproto, respectively. These all provide information about the geometry and shape of each character, as well as provide statistical information that Tesseract uses to calculate the probability that a given character is one type or another.

Finally, Tesseract renames each of the compiled data folders to be prepended by the required language name (e.g., *shapetable* is renamed to *cap.shapetable*) and compiles all of those files into the final training data file *cap.traineddata*.

Using traineddata files with Tesseract

The *traineddata* file is the main output of this entire process. This file tells Tesseract how to identify characters in the training dataset you've given it. To use the file, you need to move it to your *tessdata* root folder.

You can find this folder using the following command:

```
$ tesseract --list-langs
```

This will provide some output like:

```
List of available languages in "/opt/homebrew/share/tessdata/" (3):
eng
osd
snum
```

Then set the TESSDATA_PREFIX environment variable to this directory:

```
$ export TESSDATA_PREFIX=/opt/homebrew/share/tessdata/
```

Finally, move your new *traineddata* file to the *languages* directory:

```
$ cp data/exp/cap.traineddata $TESSDATA_PREFIX/cap.traineddata
```

After the new *traineddata* file is in place, Tesseract should recognize it automatically as a new language and be able to solve new CAPTCHAs it's presented with:

```
$ tesseract -l captcha U8DG.png -

U8DG
```

Success! A significant improvement over the previous interpretation of the image as u& DS.

This is just a quick overview of the full power of Tesseract's font training and recognition capabilities. If you are interested in extensively training Tesseract, perhaps starting your own library of CAPTCHA training files, or sharing new font recognition capabilities with the world, I recommend checking out the documentation (*https://github.com/tesseract-ocr/tesseract*).

Retrieving CAPTCHAs and Submitting Solutions

Many popular content management systems are frequently spammed with registrations by bots that are preprogrammed with the well-known location of these user registration pages. On *http://pythonscraping.com*, for instance, even a CAPTCHA (admittedly, weak) does little to put a damper on the influx of registrations.

So how do these bots do it? You've successfully solved CAPTCHAs in images sitting around on your hard drive, but how do you make a fully functioning bot? This section ties together many techniques covered in previous chapters. If you haven't already, you should at least skim Chapter 13.

Most image-based CAPTCHAs have several properties:

- They are dynamically generated images, created by a server-side program. They might have image sources that do not look like traditional images, such as <img src="WebForm.aspx?id=8AP85CQKE9TJ">, but can be downloaded and manipulated like any other image.
- The solution to the image is stored in a server-side database.
- Many CAPTCHAs time out if you take too long to solve them. This usually isn't a problem for bots, but queuing CAPTCHA solutions for later use, or other practices that may delay the time between when the CAPTCHA was requested and when the solution is submitted, may not be successful.

The general approach to this is to download the CAPTCHA image file to your hard drive, clean it, use Tesseract to parse the image, and return the solution under the appropriate form parameter.

I've created a page at *http://pythonscraping.com/humans-only* with a CAPTCHA-protected comment form for the purpose of writing a bot to defeat. This bot uses the command-line Tesseract library, rather than the pytesseract wrapper, although either could be used.

To start, load the page and find the location of a hidden token that needs to be POSTed with the rest of the form data:

```
html = urlopen('https://www.pythonscraping.com/humans-only')
bs = BeautifulSoup(html, 'html.parser')
#Gather prepopulated form values
hiddenToken = bs.find(
    'input',
    {'name':'_wpcf7_captcha_challenge_captcha-170'}
)['value']
```

This hidden token also happens to be the filename of the CAPTCHA image presented on the page, which makes writing the `getCaptchaSolution` function relatively straightforward:

```python
def getCaptchaSolution(hiddenToken):
    imageLocation = f'https://pythonscraping.com/wp-content/\
uploads/wpcf7_captcha/{hiddenToken}.png'
    urlretrieve(imageLocation, 'captcha.png')
    cleanImage('captcha.png')
    p = subprocess.Popen(
        ['tesseract','-l', 'captcha', 'captcha.png', 'output'],
        stdout=subprocess.PIPE,stderr=subprocess.PIPE
    )
    p.wait()
    f = open('output.txt', 'r')

    #Clean any whitespace characters
    captchaResponse = f.read().replace(' ', '').replace('\n', '')
    print('Captcha solution attempt: '+captchaResponse)
    return captchaResponse
```

Note that this script will fail under two conditions: if Tesseract did not extract exactly four characters from the image (because we know that all valid solutions to this CAPTCHA must have four characters), or if it submits the form but the CAPTCHA was solved incorrectly.

In the first case, you can reload the page and try again, likely with no penalty from the web server. In the second case, the server might take note that you're solving CAPTCHAs incorrectly and penalize you. Many servers, on multiple failed CAPTCHA attempts, will block the user or subject them to more rigorous screening.

Of course, as the owner of this particular server I can attest to the fact that it's extremely forgiving and unlikely to block you!

The form data itself is relatively lengthy and can be viewed in full in the GitHub repository or in your browser's network inspector tools when submitting the form yourself. Checking the length of the CAPTCHA solution and submitting it using the Requests library is fairly straightforward, however:

```python
if len(captcha_solution) == 4:
    formSubmissionUrl = 'https://pythonscraping.com/wp-json/contact-form-7/v1/\
contact-forms/93/feedback'
    headers = {'Content-Type': 'multipart/form-data;boundary=----WebKitFormBou\
ndaryBFvsPGsghJe0Esco'}
    r = requests.post(formSubmissionUrl, data=form_data, headers=headers)
    print(r.text)
else:
    print('There was a problem reading the CAPTCHA correctly!')
```

If the CAPTCHA solution was correct (and it usually is), you should expect to see something like the following printed out:

```
Captcha solution attempt: X9SU
{"contact_form_id":93,"status":"mail_sent","message":
"Thank you for your message. It has been sent.",
"posted_data_hash":"2bc8d1e0345bbfc281eac0410fc7b80d",
"into":"#wpcf7-f93-o1","invalid_fields":[],"captcha":
{"captcha-170":
"https:\/\/pythonscraping.com\/wp-content\/uploads
\/wpcf7_captcha\/3551342528.png"}}
```

While CAPTCHAs are not as common as they were 10 or 20 years ago, they are still used by many sites, and knowing how to handle them is important. In addition, the skills gained by working with CAPTCHA solving easily translate to other image-to-text scenarios you may encounter.

Avoiding Scraping Traps

Few things are more frustrating than scraping a site, viewing the output, and not seeing the data that's so clearly visible in your browser. Or submitting a form that should be perfectly fine but gets denied by the web server. Or getting your IP address blocked by a site for unknown reasons.

These are some of the most difficult bugs to solve, not only because they can be so unexpected (a script that works just fine on one site might not work at all on another, seemingly identical, site), but because they purposefully don't have any telltale error messages or stack traces to use. You've been identified as a bot, rejected, and you don't know why.

In this book, I've written about a lot of ways to do tricky things on websites, including submitting forms, extracting and cleaning difficult data, and executing JavaScript. This chapter is a bit of a catchall in that the techniques stem from a wide variety of subjects. However, they all have something in common: they are meant to overcome an obstacle put in place for the sole purpose of preventing automated scraping of a site.

Regardless of how immediately useful this information is to you at the moment, I highly recommend you at least skim this chapter. You never know when it might help you solve a difficult bug or prevent a problem altogether.

A Note on Ethics

In the first few chapters of this book, I discussed the legal gray area that web scraping inhabits, as well as some of the ethical and legal guidelines to scrape by. To be honest, this chapter is, ethically, perhaps the most difficult one for me to write. My websites have been plagued by bots, spammers, web scrapers, and all manner of unwanted virtual guests, as perhaps yours have been. So why teach people how to build better bots?

I believe this chapter is important to include for a few reasons:

- There are perfectly ethical and legally sound reasons to scrape some websites that do not want to be scraped. In a previous job I had as a web scraper, I performed automated collection of information from websites that were publishing clients' names, addresses, telephone numbers, and other personal information to the internet without their consent. I used the scraped information to make legal requests to the websites to remove this information. To avoid competition, these sites vigilantly guarded this information from scrapers. However, my work to ensure the anonymity of my company's clients (some of whom had stalkers, were the victims of domestic violence, or had other very good reasons to want to keep a low profile) made a compelling case for web scraping, and I was grateful that I had the skills necessary to do the job.

- Although it is almost impossible to build a "scraper proof" site (or at least one that can still be easily accessed by legitimate users), I hope that the information in this chapter will help those wanting to defend their websites against malicious attacks. Throughout, I will point out some of the weaknesses in each web scraping technique, which you can use to defend your own site. Keep in mind that most bots on the web today are merely doing a broad scan for information and vulnerabilities; employing even a couple of simple techniques described in this chapter likely will thwart 99% of them. However, they are getting more sophisticated every month, and it's best to be prepared.

- Like most programmers, I don't believe that withholding any sort of educational information is a net positive thing to do.

While you're reading this chapter, keep in mind that many of these scripts and described techniques should not be run against every site you can find. Not only is it not a nice thing to do, but you could wind up receiving a cease and desist letter or worse (for more information about what to do if you receive such a letter, see Chapter 2). But I'm not going to pound you over the head with this every time I discuss a new technique. So, for the rest of this chapter, as the philosopher Gump once said: "That's all I have to say about that."

Looking Like a Human

The fundamental challenge for sites that do not want to be scraped is figuring out how to tell bots from humans. Although many of the techniques sites use (such as CAPTCHAs) can be difficult to fool, you can do a few fairly easy things to make your bot look more human.

Adjust Your Headers

Throughout the book, you've used the Python Requests library to create, send, and receive HTTP requests, such as handling forms on a website in Chapter 13. The Requests library is also excellent for setting headers. HTTP headers are lists of attributes, or preferences, sent by you every time you make a request to a web server. HTTP defines dozens of obscure header types, most of which are not commonly used. The following seven fields, however, are consistently used by most major browsers when initiating any connection (shown with example data from my own browser):

Host	https://www.google.com/
Connection	keep-alive
Accept	text/html,application/xhtml+xml,application/xml;q=0.9,image/avif,image/webp,image/apng,*/*;q=0.8,application/signed-exchange;v=b3;q=0.7
User-Agent	Mozilla/5.0 (Macintosh; Intel Mac OS X 10_15_7) AppleWebKit/537.36 (KHTML, like Gecko) Chrome/113.0.0.0 Safari/537.36
Referrer	https://www.google.com/
Accept-Encoding	gzip, deflate, sdch
Accept-Language	en-US,en;q=0.8

And here are the headers that a typical Python scraper using the default urllib library might send:

Accept-Encoding	identity
User-Agent	Python-urllib/3.9

If you're a website administrator trying to block scrapers, which one are you more likely to let through?

Fortunately, headers can be completely customized using the Requests library. The website *https://www.whatismybrowser.com* is great for testing browser properties viewable by servers. You'll scrape this website to verify your cookie settings with the following script:

```
import requests
from bs4 import BeautifulSoup

session = requests.Session()

headers = {'User-Agent':'Mozilla/5.0 (Macintosh; Intel Mac OS X 10_15_7) \
AppleWebKit/537.36 (KHTML, like Gecko) Chrome/113.0.0.0 Safari/537.36',
        'Accept':'text/html,application/xhtml+xml,application/xml;q=0.9,\
image/avif,image/webp,image/apng,*/*;q=0.8,application/signed-exchange;v=b3;\
q=0.7'}
url = 'https://www.whatismybrowser.com/\
```

```
developers/what-http-headers-is-my-browser-sending'
req = session.get(url, headers=headers)

bs = BeautifulSoup(req.text, 'html.parser')
print(bs.find('table', {'class':'table-striped'}).get_text)
```

The output should show that the headers are now the same ones set in the `headers` dictionary object in the code.

Although it is possible for websites to check for "humanness" based on any of the properties in HTTP headers, I've found that typically the only setting that really matters is the `User-Agent`. It's a good idea to keep this one set to something more inconspicuous than `Python-urllib/3.9`, regardless of what project you are working on. In addition, if you ever encounter an extremely suspicious website, populating one of the commonly used but rarely checked headers such as `Accept-Language` might be the key to convincing it you're a human.

Headers Change the Way You See the World

Let's say you want to write a machine-learning language translator for a research project but lack large amounts of translated text to test with. Many large sites present different translations of the same content, based on the indicated language preferences in your headers. Simply changing `Accept-Language:en-US` to `Accept-Language:fr` in your headers might get you a "Bonjour" from websites with the scale and budget to handle translation (large international companies are usually a good bet).

Headers also can prompt websites to change the format of the content they are presenting. For instance, mobile devices browsing the web often see a pared-down version of sites, lacking banner ads, Flash, and other distractions. If you try changing your `User-Agent` to something like the following, you might find that sites get a little easier to scrape!

```
User-Agent:Mozilla/5.0 (iPhone; CPU iPhone OS 7_1_2 like Mac OS X)
AppleWebKit/537.51.2 (KHTML, like Gecko) Version/7.0 Mobile/11D257
Safari/9537.53
```

Handling Cookies with JavaScript

Handling cookies correctly can alleviate many scraping problems, although cookies can also be a double-edged sword. Websites that track your progression through a site using cookies might attempt to cut off scrapers that display abnormal behavior, such as completing forms too quickly, or visiting too many pages. Although these behaviors can be disguised by closing and reopening connections to the site, or even changing your IP address (see Chapter 20 for more information on how to do that), if your cookie gives your identity away, your efforts at disguise might be futile.

Cookies can also be necessary to scrape a site. As shown in Chapter 13, staying logged in on a site requires that you be able to hold and present a cookie from page to page. Some websites don't even require that you actually log in and get a new version of a cookie every time—merely holding an old copy of a "logged-in" cookie and visiting the site is enough.

If you are scraping a single targeted website or a small number of targeted sites, I recommend examining the cookies generated by those sites and considering which ones you might want your scraper to handle. Various browser plug-ins can show you how cookies are being set as you visit and move around a site. EditThisCookie (*http://www.editthiscookie.com*), a Chrome extension, is one of my favorites.

Check out the code samples in "Handling Logins and Cookies" on page 199 in Chapter 13 for more information about handling cookies by using the Requests library. Of course, because it is unable to execute JavaScript, the Requests library will be unable to handle many of the cookies produced by modern tracking software, such as Google Analytics, which are set only after the execution of client-side scripts (or sometimes based on page events, such as button clicks, that happen while browsing the page). To handle these, you need to use the Selenium and Chrome WebDriver packages (I covered their installation and basic usage in Chapter 14).

You can view cookies by visiting any site (*http://pythonscraping.com*, in this example) and calling get_cookies() on the webdriver:

```
from selenium import webdriver
from selenium.webdriver.chrome.options import Options
chrome_options = Options()
chrome_options.add_argument('--headless')
driver = webdriver.Chrome(
    executable_path='drivers/chromedriver',
    options=chrome_options)
driver.get('http://pythonscraping.com')
driver.implicitly_wait(1)
print(driver.get_cookies())
```

This provides the fairly typical array of Google Analytics cookies:

```
[{'domain': '.pythonscraping.com', 'expiry': 1722996491, 'httpOnly': False,
'name': '_ga', 'path': '/', 'sameSite': 'Lax', 'secure': False, 'value':
'GA1.1.285394841.1688436491'}, {'domain': '.pythonscraping.com', 'expiry':
1722996491, 'httpOnly': False, 'name': '_ga_G60J5CGY1N', 'path': '/',
'sameSite': 'Lax', 'secure': False, 'value':
'GS1.1.1688436491.1.0.1688436491.0.0.0'}]
```

To manipulate cookies, you can call the delete_cookie(), add_cookie(), and delete_all_cookies() functions. In addition, you can save and store cookies for use in other web scrapers. Here's an example to give you an idea of how these functions work together:

```
from selenium import webdriver
from selenium.webdriver.chrome.options import Options

chrome_options = Options()
chrome_options.add_argument("--headless")
driver = webdriver.Chrome(
    service=Service(CHROMEDRIVER_PATH),
    options=chrome_options
)

driver.get('http://pythonscraping.com')
driver.implicitly_wait(1)

savedCookies = driver.get_cookies()
print(savedCookies)

driver2 = webdriver.Chrome(
    service=Service(CHROMEDRIVER_PATH),
    options=chrome_options
)

driver2.get('http://pythonscraping.com')
driver2.delete_all_cookies()
for cookie in savedCookies:
    driver2.add_cookie(cookie)

driver2.get('http://pythonscraping.com')
driver.implicitly_wait(1)
print(driver2.get_cookies())
```

In this example, the first webdriver retrieves a website, prints the cookies, and then stores them in the variable savedCookies. The second webdriver loads the same website, deletes its own cookies, and adds the cookies from the first webdriver.

Note that the second webdriver must load the website first before the cookies are added. This is so Selenium knows which domain the cookies belong to, even if the act of loading the website does nothing useful for the scraper.

After this is done, the second webdriver should have the same cookies as the first. According to Google Analytics, this second webdriver is now identical to the first one, and they will be tracked in the same way. If the first webdriver was logged in to a site, the second webdriver will be as well.

TLS Fingerprinting

In the early 2000s, many large tech companies liked to ask prospective programmers riddles during job interviews. This mostly fell out of fashion when hiring managers realized two things: candidates were sharing and memorizing riddle solutions, and the "ability to solve riddles" doesn't correlate well to job performance.

However, one of these classic job interview riddles still has value as a metaphor for the Transport Layer Security protocol. It goes like this:

You need to ship a top secret message to a friend via a dangerous route where any unlocked message-containing boxes are intercepted by spies (padlocked message boxes, however, are safe if the spies do not have the keys). You place the message in a box that can be locked with multiple padlocks. While you have padlocks with corresponding keys and your friend also has their own padlocks with corresponding keys, none of your friend's keys work on your padlocks and vice versa. How do you ensure that your friend is able to unlock the box on their end and receive the message securely?

Note that shipping a key that unlocks your padlock, even as a separate shipment, will not work. The spies will intercept and make copies of these keys and save them for later use. Also, shipping a key afterwards will not work (although this is where "riddle as metaphor" breaks down a bit) because the spies can make copies of the *box itself* and, if a key is sent later, unlock their box copy.

One solution is this: you place your padlock on the box and ship it to your friend. Your friend receives the locked box, places their own padlock on it (so now the box has two padlocks), and ships it back. You remove your padlock and ship it to your friend with only their padlock remaining. Your friend receives the box and unlocks it.

This is, essentially, how secure communications are established over an untrusted network. Over a secure communication protocol, like HTTPS, all messages are encrypted and decrypted with a key. If an attacker obtains the key (represented by the secret message in the riddle), then they are able to read any messages being sent.

So how do you send your friend the key that you're going to use to encrypt and decrypt future messages without that key being intercepted and used by attackers? Encrypt it with your own "padlock," send it to the friend, the friend adds their own "padlock," you remove your "padlock," and send it back for the friend to "unlock." In this way, the secret key is exchanged securely.

This entire process of "locking," sending, adding another "lock," etc., is handled by the Transport Layer Security protocol, or TLS. This process of securely establishing a mutually known key is called the *TLS handshake*.

In addition to a establishing a mutually known key, or *master secret*, many other things are established during the handshake:

- The highest version of the TLS protocol supported by both parties (which will be the version used during the rest of the handshake)
- Which encryption library will be used
- Which compression method will be used

- The identity of the server, represented by its public certificate
- Verifications that the master secret is working for both parties and that the communication is now secure

This entire TLS handshake is done every time you contact a new web server and any time you need to establish a new HTTP session with that web server (see Chapter 1 for more information about sessions). The exact messages that are sent by your computer for the TLS handshake are determined by the application that is making the connection. For example, Chrome may support slightly different TLS versions or encryption libraries than Microsoft Edge, so the messages sent by it in the TLS handshake will be different.

Because the TLS handshake is so lengthy, and the variables involved in its negotiations so numerous, clever server administrators realized that the messages sent by clients during the TLS handshake were somewhat unique to each application. The messages created a sort of *TLS fingerprint* that revealed whether the messages were being generated by Chrome, Microsoft Edge, Safari, or even the Python Requests library.

You can see some of the information generated by your TLS handshake by visiting (or scraping) *https://tools.scrapfly.io/api/fp/ja3?extended=1*. To make TLS fingerprints more manageable and easy to compare, a hashing method called JA3 is often used, the results of which are shown in this API response. JA3 hashed fingerprints are catalogued in large databases and used for lookup when an application needs to be identified later.

A TLS fingerprint is a bit like a User-Agent cookie in that it is a long string that identifies the application you're using to send data. But, unlike a User-Agent cookie, it's not easy to modify. In Python, TLS is controlled by the SSL library (*https://github.com/python/cpython/blob/3.11/Lib/ssl.py*). In theory, perhaps you could rewrite the SSL library. With hard work and dedication, you may be able to modify the TLS fingerprint that Python is sending from your computer just enough to make the JA3 hash unrecognizable to servers seeking to block Python bots. With harder work and more dedication, you might impersonate an innocuous browser! Some projects, such as *https://github.com/lwthiker/curl-impersonate*, are seeking to do just that.

Unfortunately the nature of this TLS fingerprint problem means that any impersonation libraries will require frequent maintenance by volunteers and are prone to quick degradation. Until these projects gain more mainstream traction and reliability, there is a much easier way to subvert TLS fingerprinting and blocking: Selenium.

Throughout this book, I've warned against using an automated browser to solve your problems when alternative solutions exist. Browsers use lots of memory, often load unnecessary pages, and require extra dependencies that all need upkeep and maintenance to keep your web crawler running. But when it comes to TLS finger-printing, it just makes sense to avoid the headache and use a browser.

Keep in mind that your TLS fingerprint will be the same whether you're using the headless or nonheadless version of your browser. So feel free to turn off the graphics and use best practices to load only the data that you need—the target server isn't going to know (based on your TLS data, at least)!

Timing Is Everything

Some well-protected websites might prevent you from submitting forms or interacting with the site if you do it too quickly. Even if these security features aren't in place, downloading lots of information from a website significantly faster than a normal human might is a good way to get yourself noticed and blocked.

Therefore, although multithreaded programming might be a great way to load pages faster—allowing you to process data in one thread while repeatedly loading pages in another—it's a terrible policy for writing good scrapers. You should always try to keep individual page loads and data requests to a minimum. If possible, try to space them out by a few seconds, even if you have to add in an extra:

```
import time

time.sleep(3)
```

Whether or not you need this extra few seconds between page loads is often found experimentally. Many times I've struggled to scrape data from a website, having to prove myself as "not a robot" every few minutes (solving the CAPTCHA by hand, pasting my newly obtained cookies back over to the scraper so the website viewed the scraper itself as having "proven its humanness"), but adding a `time.sleep` solved my problems and allowed me to scrape indefinitely.

Sometimes you have to slow down to go fast!

Common Form Security Features

Many litmus tests have been used over the years, and continue to be used, with varying degrees of success, to separate web scrapers from browser-using humans. Although it's not a big deal if a bot downloads some articles and blog posts that were available to the public anyway, it is a big problem if a bot creates thousands of user accounts and starts spamming all of your site's members. Web forms, especially forms that deal with account creation and logins, pose a significant threat to security and computational overhead if they're vulnerable to indiscriminate use by bots, so it's in the best interest of many site owners (or at least they think it is) to try to limit access to the site.

These antibot security measures centered on forms and logins can pose a significant challenge to web scrapers.

Keep in mind that this is only a partial overview of some of the security measures you might encounter when creating automated bots for these forms. Review Chapter 16, on dealing with CAPTCHAs and image processing, as well as Chapter 13, on dealing with headers and IP addresses, for more information on dealing with well-protected forms.

Hidden Input Field Values

"Hidden" fields in HTML forms allow the value contained in the field to be viewable by the browser but invisible to the user (unless they look at the site's source code). With the increase in use of cookies to store variables and pass them around on websites, hidden fields fell out of a favor for a while before another excellent purpose was discovered for them: preventing scrapers from submitting forms.

Figure 17-1 shows an example of these hidden fields at work on a LinkedIn login page. Although the form has only three visible fields (Username, Password, and a Submit button), it conveys a great deal of information to the server behind the scenes.

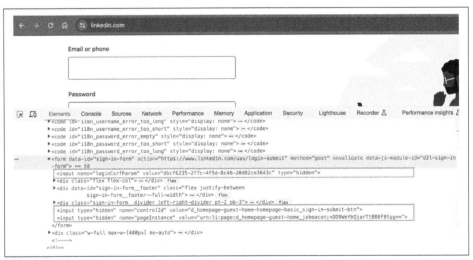

Figure 17-1. The LinkedIn login form has a few hidden fields

Hidden fields are used to prevent web scraping in two main ways: a field can be populated with a randomly generated variable on the form page that the server is expecting to be posted to the form-processing page. If this value is not present in the form, the server can reasonably assume that the submission did not originate organically from the form page but was posted by a bot directly to the processing page. The best way to get around this measure is to scrape the form page first, collect the ran-domly generated variable, and then post to the processing page from there.

The second method is a "honeypot" of sorts. If a form contains a hidden field with an innocuous name, such as Username or Email Address, a poorly written bot might fill out the field and attempt to submit it, regardless of whether it is hidden to the user. Any hidden fields with actual values (or values that are different from their defaults on the form submission page) should be disregarded, and the user may even be blocked from the site.

In short: it is sometimes necessary to check the page that the form is on to see whether you missed anything that the server might be expecting. If you see several hidden fields, often with large, randomly generated string variables, the web server likely will be checking for their existence on form submission. In addition, there might be other checks to ensure that the form variables have been used only once, are recently generated (this eliminates the possibility of simply storing them in a script and using them over and over again over time), or both.

Avoiding Honeypots

Although CSS for the most part makes life extremely easy when it comes to differen-tiating useful information from nonuseful information (e.g., by reading the id and class tags), it can occasionally be problematic for web scrapers. If a field on a web form is hidden from a user via CSS, it is reasonable to assume that the average user visiting the site will not be able to fill it out because it doesn't show up in the browser. If the form *is* populated, there is likely a bot at work and the post will be discarded.

This applies not only to forms but to links, images, files, and any other item on the site that can be read by a bot but is hidden from the average user visiting the site through a browser. A page visit to a "hidden" link on a site can easily trigger a server-side script that will block the user's IP address, log that user out of the site, or take some other action to prevent further access. In fact, many business models have been based on exactly this concept.

Take, for example, the page located at *http://pythonscraping.com/pages/itsatrap.html*. This page contains two links, one hidden by CSS and another visible. In addition, it contains a form with two hidden fields:

```html
<html>
<head>
    <title>A bot-proof form</title>
</head>
<style>
    body {
        overflow-x:hidden;
    }
    .customHidden {
```

```
            position:absolute;
            right:50000px;
        }
    </style>
    <body>
        <h2>A bot-proof form</h2>
        <a href=
          "http://pythonscraping.com/dontgohere" style="display:none;">Go here!</a>
        <a href="http://pythonscraping.com">Click me!</a>
        <form>
            <input type="hidden" name="phone" value="valueShouldNotBeModified"/><p/>
            <input type="text" name="email" class="customHidden"
                    value="intentionallyBlank"/><p/>
            <input type="text" name="firstName"/><p/>
            <input type="text" name="lastName"/><p/>
            <input type="submit" value="Submit"/><p/>
        </form>
    </body>
</html>
```

These three elements are hidden from the user in three ways:

- The first link is hidden with a simple CSS display:none attribute.
- The phone field is a hidden input field.
- The email field is hidden by moving it 50,000 pixels to the right (presumably off the screen of everyone's monitors) and hiding the telltale scroll bar.

Fortunately, because Selenium renders the pages it visits, it is able to distinguish between elements that are visually present on the page and those that aren't. Whether the element is present on the page can be determined by the is_displayed() function.

For example, the following code retrieves the previously described page and looks for hidden links and form input fields:

```
from selenium import webdriver
from selenium.webdriver.remote.webelement import WebElement
from selenium.webdriver.chrome.options import Options
from selenium.webdriver.common.by import By

driver = webdriver.Chrome(service=Service(CHROMEDRIVER_PATH))

driver.get('http://pythonscraping.com/pages/itsatrap.html')
links = driver.find_elements(By.TAG_NAME, 'a')
for link in links:
    if not link.is_displayed():
        print(f'The link {link.get_attribute("href")} is a trap')

fields = driver.find_elements(By.TAG_NAME, 'input')
for field in fields:
```

```
if not field.is_displayed():
    print(f'Do not change value of {field.get_attribute("name")}')
```

Selenium catches each hidden field, producing the following output:

```
The link http://pythonscraping.com/dontgohere is a trap
Do not change value of phone
Do not change value of email
```

Although you probably don't want to visit any hidden links you find, you will want to make sure that you submit any prepopulated hidden form values (or have Selenium submit them for you) with the rest of the form. To sum up, it is dangerous to simply ignore hidden fields, although you must be careful when interacting with them.

The Human Checklist

There's a lot of information in this chapter, and indeed in this book, about how to build a scraper that looks less like a scraper and more like a human. If you keep getting blocked by websites and you don't know why, here's a checklist you can use to remedy the problem:

- First, if the page you are receiving from the web server is blank, missing information, or is otherwise not what you expect (or have seen in your own browser), it is likely caused by JavaScript being executed on the site to create the page. Review Chapter 14.

- If you are submitting a form or making a POST request to a website, check the page to make sure that everything the website is expecting you to submit is being submitted and in the correct format. Use a tool such as Chrome's Inspector panel to view an actual POST request sent to the site to make sure you have everything, and that an "organic" request looks the same as the ones your bot is sending.

- If you are trying to log in to a site and can't make the login "stick," or the website is experiencing other strange "state" behavior, check your cookies. Make sure that cookies are being persisted correctly between each page load and that your cookies are sent to the site for every request.

- If you are getting HTTP errors from the client, especially 403 Forbidden errors, it might indicate that the website has identified your IP address as a bot and is unwilling to accept any more requests. You will need to either wait until your IP address is removed from the list or obtain a new IP address (either move to a Starbucks or see Chapter 20). To make sure you don't get blocked again, try the following:
  - Make sure that your scrapers aren't moving through the site too quickly. Fast scraping is a bad practice that places a heavy burden on the web administrator's servers, can land you in legal trouble, and is the number one cause of scrapers getting blacklisted. Add delays to your scrapers and let them run

overnight. Remember: being in a rush to write programs or gather data is a sign of bad project management; plan ahead to avoid messes like this in the first place.

— The obvious one: change your headers! Some sites will block anything that advertises itself as a scraper. Copy your own browser's headers if you're unsure about what some reasonable header values are.

— Make sure you're not clicking on or accessing anything that a human normally would not be able to (refer to "Avoiding Honeypots" on page 269 for more information).

— If you find yourself jumping through a lot of difficult hoops to gain access, consider contacting the website administrator to let them know what you're doing. Try emailing *webmaster@<domain name>* or *admin@<domain name>* for permission to use your scrapers. Admins are people too, and you might be surprised at how amenable they can be to sharing their data.

Testing Your Website with Scrapers

When working with web projects that have a large development stack, it's often only the "back" of the stack that ever gets tested regularly. Most programming languages today (including Python) have some type of test framework, but website frontends are often left out of these automated tests, although they might be the only customer-facing part of the project.

Part of the problem is that websites are often a mishmash of many markup languages and programming languages. You can write unit tests for sections of your JavaScript, but it's useless if the HTML it's interacting with has changed in such a way that the JavaScript doesn't have the intended action on the page, even if it's working correctly.

The problem of frontend website testing has often been left as an afterthought or delegated to lower-level programmers armed with, at most, a checklist and a bug tracker. However, with just a little more up-front effort, you can replace this checklist with a series of unit tests and replace human eyes with a web scraper.

Imagine: test-driven development for web development. Daily tests to make sure all parts of the web interface are functioning as expected. A suite of tests run every time someone adds a new website feature or changes the position of an element. This chapter covers the basics of testing and how to test all sorts of websites, from simple to complicated, with Python-based web scrapers.

An Introduction to Testing

If you've never written tests for your code before, there's no better time to start than now. Having a suite of tests that can be run to ensure that your code performs as expected (at least, as far as you've written tests for) saves you time and worry and makes releasing new updates easy.

What Are Unit Tests?

The words *test* and *unit test* are often used interchangeably. Often, when programmers refer to "writing tests," what they really mean is "writing unit tests." On the other hand, when some programmers refer to writing unit tests, they're really writing some other kind of test.

Although definitions and practices tend to vary from company to company, a unit test generally has the following characteristics:

- Each unit test tests one aspect of the functionality of a component. For example, it might ensure that the appropriate error message is thrown if a negative number of dollars is withdrawn from a bank account.

  Often, unit tests are grouped together in the same class, based on the component they are testing. You might have the test for a negative dollar value being withdrawn from a bank account, followed by a unit test for the behavior of an overdrawn bank account.

- Each unit test can be run completely independently, and any setup or teardown required for the unit test must be handled by the unit test itself. Similarly, unit tests must not interfere with the success or failure of other tests, and they must be able to run successfully in any order.

- Each unit test usually contains at least one *assertion*. For example, a unit test might assert that the answer to 2 + 2 is 4. Occasionally, a unit test might contain only a failure state. For example, it might fail if an exception is thrown but pass by default if everything goes smoothly.

- Unit tests are separated from the bulk of the code. Although they necessarily need to import and use the code they are testing, they are generally kept in separate classes and directories.

Although many other types of tests can be written—integration tests and validation tests, for example—this chapter primarily focuses on unit testing. Not only have unit tests become extremely popular with recent pushes toward test-driven development, but their length and flexibility make them easy to work with as examples, and Python has some built-in unit testing capabilities, as you'll see in the next section.

Python unittest

Python's unit-testing module, unittest, comes packaged with all standard Python installations. Just import and extend unittest.TestCase, and it will:

- Provide setUp and tearDown functions that run before and after each unit test
- Provide several types of "assert" statements to allow tests to pass or fail
- Run all functions that begin with test_ as unit tests and ignore functions that are not prepended as tests

The following provides a simple unit test for ensuring that 2 + 2 = 4, according to Python:

```
import unittest

class TestAddition(unittest.TestCase):
    def setUp(self):
        print('Setting up the test')

    def tearDown(self):
        print('Tearing down the test')

    def test_twoPlusTwo(self):
        total = 2+2
        self.assertEqual(4, total);

if __name__ == '__main__':
    unittest.main()
```

Although setUp and tearDown don't provide any useful functionality here, they are included for illustration purposes. Note that these functions are run before and after each individual test, not before and after all the tests in the class.

The output of the test function, when run from the command line, should look like this:

```
Setting up the test
Tearing down the test
.
----------------------------------------------------------------
Ran 1 test in 0.000s

OK
```

This indicates that the test ran successfully, and 2 + 2 does indeed equal 4.

Running unittest in Jupyter Notebooks

The unit test scripts in this chapter are all kicked off with:

```
if __name__ == '__main__':
    unittest.main()
```

The line if __name__ == '__main__' is true only if the line is executed directly in Python and not via an import statement. This allows you to run your unit test, using the unittest.TestCase class that it extends, directly from the command line.

In a Jupyter notebook, things are a little bit different. The argv parameters created by Jupyter can cause errors in the unit test, and because the unittest framework exits Python by default after the test is run (which causes problems in the notebook kernel), we also need to prevent that from happening.

In the Jupyter notebooks, you will use the following to launch unit tests:

```
if __name__ == '__main__':
    unittest.main(argv=[''], exit=False)
    %reset
```

The second line sets all of the argv variables (command-line arguments) to a single empty string, which is ignored by unnittest.main. It also prevents unittest from exiting after the test is run.

The %reset line is useful because it resets the memory and destroys all user-created variables in the Jupyter notebook. Without it, each unit test you write in the notebook will contain all of the methods from all other previously run tests that also inherited unittest.TestCase, including setUp and tearDown methods. This also means that each unit test would run all of the methods from the unit tests before it!

Using %reset does create one extra manual step for the user when running the tests. When running the test, the notebook will prompt the user if they're sure they want to reset the memory. Simply type **y** and hit Enter to do this.

Testing Wikipedia

Testing the frontend of your website (excluding JavaScript, which we'll cover next) is as simple as combining the Python unittest library with a web scraper:

```
from urllib.request import urlopen
from bs4 import BeautifulSoup
import unittest

class TestWikipedia(unittest.TestCase):
    bs = None
    def setUpClass():
        url = 'http://en.wikipedia.org/wiki/Monty_Python'
        TestWikipedia.bs = BeautifulSoup(urlopen(url), 'html.parser')

    def test_titleText(self):
        pageTitle = TestWikipedia.bs.find('h1').get_text()
        self.assertEqual('Monty Python', pageTitle);

    def test_contentExists(self):
        content = TestWikipedia.bs.find('div',{'id':'mw-content-text'})
        self.assertIsNotNone(content)


if __name__ == '__main__':
    unittest.main()
```

There are two tests this time: the first tests whether the title of the page is the expected "Monty Python," and the second makes sure that the page has a content div.

Note that the content of the page is loaded only once, and that the global object bs is shared between tests. This is accomplished by using the unittest-specified function setUpClass, which is run only once at the start of the class (unlike setUp, which is run before every individual test). Using setUpClass instead of setUp saves unnecessary page loads; you can grab the content once and run multiple tests on it.

One major architectural difference between setUpClass and setUp, besides just when and how often they're run, is that setUpClass is a static method that "belongs" to the class itself and has global class variables, whereas setUp is an instance function that belongs to a particular instance of the class. This is why setUp can set attributes on self—the particular instance of that class—while setUpClass can access only static class attributes on the class TestWikipedia.

Although testing a single page at a time might not seem all that powerful or interesting, as you may recall from Chapter 6, it is relatively easy to build web crawlers that can iteratively move through all pages of a website. What happens when you combine a web crawler with a unit test that makes an assertion about each page?

There are many ways to run a test repeatedly, but you must be careful to load each page only once for each set of tests you want to run on the page, and you must also avoid holding large amounts of information in memory at once. The following setup does just that:

```python
from urllib.request import urlopen
from bs4 import BeautifulSoup
import unittest
import re
import random
from urllib.parse import unquote

class TestWikipedia(unittest.TestCase):

    def test_PageProperties(self):
        self.url = 'http://en.wikipedia.org/wiki/Monty_Python'
        #Test the first 10 pages we encounter
        for i in range(1, 10):
            self.bs = BeautifulSoup(urlopen(self.url), 'html.parser')
            titles = self.titleMatchesURL()
            self.assertEquals(titles[0], titles[1])
            self.assertTrue(self.contentExists())
            self.url = self.getNextLink()
        print('Done!')

    def titleMatchesURL(self):
        pageTitle = self.bs.find('h1').get_text()
        urlTitle = self.url[(self.url.index('/wiki/')+6):]
        urlTitle = urlTitle.replace('_', ' ')
        urlTitle = unquote(urlTitle)
        return [pageTitle.lower(), urlTitle.lower()]

    def contentExists(self):
        content = self.bs.find('div',{'id':'mw-content-text'})
        if content is not None:
            return True
        return False

    def getNextLink(self):
        #Returns random link on page, using technique from Chapter 3
        links = self.bs.find('div', {'id':'bodyContent'}).find_all(
            'a', href=re.compile('^(/wiki/)((?!:).)*$'))
        randomLink = random.SystemRandom().choice(links)
        return 'https://wikipedia.org{}'.format(randomLink.attrs['href'])

if __name__ == '__main__':
    unittest.main()
```

There are a few things to notice. First, there is only one actual test in this class. The other functions are technically only helper functions, even though they're doing the bulk of the computational work to determine whether a test passes. Because the test function performs the assertion statements, the results of the test are passed back to the test function where the assertions happen.

Also, while `contentExists` returns a boolean, `titleMatchesURL` returns the values themselves for evaluation. To see why you would want to pass values back rather than just a boolean, compare the results of a boolean assertion:

```
======================================================================
FAIL: test_PageProperties (__main__.TestWikipedia)
----------------------------------------------------------------------
Traceback (most recent call last):
  File "15-3.py", line 22, in test_PageProperties
    self.assertTrue(self.titleMatchesURL())
AssertionError: False is not true
```

with the results of an `assertEquals` statement:

```
======================================================================
FAIL: test_PageProperties (__main__.TestWikipedia)
----------------------------------------------------------------------
Traceback (most recent call last):
  File "15-3.py", line 23, in test_PageProperties
    self.assertEquals(titles[0], titles[1])
AssertionError: 'lockheed u-2' != 'u-2 spy plane'
```

Which one is easier to debug? (In this case, the error is occurring because of a redirect, when the article *http://wikipedia.org/wiki/u-2%20spy%20plane* redirects to an article titled "Lockheed U-2.")

Testing with Selenium

As with Ajax scraping in Chapter 14, JavaScript presents particular challenges when doing website testing. Fortunately, Selenium has an excellent framework in place for handling particularly complicated websites; in fact, the library was originally designed for website testing!

Although obviously written in the same language, the syntaxes of Python unit tests and Selenium unit tests have surprisingly little in common. Selenium does not require that its unit tests be contained as functions within classes; its `assert` statements do not require parentheses; and tests pass silently, producing some kind of message only on a failure:

```
driver = webdriver.Chrome()
driver.get('http://en.wikipedia.org/wiki/Monty_Python')
assert 'Monty Python' in driver.title
driver.close()
```

When run, this test should produce no output.

In this way, Selenium tests can be written more casually than Python unit tests, and `assert` statements can even be integrated into regular code, where it is desirable for code execution to terminate if some condition is not met.

Interacting with the Site

Recently, I wanted to contact a local small business through its website's contact form but found that the HTML form was broken; nothing happened when I clicked the Submit button. After a little investigation, I saw they were using a simple mailto form that was designed to send them an email with the form's contents. Fortunately, I was able to use this information to send them an email, explain the problem with their form, and hire them, despite the technical issue.

If I were to write a traditional scraper that used or tested this form, my scraper would likely just copy the layout of the form and send an email directly—bypassing the form altogether. How could I test the functionality of the form and ensure that it was working perfectly through a browser?

Although previous chapters have discussed navigating links, submitting forms, and other types of interaction-like activity, at its core everything we've done is designed to *bypass* the browser interface, not use it. Selenium, on the other hand, can literally enter text, click buttons, and do everything through the browser (in this case, the headless Chrome browser), and detect things like broken forms, badly coded JavaScript, HTML typos, and other issues that might stymie actual customers.

Key to this sort of testing is the concept of Selenium elements. This object was briefly encountered in Chapter 14, and is returned by calls like this:

```
usernameField = driver.find_element_by_name('username')
```

Just as there are numerous actions you can take on various elements of a website in your browser, there are many actions Selenium can perform on any given element. Among these are:

```
myElement.click()
myElement.click_and_hold()
myElement.release()
myElement.double_click()
myElement.send_keys_to_element('content to enter')
```

In addition to performing a one-time action on an element, strings of actions can be combined into *action chains*, which can be stored and executed once or multiple times in a program. Action chains are useful in that they can be a convenient way to string long sets of multiple actions, but they are functionally identical to calling the action explicitly on the element, as in the preceding examples.

To see this difference, take a look at the form page at *http://pythonscraping.com/pages/files/form.html* (which was previously used as an example in Chapter 13). We can fill out the form and submit it in this way:

```python
from selenium import webdriver
from selenium.webdriver.remote.webelement import WebElement
from selenium.webdriver.common.keys import Keys
from selenium.webdriver import ActionChains
from selenium.webdriver.chrome.options import Options

chrome_options = Options()
chrome_options.add_argument('--headless')

driver = webdriver.Chrome(
    executable_path='drivers/chromedriver', options=chrome_options)
driver.get('http://pythonscraping.com/pages/files/form.html')

firstnameField = driver.find_element_by_name('firstname')
lastnameField = driver.find_element_by_name('lastname')
submitButton = driver.find_element_by_id('submit')

### METHOD 1 ###
#firstnameField.send_keys('Ryan')
lastnameField.send_keys('Mitchell')
submitButton.click()
################

### METHOD 2 ###
actions = ActionChains(driver).click(firstnameField)
    .send_keys('Ryan')
    .click(lastnameField)
    .send_keys('Mitchell')
    .send_keys(Keys.RETURN)
actions.perform()
###############

print(driver.find_element_by_tag_name('body').text)

driver.close()
```

Method 1 calls send_keys on the two fields and then clicks the Submit button. Method 2 uses a single action chain to click and enter text in each field, which happens in a sequence after the perform method is called. This script operates in the same way, whether the first method or the second method is used, and prints this line:

```
Hello there, Ryan Mitchell!
```

There is another variation in the two methods, in addition to the objects they use to handle the commands: notice that the first method clicks the Submit button, while the second uses the Return keystroke to submit the form while the text box is submitted. Because there are many ways to think about the sequence of events that complete the same action, there are many ways to complete the same action using Selenium.

Drag and drop

Clicking buttons and entering text is one thing, but where Selenium really shines is in its ability to deal with relatively novel forms of web interaction. Selenium allows for the manipulation of drag-and-drop interfaces with ease. Using its drag-and-drop function requires you to specify a *source* element (the element to be dragged) and either an offset to drag it across, or a target element to drag it to.

The demo page located at *http://pythonscraping.com/pages/javascript/draggable-Demo.html* presents an example of this type of interface:

```
from selenium import webdriver
from selenium.webdriver.remote.webelement import WebElement
from selenium.webdriver import ActionChains
from selenium.webdriver.chrome.options import Options
import unittest

class TestDragAndDrop(unittest.TestCase):
    driver = None

    def setUp(self):
        chrome_options = Options()
        chrome_options.add_argument('--headless')
        self.driver = webdriver.Chrome(
            executable_path='drivers/chromedriver', options=chrome_options)
        url = 'http://pythonscraping.com/pages/javascript/draggableDemo.html'
        self.driver.get(url)

    def tearDown(self):
        driver.close()

    def test_drag(self):
        element = self.driver.find_element_by_id('draggable')
        target = self.driver.find_element_by_id('div2')
        actions = ActionChains(self.driver)
        actions.drag_and_drop(element, target).perform()
        self.assertEqual('You are definitely not a bot!',
                    self.driver.find_element_by_id('message').text)
```

Two messages are printed out from the `message` div on the demo page. The first says:

```
Prove you are not a bot, by dragging the square from the blue area to the red
area!
```

Then, quickly, after the task is completed, the content is printed out again, which now reads:

```
You are definitely not a bot!
```

As the demo page suggests, dragging elements to prove you're not a bot is a common theme in many CAPTCHAs. Although bots have been able to drag objects around for a long time (it's just a matter of clicking, holding, and moving), somehow the idea of using "drag this" as a verification of humanity just won't die.

In addition, these draggable CAPTCHA libraries rarely use any difficult-for-bots tasks, like "drag the picture of the kitten onto the picture of the cow" (which requires you to identify the pictures as "a kitten" and "a cow," while parsing instructions); instead, they often involve number ordering or some other fairly trivial task like the one in the preceding example.

Of course, their strength lies in the fact that there are so many variations, and they are so infrequently used; no one will likely bother making a bot that can defeat all of them. At any rate, this example should be enough to illustrate why you should never use this technique for large-scale websites.

Taking screenshots

In addition to the usual testing capabilities, Selenium has an interesting trick up its sleeve that might make your testing (or impressing your boss) a little easier: screenshots. Yes, photographic evidence can be created from unit tests run without the need for actually pressing the PrtScn key:

```
driver = webdriver.Chrome()
driver.get('http://www.pythonscraping.com/')
driver.get_screenshot_as_file('tmp/pythonscraping.png')
```

This script navigates to *http://pythonscraping.com* and then stores a screenshot of the home page in the local *tmp* folder (the folder must already exist for this to store correctly). Screenshots can be saved as a variety of image formats.

Web Scraping in Parallel

Web crawling is fast. At least, it's usually much faster than hiring a dozen interns to copy data from the internet by hand! Of course, the progression of technology and the hedonic treadmill demand that at a certain point even this will not be "fast enough." That's the point at which people generally start to look toward distributed computing.

Unlike most other technology fields, web crawling cannot often be improved simply by "throwing more cycles at the problem." Running one process is fast; running two processes is not necessarily twice as fast. Running three processes might get you banned from the remote server you're hammering on with all your requests!

However, in some situations parallel web crawling, or running parallel threads or processes, can still be of benefit:

- Collecting data from multiple sources (multiple remote servers) instead of just a single source

- Performing long or complex operations on the collected data (such as doing image analysis or OCR) that could be done in parallel with fetching the data

- Collecting data from a large web service where you are paying for each query, or where creating multiple connections to the service is within the bounds of your usage agreement

Processes Versus Threads

Threads and processes are not a Python-specific concept. While the exact implementation details differ between (and are dependent on) operating systems, the general consensus in computer science is that processes are larger and have their own memory, while threads are smaller and share memory within the process that contains them.

Generally, when you run a simple Python program, you are running it within its own process which contains a single thread. But Python supports both multiprocessing and multithreading. Both multiprocessing and multithreading achieve the same ultimate goal: performing two programming tasks in parallel instead of running one function after another in a more traditional linear way.

However, you must consider the pros and cons of each carefully. For example, each process has its own memory allocated separately by the operating system. This means that memory is not shared between processes. While multiple threads can happily write to the same shared Python queues, lists, and other objects, processes cannot and must communicate this information more explicitly.

Using multithreaded programming to execute tasks in separate threads with shared memory is often considered easier than multiprocess programming. But this convenience comes at a cost.

Python's global interpreter lock (or GIL) acts to prevent threads from executing the same line of code at once. The GIL ensures that the common memory shared by all processes does not become corrupted (for instance, bytes in memory being half written with one value and half written with another value). This locking makes it possible to write a multithreaded program and know what you're getting, within the same line, but it also has the potential to create bottlenecks.

Multithreaded Crawling

The following example illustrates using multiple threads to perform a task:

```python
import threading
import time

def print_time(threadName, delay, iterations):
    start = int(time.time())
    for i in range(0,iterations):
        time.sleep(delay)
        print(f'{int(time.time() - start)} - {threadName}')

threads = [
    threading.Thread(target=print_time, args=('Fizz', 3, 33)),
    threading.Thread(target=print_time, args=('Buzz', 5, 20)),
    threading.Thread(target=print_time, args=('Counter', 1, 100))
]

[t.start() for t in threads]
[t.join() for t in threads]
```

This is a reference to the classic FizzBuzz programming test (*http://wiki.c2.com/?Fizz BuzzTest*), with a somewhat more verbose output:

```
1 Counter
2 Counter
3 Fizz
3 Counter
4 Counter
5 Buzz
5 Counter
6 Fizz
6 Counter
```

The script starts three threads, one that prints "Fizz" every three seconds, another that prints "Buzz" every five seconds, and a third that prints "Counter" every second.

Rather than printing fizzes and buzzes, you can perform a useful task in the threads, such as crawling a website:

```python
from urllib.request import urlopen
from bs4 import BeautifulSoup
import re
import random
import threading
import time

# Recursively find links on a Wikipedia page,
# then follow a random link, with artificial 5 sec delay
def scrape_article(thread_name, path):
    time.sleep(5)
    print(f'{thread_name}: Scraping {path}')
    html = urlopen('http://en.wikipedia.org{}'.format(path))
    bs = BeautifulSoup(html, 'html.parser')
    title = bs.find('h1').get_text()
    links = bs.find('div', {'id':'bodyContent'}).find_all('a',
        href=re.compile('^(/wiki/)((?!:).)*$'))
    if len(links) > 0:
        newArticle = links[random.randint(0, len(links)-1)].attrs['href']
        scrape_article(thread_name, newArticle)


threads = [
    threading.Thread(
        target=scrape_article,
        args=('Thread 1', '/wiki/Kevin_Bacon',)
    ),
    threading.Thread(
        target=scrape_article,
        args=('Thread 2', '/wiki/Monty_Python',)
    ),
]
[t.start() for t in threads]
[t.join() for t in threads]
```

Note the inclusion of this line:

```
time.sleep(5)
```

Because you are crawling Wikipedia almost twice as fast as you would with just a single thread, the inclusion of this line prevents the script from putting too much of a load on Wikipedia's servers. In practice, when running against a server where the number of requests is not an issue, this line should be removed.

What if you want to rewrite this slightly to keep track of the articles the threads have collectively seen so far, so that no article is visited twice? You can use a list in a multi-threaded environment in the same way that you use it in a single-threaded environment:

```
visited = []
def get_links(thread_name, bs):
    print('Getting links in {}'.format(thread_name))
    links = bs.find('div', {'id':'bodyContent'}).find_all('a',
        href=re.compile('^(/wiki/)((?!:).)*$')
    )
    return [link for link in links if link not in visited]

def scrape_article(thread_name, path):
    visited.append(path)
    ...
    links = get_links(thread_name, bs)
    ...
```

Note that you are appending the path to the list of visited paths as the first action that scrape_article takes. This reduces, but does not entirely eliminate, the chances that it will be scraped twice.

If you are unlucky, both threads might still stumble across the same path at the same instant, both will see that it is not in the visited list, and both will subsequently add it to the list and scrape at the same time. However, in practice this is unlikely to happen because of the speed of execution and the number of pages that Wikipedia contains.

This is an example of a *race condition*. Race conditions can be tricky to debug, even for experienced programmers, so it is important to evaluate your code for these potential situations, estimate their likelihood, and anticipate the seriousness of their impact.

In the case of this particular race condition, where the scraper goes over the same page twice, it may not be worth writing around.

Race Conditions and Queues

Although you can communicate between threads with lists, lists are not specifically designed for communication between threads, and their misuse can easily cause slow program execution or even errors resulting from race conditions.

Lists are great for appending to or reading from, but they're not so great for removing items at arbitrary points, especially from the beginning of the list. Using a line like:

```
myList.pop(0)
```

actually requires Python to rewrite the entire list, slowing program execution.

More dangerous, lists also make it convenient to accidentally write in a line that isn't thread-safe. For instance:

```
myList[len(myList)-1]
```

may not actually get you the last item in the list in a multithreaded environment, or it may even throw an exception if the value for `len(myList)-1` is calculated immediately before another operation modifies the list.

One might argue that the preceding statement can be more "Pythonically" written as `myList[-1]`, and of course, no one has *ever* accidentally written non-Pythonic code in a moment of weakness (especially not former Java developers like myself, thinking back to their days of patterns like `myList[myList.length-1]`)! But even if your code is beyond reproach, consider these other forms of nonthread-safe lines involving lists:

```
my_list[i] = my_list[i] + 1
my_list.append(my_list[-1])
```

Both of these may result in a race condition that can cause unexpected results. You might be tempted to try another approach and use some other variable types besides lists. For example:

```
# Read the message in from the global list
my_message = global_message
# Write a message back
global_message = 'I've retrieved the message'
# do something with my_message
```

This seems like an excellent solution until you realize that you might have inadvertently overwritten another message coming in from another thread, in the instant between the first and second lines, with the text "I've retrieved the message." So now you just need to construct an elaborate series of personal message objects for each thread with some logic to figure out who gets what...or you could use the Queue module built for this exact purpose.

Queues are list-like objects that operate on either a first in, first out (FIFO) or a last in, first out (LIFO) approach. A queue receives messages from any thread via `queue.put('My message')` and can transmit the message to any thread that calls `queue.get()`.

Queues are not designed to store static data but to transmit it in a thread-safe way. After the data is retrieved from the queue, it should exist only in the thread that retrieved it. For this reason, they are commonly used to delegate tasks or send temporary notifications.

This can be useful in web crawling. For instance, let's say that you want to persist the data collected by your scraper into a database, and you want each thread to be able to persist its data quickly. A single shared connection for all threads might cause issues (a single connection cannot handle requests in parallel), but it makes no sense to give every single scraping thread its own database connection. As your scraper grows in size (eventually you may be collecting data from a hundred different websites in a hundred different threads), this might translate into a lot of mostly idle database connections doing only an occasional write after a page loads.

Instead, you can have a smaller number of database threads, each with its own connection, sitting around taking items from a queue and storing them. This provides a much more manageable set of database connections:

```python
def storage(queue):
    conn = pymysql.connect(host='127.0.0.1', unix_socket='/tmp/mysql.sock',
    user='root', passwd='password', db='mysql', charset='utf8')
    cur = conn.cursor()
    cur.execute('USE wikipedia')
    while 1:
        if not queue.empty():
            path = queue.get()
            cur.execute('SELECT * FROM pages WHERE url = %s', (path))
            if cur.rowcount == 0:
                print(f'Storing article {path}')
                cur.execute('INSERT INTO pages (url) VALUES (%s)', (path))
                conn.commit()
            else:
                print("Article already exists: {}".format(path))

visited = set()
def get_links(thread_name, bs):
    print('Getting links in {}'.format(thread_name))
    links = bs.find('div', {'id':'bodyContent'}).find_all(
        'a',
        href=re.compile('^(/wiki/)((?!:).)*$')
    )
    links = [link.get('href') for link in links]
    return [link for link in links if link and link not in visited]
```

```
def scrape_article(thread_name, path):
    time.sleep(5)
    visited.add(path)
    print(f'{thread_name}: Scraping {path}')
    bs = BeautifulSoup(
        urlopen('http://en.wikipedia.org{}'.format(path)),
        'html.parser'
    )
    links = get_links(thread_name, bs)
    if len(links) > 0:
        [queue.put(link) for link in links]
        newArticle = links[random.randint(0, len(links)-1)].attrs['href']
        scrape_article(thread_name, newArticle)


queue = Queue()


threads = [
    threading.Thread(
        target=scrape_article,
        args=('Thread 1', '/wiki/Kevin_Bacon',)
    ),
    threading.Thread(
        target=scrape_article,
        args=('Thread 2', '/wiki/Monty_Python',)
    ),
    threading.Thread(
        target=storage,
        args=(queue,)
    )
]
[t.start() for t in threads]
[t.join() for t in threads]
```

This script creates three threads: two to scrape pages from Wikipedia in a random walk, and a third to store the collected data in a MySQL database. For more information about MySQL and data storage, see Chapter 9.

This scraper is also simplified somewhat from the previous one. Rather than deal with both the title and the page's URL, it concerns itself with the URL only. Also, as an acknowledgement to the fact that both threads might attempt to add the exact same URL to the visited list at the exact same time, I've turned this list into a set. Although it is not strictly thread-safe, the redundancies are built in so that any duplicates won't have any effect on the end result.

More Features of the Threading Module

The Python `threading` module is a higher-level interface built on the lower-level `_thread` module. Although `_thread` is perfectly usable all on its own, it takes a little more effort and doesn't provide the little things that make life so enjoyable—like convenience functions and nifty features.

For example, you can use static functions like `enumerate` to get a list of all active threads initialized through the `threading` module without needing to keep track of them yourself. The `activeCount` function, similarly, provides the total number of threads. Many functions from `_thread` are given more convenient or memorable names, like `currentThread` instead of `get_ident` to get the name of the current thread.

One of the nice things about the threading module is the ease of creating local thread data that is unavailable to the other threads. This might be a nice feature if you have several threads, each scraping a different website, and each keeping track of its own local list of visited pages.

This local data can be created at any point within the thread function by calling `threading.local()`:

```
import threading

def crawler(url):
    data = threading.local()
    data.visited = []
    # Crawl site

threading.Thread(target=crawler, args=('http://brookings.edu')).start()
```

This solves the problem of race conditions happening between shared objects in threads. Whenever an object does not need to be shared, it should not be, and should be kept in local thread memory. To safely share objects between threads, the `Queue` from the previous section can still be used.

The threading module acts as a thread babysitter of sorts, and it can be highly customized to define what that babysitting entails. The `isAlive` function by default looks to see if the thread is still active. It will be true until a thread completes crawling (or crashes).

Often, crawlers are designed to run for a very long time. The `isAlive` method can ensure that, if a thread crashes, it restarts:

```
threading.Thread(target=crawler)
t.start()

while True:
    time.sleep(1)
    if not t.isAlive():
        t = threading.Thread(target=crawler)
        t.start()
```

Other monitoring methods can be added by extending the `threading.Thread` object:

```
import threading
import time

class Crawler(threading.Thread):
    def __init__(self):
        threading.Thread.__init__(self)
        self.done = False

    def isDone(self):
        return self.done

    def run(self):
        time.sleep(5)
        self.done = True
        raise Exception('Something bad happened!')

t = Crawler()
t.start()

while True:
    time.sleep(1)
    if t.isDone():
        print('Done')
        break
    if not t.isAlive():
        t = Crawler()
        t.start()
```

This new `Crawler` class contains an `isDone` method that can be used to check if the crawler is done crawling. This may be useful if there are some additional logging methods that need to be finished so the thread cannot close, but the bulk of the crawling work is done. In general, `isDone` can be replaced with some sort of status or progress measure—how many pages logged, or the current page, for example.

Any exceptions raised by `Crawler.run` will cause the class to be restarted until `isDone` is `True` and the program exits.

Extending `threading.Thread` in your crawler classes can improve their robustness and flexibility, as well as your ability to monitor any property of many crawlers at once.

Multiple Processes

The Python `Processing` module creates new process objects that can be started and joined from the main process. The following code uses the FizzBuzz example from the section on threading processes to demonstrate:

```
from multiprocessing import Process
import time

def print_time(threadName, delay, iterations):
    start = int(time.time())
    for i in range(0,iterations):
        time.sleep(delay)
        seconds_elapsed = str(int(time.time()) - start)
        print (threadName if threadName else seconds_elapsed)

processes = [
    Process(target=print_time, args=('Counter', 1, 100)),
    Process(target=print_time, args=('Fizz', 3, 33)),
    Process(target=print_time, args=('Buzz', 5, 20))
]

[p.start() for p in processes]
[p.join() for p in processes]
```

Remember that each process is treated as an individual independent program by the OS. If you view your processes through your OS's activity monitor or task manager, you should see this reflected, as shown in Figure 19-1.

Process Name	Bytes Written	Bytes Read	Kind	PID	User
python3.6	0 bytes	0 bytes	64 bit	83561	rmitchell
python3.6	0 bytes	0 bytes	64 bit	83562	rmitchell
python3.6	0 bytes	0 bytes	64 bit	83563	rmitchell
python3.6	4 KB	14.0 MB	64 bit	76154	rmitchell
python3.6	0 bytes	0 bytes	64 bit	83560	rmitchell

Figure 19-1. Five Python processes running while running FizzBuzz

The fourth process with PID 76154 is a running Jupyter notebook instance, which should appear if you are running this from the IPython notebook. The fifth process, 83560, is the main thread of execution, which starts up when the program is first executed. The PIDs are allocated by the OS sequentially. Unless you happen to have another program that quickly allocates a PID while the FizzBuzz script is running, you should see three more sequential PIDs—in this case 83561, 83562, and 83563.

These PIDs also can be found in code by using the os module:

```
import os
...
# prints the child PID
os.getpid()
# prints the parent PID
os.getppid()
```

Each process in your program should print a different PID for the line os.getpid(), but will print the same parent PID on os.getppid().

Technically, a couple of lines of code are not needed for this particular program. If the ending join statement is not included:

```
[p.join() for p in processes]
```

the parent process will still end and terminate the child processes with it automatically. However, this joining is needed if you wish to execute any code after these child processes complete.

For example:

```
[p.start() for p in processes]
print('Program complete')
```

If the join statement is not included, the output will be as follows:

```
Program complete
1
2
```

If the join statement is included, the program waits for each process to finish before continuing:

```
[p.start() for p in processes]
[p.join() for p in processes]
print('Program complete')

...
Fizz
99
Buzz
100
Program complete
```

If you want to stop program execution prematurely, you can of course use Ctrl-C to terminate the parent process. The termination of the parent process will also terminate any child processes that have been spawned, so using Ctrl-C is safe to do without worrying about accidentally leaving processes running in the background.

Multiprocess Crawling

The multithreaded Wikipedia crawling example can be modified to use separate processes rather than separate threads:

```
from urllib.request import urlopen
from bs4 import BeautifulSoup
import re
import random

from multiprocessing import Process
import os
import time

visited = []
def get_links(bs):
    links = bs.find('div', {'id':'bodyContent'})
        .find_all('a', href=re.compile('^(/wiki/)((?!:).)*$'))
    return [link for link in links if link not in visited]

def scrape_article(path):
    visited.append(path)
    html = urlopen('http://en.wikipedia.org{}'.format(path))
    time.sleep(5)
    bs = BeautifulSoup(html, 'html.parser')
    print(f'Scraping {bs.find("h1").get_text()} in process {os.getpid()}')
    links = get_links(bs)
    if len(links) > 0:
        scrape_article(links[random.randint(0, len(links)-1)].attrs['href'])

processes = [
    Process(target=scrape_article, args=('/wiki/Kevin_Bacon',)),
    Process(target=scrape_article, args=('/wiki/Monty_Python',))
]
[p.start() for p in processes]
```

Again, you are artificially slowing the process of the scraper by including a time.sleep(5) so that this can be used for example purposes without placing an unreasonably high load on Wikipedia's servers.

Here, you are replacing the user-defined thread_name, passed around as an argument, with os.getpid(), which does not need to be passed as an argument and can be accessed at any point.

This produces output like this:

```
Scraping Kevin Bacon in process 4067
Scraping Monty Python in process 4068
Scraping Ewan McGregor in process 4067
Scraping Charisma Records in process 4068
Scraping Renée Zellweger in process 4067
Scraping Genesis (band) in process 4068
Scraping Alana Haim in process 4067
Scraping Maroon 5 in process 4068
```

Crawling in separate processes is, in theory, slightly faster than crawling in separate threads for two major reasons:

- Processes are not subject to locking by the GIL and can execute the same lines of code and modify the same (really, separate instantiations of the same) object at the same time.

- Processes can run on multiple CPU cores, which may provide speed advantages if each of your processes or threads is processor intensive.

However, these advantages come with one major disadvantage. In the preceding program, all found URLs are stored in a global `visited` list. When you were using multiple threads, this list was shared among all threads; and one thread, in the absence of a rare race condition, could not visit a page that had already been visited by another thread. However, each process now gets its own independent version of the visited list and is free to visit pages that have already been visited by other processes.

Communicating Between Processes

Processes operate in their own independent memory, which can cause problems if you want them to share information.

Modifying the previous example to print the current output of the visited list, you can see this principle in action:

```
def scrape_article(path):
    visited.append(path)
    print("Process {} list is now: {}".format(os.getpid(), visited))
```

This results in output like the following:

```
Process 84552 list is now: ['/wiki/Kevin_Bacon']
Process 84553 list is now: ['/wiki/Monty_Python']
Scraping Kevin Bacon in process 84552
/wiki/Desert_Storm
Process 84552 list is now: ['/wiki/Kevin_Bacon', '/wiki/Desert_Storm']
Scraping Monty Python in process 84553
/wiki/David_Jason
Process 84553 list is now: ['/wiki/Monty_Python', '/wiki/David_Jason']
```

But there is a way to share information between processes on the same machine through two types of Python objects: queues and pipes.

A *queue* is similar to the threading queue seen previously. Information can be put into it by one process and removed by another process. After this information has been removed, it's gone from the queue. Because queues are designed as a method of "temporary data transmission," they're not well suited to hold a static reference such as a "list of web pages that have already been visited."

But what if this static list of web pages was replaced with some sort of a scraping delegator? The scrapers could pop off a task from one queue in the form of a path to scrape (for example, */wiki/Monty_Python*) and in return, add a list of "found URLs" back onto a separate queue that would be processed by the scraping delegator so that only new URLs were added to the first task queue:

```python
def task_delegator(taskQueue, urlsQueue):
    #Initialize with a task for each process
    visited = ['/wiki/Kevin_Bacon', '/wiki/Monty_Python']
    taskQueue.put('/wiki/Kevin_Bacon')
    taskQueue.put('/wiki/Monty_Python')

    while 1:
        # Check to see if there are new links in the urlsQueue
        # for processing
        if not urlsQueue.empty():
            links = [link for link in urlsQueue.get() if link not in visited]
            for link in links:
                #Add new link to the taskQueue
                taskQueue.put(link)

def get_links(bs):
    links = bs.find('div', {'id':'bodyContent'}).find_all('a',
        href=re.compile('^(/wiki/)((?!:).)*$'))
    return [link.attrs['href'] for link in links]

def scrape_article(taskQueue, urlsQueue):
    while 1:
        while taskQueue.empty():
            #Sleep 100 ms while waiting for the task queue
            #This should be rare
            time.sleep(.1)
        path = taskQueue.get()
        html = urlopen('http://en.wikipedia.org{}'.format(path))
        time.sleep(5)
        bs = BeautifulSoup(html, 'html.parser')
        title = bs.find('h1').get_text()
        print(f'Scraping {bs.find('h1').get_text()} in process {os.getpid()}')
        links = get_links(bs)
        #Send these to the delegator for processing
        urlsQueue.put(links)
```

```
processes = []
taskQueue = Queue()
urlsQueue = Queue()
processes.append(Process(target=task_delegator, args=(taskQueue, urlsQueue,)))
processes.append(Process(target=scrape_article, args=(taskQueue, urlsQueue,)))
processes.append(Process(target=scrape_article, args=(taskQueue, urlsQueue,)))

for p in processes:
    p.start()
```

Some structural differences exist between this scraper and the ones originally created. Rather than each process or thread following its own random walk from the starting point they were assigned, they work together to do a complete coverage crawl of the website. Each process can pull any "task" from the queue, not just links that they have found themselves.

You can see this in action, as process 97024 scrapes both *Monty Python* and *Philadelphia* (a Kevin Bacon movie):

```
Scraping Kevin Bacon in process 97023
Scraping Monty Python in process 97024
Scraping Kevin Bacon (disambiguation) in process 97023
Scraping Philadelphia in process 97024
Scraping Kevin Bacon filmography in process 97023
Scraping Kyra Sedgwick in process 97024
Scraping Sosie Bacon in process 97023
Scraping Edmund Bacon (architect) in process 97024
Scraping Michael Bacon (musician) in process 97023
Scraping Holly Near in process 97024
Scraping Leading actor in process 97023
```

Multiprocess Crawling—Another Approach

All of the approaches discussed for multithreaded and multiprocess crawling assume that you require some sort of "parental guidance" over the child threads and processes. You can start them all at once, you can end them all at once, and you can send messages or share memory between them.

But what if your scraper is designed in such a way that no guidance or communication is required? There may be very little reason to start going crazy with `import _thread` just yet.

For example, let's say you want to crawl two similar websites in parallel. You have a crawler written that can crawl either of these websites, determined by a small configuration change or perhaps a command-line argument. There's absolutely no reason you can't simply do the following:

```
$ python my_crawler.py website1
$ python my_crawler.py website2
```

And voilà, you've just kicked off a multiprocess web crawler, while saving your CPU the overhead of keeping around a parent process to boot!

Of course, this approach has downsides. If you want to run two web crawlers on the *same* website in this way, you need some way of ensuring that they won't accidentally start scraping the same pages. The solution might be to create a URL rule ("crawler 1 scrapes the blog pages, crawler 2 scrapes the product pages") or divide the site in some way.

Alternatively, you may be able to handle this coordination through some sort of intermediate database, such as Redis (*https://redis.io/*). Before going to a new link, the crawler may make a request to the database to ask, "Has this page been crawled?" The crawler is using the database as an interprocess communication system. Of course, without careful consideration, this method may lead to race conditions or lag if the database connection is slow (likely only a problem if connecting to a remote database).

You may also find that this method isn't quite as scalable. Using the Process module allows you to dynamically increase or decrease the number of processes crawling the site or even storing data. Kicking them off by hand requires either a person physically running the script or a separate managing script (whether a bash script, a cron job, or something else) doing this.

However, I have used this method with great success in the past. For small, one-off projects, it is a great way to get a lot of information quickly, especially across multiple websites.

Web Scraping Proxies

That this is the last chapter in the book is somewhat appropriate. Until now you have been running all the Python applications from the command line, within the confines of your home computer. As the saying goes: "If you love something, set it free."

Although you might be tempted to put off this step as something you don't *need* right now, you might be surprised at how much easier your life becomes when you stop trying to run Python scrapers from your laptop.

What's more, since the first edition of this book was published in 2015, a whole industry of web scraping proxy companies has emerged and flourished. Paying someone to run a web scraper for you used to be a matter of paying for the cloud server instance and running your scraper on it like you would any other software. Now, you can make an API request to, essentially, say "fetch this website," and a remote program will take care of the details, handle any security issues, and return the data to you (for a fee, of course!).

In this chapter, we'll look at some methods that will allow you to route your requests through remote IP addresses, host and run your software elsewhere, and even offload the work to a web scraping proxy entirely.

Why Use Remote Servers?

Although using a remote server might seem like an obvious step when launching a web application intended for use by a wide audience, often the tools programmers build for their own purposes are left running locally. In the absence of a motivation for moving the program elsewhere, why do anything? A reason to move it usually falls into one of two camps: the need for an alternate IP address (either because yours is blocked, or to prevent it from getting blocked), and the need for greater power and flexibility.

Avoiding IP Address Blocking

When building web scrapers, the rule of thumb is: almost everything can be faked. You can send emails from addresses you don't own, automate mouse-movement data from a command line, or even horrify web administrators by sending their website traffic from Internet Explorer 9.0.

The one thing that cannot be faked is your IP address. In the real world, anyone can send you a letter with the return address: "The President, 1600 Pennsylvania Avenue Northwest, Washington, DC 20500." However, if the letter is postmarked from Albuquerque, NM, you can be fairly certain you're not corresponding with the President of the United States.[1]

Most efforts to stop scrapers from accessing websites focus on detecting the difference between humans and bots. Going so far as to block IP addresses is a little like a farmer giving up spraying pesticides in favor of just torching the field. It's a last-ditch but effective method of discarding packets sent from troublesome IP addresses. However, there are problems with this solution:

- IP address access lists are painful to maintain. Although large websites most often have their own programs automating some of the routine management of these lists (bots blocking bots!), someone has to occasionally check them or at least monitor their growth for problems.

- Each address adds a tiny amount of processing time to receive packets, as the server must check received packets against the list to decide whether to approve them. Many addresses multiplied by many packets can add up quickly. To save on processing time and complexity, admins often group these IP addresses into blocks and make rules such as "all 256 addresses in this range are blocked" if there are a few tightly clustered offenders. Which leads us to the third point.

- IP address blocking can lead to blocking the "good guys" as well. For example, while I was an undergrad at Olin College of Engineering, one student wrote some software that attempted to rig votes for content on the then-popular *http:// digg.com*. This software was blocked, and that single blocked IP address led to an entire dormitory being unable to access the site. The student simply moved his software to another server; in the meantime, Digg lost page visits from many regular users in its prime target demographic.

---

1 Technically, IP addresses can be spoofed in outgoing packets, which is a technique used in distributed denial-of-service attacks, where the attackers don't care about receiving return packets (which, if sent, will be sent to the wrong address). But web scraping is, by definition, an activity in which a response from the web server is required, so we think of IP addresses as one thing that can't be faked.

Despite its drawbacks, IP address blocking remains an extremely common method for server administrators to stop suspected web scrapers from accessing servers. If an IP address is blocked, the only real solution is to scrape from a different IP address. This can be accomplished by moving the scraper to a new server or routing your traffic through a different server using a service such as Tor.

Portability and Extensibility

Some tasks are too large for a home computer and internet connection. Although you don't want to put a large load on any single website, you might be collecting data across a wide range of sites and thus require a lot more bandwidth and storage than your current setup can provide.

Moreover, by offloading computationally intensive processing, you can free up your home machine's cycles for more important tasks (*World of Warcraft*, anyone?). You don't have to worry about maintaining power and an internet connection. You can launch your app at a Starbucks, pack up your laptop, and leave knowing that everything's still running safely. Similarly, later on you can access your collected data anywhere there's an internet connection.

If you have an application that requires so much computing power that a single Amazon extra-large computing instance won't satisfy you, you can also look into *distributed computing*. This allows multiple machines to work in parallel to accomplish your goals. As a simple example, you might have one machine crawl one set of sites and another crawl a second set of sites, and have both of them store collected data in the same database.

Of course, as noted in previous chapters, many can replicate what Google search does, but few can replicate the scale at which Google search does it. Distributed computing is a large field of computer science that is outside the scope of this book. However, learning how to launch your application onto a remote server is a necessary first step, and you might be surprised at what computers are capable of these days.

Tor

The Onion Router network, better known by the acronym *Tor*, is a network of volunteer servers set up to route and reroute traffic through many layers (hence the onion reference) of different servers in order to obscure its origin. Data is encrypted before it enters the network so that if any particular server is eavesdropped on, the nature of the communication cannot be revealed. In addition, although the inbound and outbound communications of any particular server can be compromised, one would need to know the details of inbound and outbound communication for *all* the servers along the path of communication in order to decipher the true start and endpoints of a communication—a near-impossible feat.

Tor is commonly used by human rights workers and political whistleblowers to communicate with journalists, and it receives much of its funding from the US government. Of course, it is also commonly used for illegal activities, and so remains a constant target for government surveillance—although it's unclear how useful this surveillance is.

Limits of Tor Anonymity

Although the reason you are using Tor in this book is to change your IP address, not achieve complete anonymity per se, it is worth taking a moment to address some of the strengths and limitations of Tor's ability to anonymize traffic.

Although you can assume when using Tor that the IP address you are coming from, according to a web server, is not an IP address that can be traced back to you, any information you share with that web server might expose you. For instance, if you log in to your own Gmail account and then make incriminating Google searches, those searches can now be tied back to your identity.

Beyond the obvious, however, even the act of logging in to Tor might be hazardous to your anonymity. In December 2013, a Harvard undergraduate student, in an attempt to get out of final exams, emailed a bomb threat to the school through the Tor network, using an anonymous email account. When the Harvard IT team looked at their logs, they found traffic going out to the Tor network from only a single machine, registered to a known student, during the time that the bomb threat was sent. Although they could not identify the eventual destination of this traffic (only that it was sent across Tor), the fact that the times matched up and only a single machine was logged in at the time was damning enough to prosecute the student.[2]

Logging in to Tor is not an automatic invisibility cloak, nor does it give you free rein to do as you please on the internet. Although it is a useful tool, be sure to use it with caution, intelligence, and, of course, morality.

Having Tor installed and running is a requirement for using Python with Tor, as you will see in the next section. Fortunately, the Tor service is extremely easy to install and start running with. Just go to the Tor downloads page (*https://www.torproject.org/download*) and download, install, open, and connect. Keep in mind that your internet

---

2 See Nicholas P. Fandos, "Harvard Sophomore Charged in Bomb Threat," *The Harvard Crimson*, December 17, 2023, *https://www.thecrimson.com/article/2013/12/17/student-charged-bomb-threat*.

speed might appear to be slower while using Tor. Be patient—it might be going around the world several times!

PySocks

PySocks is a remarkably simple Python module that is capable of routing traffic through proxy servers and works fantastically in conjunction with Tor. You can download it from its website (*https://pypi.python.org/pypi/PySocks/1.5.0*) or use any number of third-party module managers to install it.

Although not much in the way of documentation exists for this module, using it is extremely straightforward. The Tor service must be running on port 9150 (the default port) while running this code:

```
import socks
import socket
from urllib.request import urlopen


socks.set_default_proxy(socks.PROXY_TYPE_SOCKS5, "localhost", 9150)
socket.socket = socks.socksocket
print(urlopen('http://icanhazip.com').read())
```

The website *http://icanhazip.com* displays only the IP address for the client connecting to the server and can be useful for testing purposes. When this script is run, it should display an IP address that is not your own.

If you want to use Selenium and ChromeDriver with Tor, you don't need PySocks at all—just make sure that Tor is currently running and add the optional proxy-server Chrome option, specifying that Selenium should connect on the socks5 protocol on port 9150:

```
from selenium import webdriver
from selenium.webdriver.chrome.service import Service
from selenium.webdriver.chrome.options import Options
from webdriver_manager.chrome import ChromeDriverManager

CHROMEDRIVER_PATH = ChromeDriverManager().install()
driver = webdriver.Chrome(service=Service(CHROMEDRIVER_PATH))
chrome_options = Options()
chrome_options.add_argument('--headless')
chrome_options.add_argument('--proxy-server=socks5://127.0.0.1:9150')
driver = webdriver.Chrome(
    service=Service(CHROMEDRIVER_PATH),
    options=chrome_options
)

driver.get('http://icanhazip.com')
print(driver.page_source)
driver.close()
```

Again, this should print out an IP address that is not your own but the one that your running Tor client is currently using.

Remote Hosting

Although complete anonymity is lost after you pull out your credit card, hosting your web scrapers remotely may dramatically improve their speed. This is because you're able to purchase time on much larger machines than you likely own, but also because the connection no longer has to bounce through layers of a Tor network to reach its destination.

Running from a Website-Hosting Account

If you have a personal or business website, you might already likely have the means to run your web scrapers from an external server. Even with relatively locked-down web servers, where you have no access to the command line, it is possible to trigger scripts to start and stop through a web interface.

If your website is hosted on a Linux server, the server likely already runs Python. If you're hosting on a Windows server, you might be out of luck; you'll need to check specifically to see if Python is installed, or if the server administrator is willing to install it.

Most small web-hosting providers come with software called *cPanel*, used to provide basic administration services and information about your website and related services. If you have access to cPanel, you can make sure that Python is set up to run on your server by going to Apache Handlers and adding a new handler (if it is not already present):

```
Handler: cgi-script
Extension(s): .py
```

This tells your server that all Python scripts should be executed as a *CGI-script*. CGI, which stands for *Common Gateway Interface*, is any program that can be run on a server and dynamically generate content that is displayed on a website. By explicitly defining Python scripts as CGI scripts, you're giving the server permission to execute them, rather than just display them in a browser or send the user a download.

Write your Python script, upload it to the server, and set the file permissions to 755 to allow it to be executed. To execute the script, navigate to the place you uploaded it to through your browser (or even better, write a scraper to do it for you). If you're worried about the general public accessing and executing the script, you have two options:

- Store the script at an obscure or hidden URL and make sure to never link to the script from any other accessible URL to avoid search engines indexing it.

- Protect the script with a password, or require that a password or secret token be sent to it before it can execute.

Of course, running a Python script from a service that is specifically designed to display websites is a bit of a hack. For instance, you'll probably notice that your web scraper-cum-website is a little slow to load. In fact, the page doesn't actually load (complete with the output of all `print` statements you might have written in) until the entire scrape is complete. This might take minutes, hours, or never complete at all, depending on how it is written. Although it certainly gets the job done, you might want more real-time output. For that, you'll need a server that's designed for more than just the web.

Running from the Cloud

Back in the olden days of computing, programmers paid for or reserved time on computers in order to execute their code. With the advent of personal computers, this became unnecessary—you simply write and execute code on your own computer. Now programmers are once again moving to pay-per-hour computing instances.

This time around, however, users aren't paying for time on a single, physical machine but on its equivalent computing power, often spread among many machines. The nebulous structure of this system allows computing power to be priced according to times of peak demand. For instance, Amazon allows for bidding on "spot instances" when low costs are more important than immediacy.

Compute instances are also more specialized and can be selected based on the needs of your application, with options like "high memory," "fast computing," and "large storage." Although web scrapers don't typically use much in the way of memory, you may want to consider large storage or fast computing in lieu of a more general-purpose instance for your scraping application. If you're doing large amounts of natural language processing, OCR work, or path finding (such as with the Six Degrees of Wikipedia problem), a fast computing instance might work well. If you're scraping large amounts of data, storing files, or doing large-scale analytics, you might want to go for an instance with storage optimization.

Although the sky is the limit as far as spending goes, at the time of this writing, instances start at just 0.9 cents (less than a penny) an hour for the cheapest Google instance, the f1-micro, and 0.8 cents an hour for a comparable Amazon EC2 micro instance. Thanks to the economies of scale, buying a small compute instance with a large company is almost always cheaper than buying your own physical, dedicated machine. Because now you don't need to hire an IT guy to keep it running.

Of course, step-by-step instructions for setting up and running cloud computing instances are somewhat outside the scope of this book, but you will likely find that step-by-step instructions are not needed. With both Amazon and Google (not to mention the countless smaller companies in the industry) vying for cloud computing dollars, they've made setting up new instances as easy as following a simple prompt, thinking of an app name, and providing a credit card number. As of this writing, both Amazon and Google also offer hundreds of dollars' worth of free computing hours to further tempt new clients.

If you're new to cloud computing, DigitalOcean is also a great provider of compute instances (which they call droplets), starting at 0.6 cents an hour. They have an incredibly easy user interface and simply email you the IP address and credentials for any new droplet they create so that you can log in and start running. Although they specialize more in web app hosting, DNS management, and load balancing, you can run anything you want from your instance!

Once you have an instance set up, you should be the proud new owner of an IP address, username, and public/private keys that can be used to connect to your instance through SSH. From there, everything should be the same as working with a server that you physically own—except, of course, you no longer have to worry about hardware maintenance or running your own plethora of advanced monitoring tools.

For quick and dirty jobs, especially if you don't have a lot of experience dealing with SSH and key pairs, I've found that Google's Cloud Platform instances can be easier to get up and running right away. They have a simple launcher and even have a button available after launch to view an SSH terminal right in the browser, as shown in Figure 20-1.

Figure 20-1. Browser-based terminal from a running Google Cloud Platform VM instance

Moving Forward

The web is constantly changing. The technologies that bring us images, video, text, and other data files are constantly being updated and reinvented. To keep pace, the collection of technologies used to scrape data from the internet must also change.

Who knows? Future versions of this text may omit JavaScript entirely as an obsolete and rarely used technology and instead focus on HTML8 hologram parsing. However, what won't change is the mindset and general approach needed to successfully scrape any website (or whatever we use for "websites" in the future).

When encountering any web scraping project, you should always ask yourself:

- What is the question I want answered or the problem I want solved?
- What data will help me achieve this and where is it?
- How is the website displaying this data? Can I identify exactly which part of the website's code contains this information?
- How can I isolate the data and retrieve it?
- What processing or analysis needs to be done to make it more useful?
- How can I make this process better, faster, and more robust?

In addition, you need to understand not just how to use the tools presented in this book in isolation but how they can work together to solve a larger problem. Sometimes the data is easily available and well formatted, allowing a simple scraper to do the trick. Other times you have to put some thought into it.

In Chapter 16, for example, you combined the Selenium library to identify Ajax-loaded images on Amazon and Tesseract to use OCR to read them. In the Six Degrees of Wikipedia problem, you used regular expressions to write a crawler that stored link information in a database, and then used a graph-solving algorithm to answer the question, "What is the shortest path of links between Kevin Bacon and Eric Idle?"

There is rarely an unsolvable problem when it comes to automated data collection on the internet. Just remember: the internet is one giant API with a somewhat poor user interface.

Web Scraping Proxies

This book discusses many products and technologies, with a focus on free and open-source software. In cases where paid products are discussed, it's generally because a free alternative doesn't exist, isn't practical, and/or the paid products are so ubiquitous I'd feel remiss not to mention them.

The web scraping proxy and API service industry is an odd one, as far as industries go. It's new, relatively niche, but still extremely crowded with a low barrier to entry. Because of this, there aren't any big "household names" yet that all programmers would agree *require* discussion. Yes, some names are bigger than others, and some services are better than others, but it's still quite the jungle out there.

Also, because web scraping proxying requires vast amounts of equipment and electricity to run, a viable free alternative does not exist and is unlikely to exist in the future.

This puts me in the precarious position of writing about an assortment of companies that you may not have heard of but that want your money. Rest assured, while I have opinions about these companies, I have not been paid for those opinions. I have used their services, spoken with their representatives, and in several cases been given free account credits for research purposes, but I do not have any incentive to promote them. I am not invested, either financially or emotionally, in any of these companies.

When you read this section, I suggest that you think more generally about the attributes of web scraping proxies and API services, their specialties, your budget, and your project requirements. These profiles are designed to be read as case studies and examples of "what's out there" rather than specific endorsements. And if you do feel like giving any of these particular companies money, that's between you and them!

ScrapingBee

ScrapingBee is the smallest of the companies in this list. It has a strong focus on JavaScript automation, headless browsers, and innocuous-looking IP addresses. Its API is well documented but, if you prefer not to do any reading, ScrapingBee also has an API request generation tool on its website that reduces the problem to button clicking and copy/pasting.

An important feature to consider when evaluating proxy services is the amount of time it takes to return request data to you. Not only does the request have to be routed from your computer to their server to the target's server and back again, but the proxy service may actually be buffering these requests on its end and not sending them out immediately. It's not unusual for a request to take a minute or longer to return. During a formal evaluation, it's important to time these requests throughout the day and time multiple types of requests for any features you might want to use.

Using ScrapingBee's API directly, we can scrape a product page and print both the results and the time it took to fetch them:

```
import requests
import time

start = time.time()
params = {
    'api_key': SCRAPING_BEE_KEY,
    'url': 'https://www.target.com/p/-/A-83650487',
}
response = requests.get('https://app.scrapingbee.com/api/v1/', params=params)
```

```
print(f'Time: {time.time() - start}')
print(f'HTTP status: {response.status_code}')
print(f'Response body: {response.content}')
```

ScrapingBee also has a Python package (*https://pypi.org/project/scrapingbee/*) that can be installed with pip:

```
$ pip install scrapingbee
```

This is a Software Development Kit (SDK) that let you use various features of the API in a slightly more convenient way. For example, the request above can be written as:

```
from scrapingbee import ScrapingBeeClient

start = time.time()
client = ScrapingBeeClient(api_key=SCRAPING_BEE_KEY)
response = client.get('https://www.target.com/p/-/A-83650487')

print(f'Time: {time.time() - start}')
print(f'HTTP status: {response.status_code}')
print(f'Response body: {response.content}')
```

Notice that the response is a Python requests response, and it can be used in the same way as in the previous example.

Scraping API services usually deal in units of "credits," where one basic API request costs one credit. Features such as JavaScript rendering with a headless browser or a residential IP address may cost anywhere from 5 credits to 75 credits. Each paid account level gives you a certain number of credits per month.

While there is a free trial with 1,000 credits, ScrapingBee's paid subscriptions start at $50/month for 150,000 credits, or 3,000 credits per dollar. Like with most of these services, there are large volume discounts—credits can be 13,000 per dollar or less with greater monthly spend.

If you want to maximize your requests, keep in mind that ScrapingBee charges 5 credits for JavaScript rendering and turns it on by default. This means that the requests above will cost 5 credits each, not 1.

This makes it convenient for customers who may not have read Chapter 14 of this book and do not understand why the data appearing in their web browser does not appear in the scraping results coming back from ScrapingBee. If those customers read Chapter 15, they would also understand how to get the data they want without JavaScript rendering at all. If you have read both of these chapters, you can turn off JavaScript rendering and reduce request costs by 80% using:

```
client = ScrapingBeeClient(api_key=SCRAPING_BEE_KEY)
params = {'render_js': 'false'}
response = client.get('https://www.target.com/p/-/A-83650487', params=params)
```

Like many of these services, ScrapingBee offers the option of using "premium" IP addresses, which may prevent your scrapers from getting blocked by websites wary of IP addresses frequently used by bots. These IP addresses are reported as residential addresses owned by smaller telecommunication companies. If that's not enough, ScrapingBee also offers a "stealth" IP address for 75 credits per request. The stealth IP addresses I was given were listed as datacenters and VPN servers, so it's unclear what, exactly, the stealth IP addresses are and what real advantages they offer over the premium addresses.

ScraperAPI

ScraperAPI, true to its name, has a mostly clean and REST-ful API with tons of features. It supports asynchronous requests, which allow you to make the scraping request and fetch the results later in a separate API call. Alternatively, you can provide a webhook endpoint that the results are sent to after the request is complete.

A simple one-credit call with ScraperAPI looks like this:

```
import requests
import time

start = time.time()
params = {
    'api_key': SCRAPER_API_KEY,
    'url': 'https://www.target.com/p/-/A-83650487'
}
response = requests.get('http://api.scraperapi.com', params=params)
print(f'Time: {time.time() - start}')
print(f'HTTP status: {response.status_code}')
print(f'Response body: {response.content}')
```

ScraperAPI also has an SDK that can be installed with pip:

```
$ pip install scraperapi-sdk
```

Like with most of these SDKs, it is a very thin wrapper around the Python requests library. As with the ScrapingBee API, a Python Requests response is returned:

```
from scraper_api import ScraperAPIClient

client = ScraperAPIClient(SCRAPER_API_KEY)
start = time.time()
result = client.get('https://www.target.com/p/-/A-83650487')
print(f'Time: {time.time() - start}')
print(f'HTTP status: {response.status_code}')
print(f'Response body: {response.content}')
```

When evaluating web scraping services, it may be tempting to prefer those that have Python SDKs built around their APIs. However, you should carefully consider how much programming effort it will reduce or convenience it will provide. Technically, a

Python "SDK" can be written around any scraping API with very little effort, including your own. This example SDK is written around an imaginary API in just a few lines of code:

```python
class RyansAPIClient:
    def __init__(self, key):
        self.key = key
        self.api_root = 'http://api.pythonscraping.com/ryansApiPath'

    def get(url):
        params = {'key': self.key, 'url': url}
        return requests.get(self.api_root, params=params)
```

But one unique feature of ScraperAPI is its auto-parsing tools for Amazon products and Google search results. A request for an Amazon product page or an Amazon or Google search results page has a cost of 5 credits, rather the 1 credit for most requests. Although the documentation does mention an explicit call to the Amazon Product Endpoint at *https://api.scraperapi.com/structured/amazon/product*, this service appears to be turned on by default:

```python
from scraper_api import ScraperAPIClient

client = ScraperAPIClient(SCRAPER_API_KEY)
start = time.time()
result = client.get('https://www.amazon.com/Web-Scraping-Python-Collecting\
-Modern/dp/1491985577')
print(f'Time: {time.time() - start}')
print(f'HTTP status: {response.status_code}')
print(f'Response body: {response.text}')
```

With the response:

```
Time: 4.672130823135376
HTTP status: 200
Response body: {"name":"Web Scraping with Python: Collecting More
Data from the Modern Web","product_information":{"publisher":
"O'Reilly Media; 2nd edition (May 8, 2018)","language":"English",
"paperback":"306 pages","isbn_10":"1491985577","isbn_13":
"978-1491985571","item_weight":"1.21 pounds" ...
```

While writing an Amazon product parsing tool is hardly an insurmountable challenge, offloading the responsibility of testing and maintaining that parsing tool over the years may be well worth the costs.

As mentioned before, ScraperAPI also allows you to make asynchronous requests to its API and fetch the results at a later time. This request takes less than 100 ms to return:

```python
start = time.time()
params = {
    'apiKey': SCRAPER_API_KEY,
    'url': 'https://www.target.com/p/-/A-83650487'
```

```
}
response = requests.post('https://async.scraperapi.com/jobs', json=params)
print(f'Time: {time.time() - start}')
print(f'HTTP status: {response.status_code}')
print(f'Response body: {response.content}')
```

Note that this is a POST request rather than a GET request, as shown in previous examples. We are, in a sense, posting data for the creation of a stored entity on Scraper API's server. Also, the attribute used to send the key changes from api_key to apiKey.

The response body contains only a URL where the job can be fetched:

```
Time: 0.09664416313171387
HTTP status: 200
Response body: b'{"id":"728a365b-3a2a-4ed0-9209-cc4e7d88de96",
"attempts":0,"status":"running","statusUrl":"https://async.
scraperapi.com/jobs/728a365b-3a2a-4ed0-9209-cc4e7d88de96",
"url":"https://www.target.com/p/-/A-83650487"}'
```

Calling it does not require an API key—the UUID is sufficient security here—and, assuming the request has been completed on their end, it returns the target's body:

```
response = requests.get('https://async.scraperapi.com/jobs/\
    728a365b-3a2a-4ed0-9209-cc4e7d88de96')
print(f'Response body: {response.content}')
```

The results of these async requests are stored for up to four hours, or until you retrieve the data. While you could accomplish a similar result at home with a multithreaded scraper and a little code, you could not easily do it while rotating residential and mobile IP addresses, changing countries of origin, managing session data, rendering all the JavaScript (which will quickly bog down a machine), and tracking all successes and failures in a dashboard.

Asynchronous requests and webhooks (where the proxy service returns the results to the URL you provide) are excellent features in an API service, especially for larger and longer-running scraping projects. ScraperAPI provides this at no extra cost per request, which is especially nice.

Oxylabs

Oxylabs is a large Lithuanian-based company with a focus on search engine results page (SERP) and product page scraping. Its product ecosystem and API have a bit of a learning curve. After creating an account, you must activate (either with a one-week trial or paid subscription) every "product" that you want to use and create separate username/password credentials specific to each product. These username/password credentials work a bit like an API key.

The Web Scraper API product allows you to make calls that look like this, with a Web Scraper API username and password:

```python
import requests
import time

start = time.time()
data = {
    'url': 'https://www.target.com/p/-/A-83650487',
    'source': 'universal',
}

response = requests.post(
    'https://realtime.oxylabs.io/v1/queries',
    auth=(OXYLABS_USERNAME, OXYLABS_PASSWORD),
    json=data
)

response = response.json()['results'][0]

print(f'Time: {time.time() - start}')
print(f'HTTP status: {response["status_code"]}')
print(f'Response body: {response["content"]}')
```

However, the user may be in for a surprise if the target URL is switched to one from the amazon.com domain:

```python
data = {
    'url': 'https://www.amazon.com/Web-Scraping-Python-Collecting-Modern\
-dp-1491985577/dp/1491985577',
    'source': 'universal',
}

response = requests.post(
    'https://realtime.oxylabs.io/v1/queries',
    auth=(OXYLABS_USERNAME, OXYLABS_PASSWORD),
)
print(response.json())
```

This code prints an error message:

```python
{'message': 'provided url is not supported'}
```

Like ScraperAPI, Oxylabs has parsing tools predesigned for sites like Amazon and Google. However, to scrape those domains—with or without the special parsing tools—you must subscribe specifically to the SERP Scraper API product (to scrape Google, Bing, Baidu, or Yandex) or the E-Commerce Scraper API product (to scrape Amazon, Aliexpress, eBay, and many others).

If subscribed to the E-Commerce Scraper API product, the Amazon domain can be successfully scraped by changing the source attribute to amazon and passing in the E-Commerce-specific credentials:

```
data = {
    'url': 'https://www.amazon.com/Web-Scraping-Python-Collecting-Modern\
-dp-1491985577/dp/1491985577',
    'source': 'amazon',
}

response = requests.post(
    'https://realtime.oxylabs.io/v1/queries',
    auth=(OXYLABS_USERNAME_ECOMMERCE, OXYLABS_PASSWORD),
    json=data
)
```

This does not do anything special; it simply returns the content of the page as usual. To use the product information formatting templates, we must also set the attribute parse to True:

```
data = {
    'url': 'https://www.amazon.com/Web-Scraping-Python-Collecting-Modern\
-dp-1491985577/dp/1491985577',
    'source': 'amazon',
    'parse': True
}
```

This parses the website and returns formatted JSON data:

```
...
'page': 1,
'price': 32.59,
'stock': 'Only 7 left in stock - order soon',
'title': 'Web Scraping with Python: Collecting More Data from the Modern Web',
'buybox': [{'name': 'buy_new', 'price': 32.59, 'condition': 'new'},
...
```

It's important to keep in mind that parsing tools themselves are not specific to the E-Commerce Scraper API product. We can also parse the target.com domain using the regular Web Scraper API product, setting the source back to universal and using the Web Scraper API credentials:

```
data = {
    'url': 'https://www.target.com/p/-/A-83650487',
    'source': 'universal',
    'parse': True
}

response = requests.post(
    'https://realtime.oxylabs.io/v1/queries',
    auth=(OXYLABS_USERNAME, OXYLABS_PASSWORD),
    json=data
)
```

Which returns JSON-formatted product data:

```
'url': 'https://www.target.com/p/-/A-83650487',
'price': 44.99,
'title': 'Web Scraping with Python - 2nd Edition by  Ryan Mitchell (Paperback)',
'category': 'Target/Movies, Music & Books/Books/All Book Genres/Computers & Techn
ology Books',
'currency': 'USD',
'description': 'Error while parsing `description`: `(<class \'AttributeError\'>,
AttributeError("\'NoneType\' object has no attribute \'xpath\'"))`.', 'rating_sco
re': 0, 'parse_status_code': 12004
```

Because it was attempting to parse pages at the domain target.com automatically, it is liable to run into errors here and there, like it did with the description. Fortunately, users can also write custom parsers, which are compatible with any API product type (Web Scraper API, SERP Scraper API, E-Commerce Scraper API, etc.). These custom parsers take the form of JSON files with a format specified by Oxylabs, which defines the various fields and the XPath selectors that collect data for them.

These custom parsers are essentially the "business logic" of the web scraper itself. It may be worth considering that, if you move to another web scraping API or proxy platform, these templates would be essentially useless and would need to be heavily modified, rewritten, or your new code base would need to be written specifically to work with them. Writing web scraping templates in the Oxylabs-specific language may be somewhat limiting if you choose to go elsewhere.

It's also important to stress that these different API "products" (which, in fact, use the same API endpoint and call structure) are defined, based not on their particular features but on the domains they're allowed to send requests to, which could change at any time.

The domains under the purview of a specific product may not necessarily be well-supported by that product either. Oxylab's SERP Scraping API advertises support for sites such as Baidu and Bing, but it does not have parsing templates developed for them. This "support" may be as simple as the ability to specify a search like:

```
data = {
    'query': 'foo',
    'source': 'bing_search',
}
```

instead of writing out the full URL:

```
data = {
    'url': 'https://bing.com?q=foo',
    'source': 'bing',
}
```

Note that, while I am critical of some aspects of Oxylab's API products, this criticism is not directed at the company per se and should not be interpreted as a comprehensive review or recommendation. I intend it only as a case study, or as an example for consideration, for those who might be evaluating similar products in the future.

When evaluating APIs and web scraping services, it's always important to consider what is being advertised, what is being provided, and who the target audience is. The structure of an API call may reveal important information about the actual construction of a product, and even the documentation can be misleading.

Oxylabs has many excellent qualities as well. It is one of the best providers of proxy IP addresses. Oxylabs continuously sources a wide variety and large number of IP addresses, listed publicly as being residential, mobile, and data centers. Like other proxy services, these IP addresses are available at a higher cost, depending on the type. However, Oxylabs charges by the gigabyte for these proxy services, rather than the request. Currently, costs range from \$22/GB (low-volume mobile IP addresses) to \$8/GB (high-volume residential IP addresses).

Zyte

Zyte, formerly Scrapinghub, is another large web scraping proxy and API service company. It's also one of the oldest, founded in 2010. While I have no particular attachment to any of these companies, I would be lying if I said that, as the maintainers of Scrapy, Zyte doesn't stand out from the crowd somewhat. And, beginning in 2019, it also hosts the Web Data Extraction Summit (*https://www.extractsummit.io*).

As a large company, Zyte has most of the features of the previous companies mentioned, and more. Unlike most others, it also sells data outright. If you need, for example, job postings, real estate data, or product information, it can provide those datasets or provide consultants who can build custom datasets.

Zyte maintains Scrapy and has incorporated it into its product lineup in the form of Scrapy Cloud. This tool allows you to deploy and run Scrapy projects in the cloud from either a GitHub repository or from your local machine using the Scrapinghub command-line client (*https://pypi.org/project/shub/*). This allows you to keep your web scrapers platform agnostic and portable but still interface tightly with the Zyte ecosystem.

Once a Scrapy project is deployed, Zyte finds all of the spider classes in the project and automatically loads them into your dashboard. You can use Zyte's dashboard UI to launch and monitor these spiders as they run in the cloud, then view or download the resulting data.

Of course, Zyte also has an API. It is somewhat similar to the other APIs in that it heavily relies on the Python requests package. It is also similar to Oxylab's API in that it uses the POST method entirely along with HTTP Basic Authentication. However, unlike Oxylab, only a Zyte key is sent over Basic Auth, rather than the username and password:

```python
import time
from base64 import b64decode
import requests

json_data = {
    'url': 'https://www.target.com/p/-/A-83650487',
    'httpResponseBody': True,
}
start = time.time()
response = requests.post('https://api.zyte.com/v1/extract',
    auth=(ZYTE_KEY, ''), json=json_data)

response = response.json()
print(f'Time: {time.time() - start}')
print(f'HTTP status: {response["statusCode"]}')
body = b64decode(response["httpResponseBody"])
print(f'Response body: {body}')
```

The other major difference is that all response bodies are returned as base64 encoded strings, rather than HTML or JSON text. This is trivial to handle with Python's base64 package. It also allows you to retrieve binary data, images, and other files just like any other request response by simply decoding the response as that file type.

If you don't feel like using Scrapy and have a fairly straightforward project, Zyte's Automatic Extraction API uses AI to detect various fields on a page and return them as JSON-formatted data. Currently, it works with both articles and product types. Obviously, it does not need to use base64 encoding because all the pages it parses must be text:

```python
json_data = [{
    'url': 'https://www.target.com/p/-/A-83650487',
    'pageType': 'product',
}]

response = requests.post(
    'https://autoextract.zyte.com/v1/extract',
    auth=(ZYTE_KEY, ''),
    json=json_data
)

print(response.json())
```

The documentation for Zyte's Automatic Extraction API provides the URL *https:// autoextract.scrapinghub.com/v1/extract,* as an artifact of their previous name, ScrapingHub. If you see this, know that you can usually replace `zyte.com` with `scraping hub.com` and give your code some backwards compatibility if Zyte decides to shut down the old domain.

Zyte's products are heavily geared toward developers working in an enterprise environment who want full transparency and control over their scrapers. However, Zyte prefers to take IP address management out of the hands of users with its Zyte Smart Proxy Manager. Zyte controls which IP addresses the traffic is proxied through. IP addresses are maintained between sessions, but IP addresses are switched if one is being blocked. Zyte attempts to use IP address switching to create an organic-looking flow of traffic to a site that avoids suspicion.

Using the Smart Proxy Manager is straightforward, although installing certificates on your machine may add complexity:

```
response = requests.get(
    'https://www.target.com/p/-/A-83650487',
    proxies={
        'http': f'http://{ZYTE_KEY}:@proxy.crawlera.com:8011/',
        'https': f'http://{ZYTE_KEY}:@proxy.crawlera.com:8011/',
    },
    verify='/path/to/zyte-proxy-ca.crt'
)
print(response.text)
```

If you don't want to use a certificate (although this is not recommended) you can turn off verification in the requests module:

```
response = requests.get(
    ...
    verify=False
)
```

Of course, Zyte also has instructions for integrating its proxy services with Scrapy (*https://scrapy-zyte-smartproxy.readthedocs.io/en/latest/*), which can then be run in its Scrapy Cloud.

Proxy requests are around 1,600 per dollar (or less with more expensive monthly plans), API requests start around 12,000 per dollar. The Scrapy Cloud plans are relatively inexpensive, with a generous free tier and a $9/month "Professional" tier. This is likely to encourage the use of Scrapy and promote integration with the Zyte platform.

Additional Resources

Many years ago, running "in the cloud" was mostly the domain of those who felt like slogging through the documentation and already had some server administration experience. Today, the tools have improved dramatically due to increased popularity and competition among cloud computing providers.

Still, for building large-scale or more-complex scrapers and crawlers, you might want a little more guidance on creating a platform for collecting and storing data.

Google Compute Engine by Marc Cohen, Kathryn Hurley, and Paul Newson (O'Reilly) is a straightforward resource on using Google Cloud Computing with both Python and JavaScript. It covers not only Google's user interface but also the command-line and scripting tools that you can use to give your application greater flexibility.

If you prefer to work with Amazon, Mitch Garnaat's *Python and AWS Cookbook* (O'Reilly) is a brief but extremely useful guide that will get you started with Amazon Web Services and show you how to get a scalable application up and running.

Index

C

CAPTCHAs, 202, 235
  reading, 248
  retrieving, 256-258
Cascading Style Sheets (CSS) (see CSS (Cascading Style Sheets))
CFAA (Computer Fraud and Abuse Act), 23-24
CGI (Common Gateway Interface), 306
CGI-scripts, 306
chattels, 21
checkboxes, 197
ChromeDriver, 305
classes, 56
cleaning data, pandas, 166-172
cleaning text, 160-164
client-side code, 12, 203
  JavaScript (see JavaScript)
client-side redirects, 80
cloud, running from, 307-308
code optimization, 48
communication between processes
Completely Automated Public Turing Test to Tell Computers and Human Apart (see CAPTCHAs)
Computer Fraud and Abuse Act (CFAA), 23-24
cookies
  functions for manipulating, 263
  Google Analytics, 263
  headers and, 262-264
  JavaScript and, 262-264
  logins and, 199-201
  plug-ins, 263
  Requests library, 199
  viewing, 263
copyright law, 18, 19-21
Corpus of Contemporary American English, 176
CSS (Cascading Style Sheets), 9-11, 53
  as programming language, 203
CSV (comma-separated values)
  file storage, 124-126
  reading files, 151-153
  Scrapy and, 115
csv library, 125, 151-153

D

dark web, 76-78
darknet, 76

data collection, web crawlers, 78-80
data extraction, ETL (extract, transform, load), 159
data link layer, OSI model, 5
data summaries, 174-178
databases, 135
  (see also MySQL)
  connection/cursor model, 132
  id columns, 135
  scraping results, 133
DataFrames, pandas and, 167-168
deactivate command, virtual environments, 46
deep web, 76-78
developer tools
  accessing, 13-15
  Network tab, 15-16
DHTML (dynamic HTML), 208
DigitalOcean, 308
directed graphs, 181
DMCA (Digital Millennium Copyright Act) of 1988, 19
documents, encoding, 145-151
.docx files (Microsoft Word), 155-157
downloads, security, 124
Dux-Soup, 39

E

e-commerce, 34-36
  (see also marketing applications)
eBay v. Bidder's Edge, 28
EditThisCookie plug-in, 263
email
  email package, 141
  MIME (Multipurpose Internet Mail Extensions), 141
  SMTP (Simple Mail Transfer Protocol), 140-142
  smtplib package, 141
encoding documents, 145-151
endpoints, 222
ethics, 259-260
ETL (extract, transform, and load), 159
exception handling, 49-51, 75
.exe files download security, 124
expressions
  lambda expressions, 68-69
  nonregular expressions, 63
  regular expressions, 62

J

JavaScript, 11, 204
  Ajax, 208
  const keyword, 205
  cookies and, 262-264
  libraries, 205-207
  Selenium (see Selenium)
  syntax, 204
  var, 204
JavaScript ES6, 205
jQuery, 206
JSON (JavaScript Object Notation)
  API response, 222, 224-225
  parsing, 226-227
  parsing library, 226
Jupyter
  installing, 41-42
  Notebooks
    .ipynb files, 41
    cells, 42
    Processing module, 295
    unit testing, 276
  Project Jupyter, 42

L

lambda expressions, 68-69
lambda functions, 124
last in, last out (LILO), 290
legal issues
  CFAA (Computer Fraud and Abuse Act),
    23-24
  copyright law, 18
  eBay v. Bidder's Edge, 28-29
  Field v. Google, 31-32
  intellectual property, 18-19
  trespass to chattels, 21-23
  United States v. Auernheimer, 29-31
lexicographical analysis, NLTK, 188
libraries
  JavaScript, 205
    Google Analytics, 206
    Google Maps, 207
    jQuery, 206
  NumPy, 239
  Pillow, 236
  pytesseract, well-formatted text and, 241
  Python
    global installation, 46

installing, 44-46
PIL (Python Imaging Library), 236
virtual environments and, 45-51
  Requests, 193
    urllib2 module, 194
  Selenium, 211
  Tesseract, 237
    installing, 237-239
LIFO (last in, last out), 290
LinkExtractor class, 111-112
links
  rules, 111
  webcrawlers and, 99-101
logging, Scrapy and, 119
logins
  cookies and, 199-201
  forms, submitting, 194
  security, 267-271
lxml parser, 48

M

machine training, NLTK and, 190
macOS, MySQL installation, 127
malware, 124
marketing applications, 35-36
Markov models, 178-181
  Six Degrees of Wikipedia, 181-184
MarqVision, 35
media file storage, 121-124
Mersenne Twister algorithm, 75
Microsoft Word, 155-157
MIME (Multipurpose Internet Mail Extensions), 141
ML (machine learning), NLTK and, 190
multiprocess web crawling, 296-300
multithreaded web crawling, 286-294
  Processing module, 294-299
  queues, 289-291
  race conditions, 289-291
  threading module, 292-294
MySQL, 126
  (see also PyMySQL)
  commands, 129-132
  Debian-based Linux, 127
  installing, 127
  macOS installation, 127
  Six Degrees of Wikipedia, 137-140
  table keys, 130

lowercase, converting to, 161
Markov models, 178-181
    Six Degrees of Wikipedia, 181-184
n-grams, 164
newline characters, 161
normalized, 164-166
parenthesized, 162
PDF files, 153-154
statistical analysis, NLTK, 185-188
Unicode Consortium, 147
well-formatted, 239
Word (Microsoft), 155-157
text files, 146
  encoding, 147-151
  IETF (Internet Engineering Task Force), 146
text generators, Markov models and, 178
text objects, 187
threading module
  paths, appending, 288
  static functions, 292
TLS (Transport Layer Security), 264-266
  fingerprint, 266-267
Tor, 303
  anonymity, 304
    PySocks, 305
  ChromeDriver and, 305
  dark web, 76
  Selenium and, 305
TOS (Terms of Service), 24-27
trademark use, 35
trademarks, 18
traineddata files, Tesseract, 255
training, Tesseract, 245-249
  box files, 251-255
  image scraping, 250-251
  traineddata files, 255
transport layer, OSI model, 6
travel applications, 38-39
travel sites, 37
trees, 58-59
  children, 59-60
  parents, 61
  siblings, 60
trespass to chattels, 21-23, 28-29
Turing test, 248
Turing, Alan, 248
Twitter, robots.txt file, 26

U
UDP (User Datagram Protocol), 6
undirected graphs, 182
Unicode, 133
Unicode Consortium, 147
unicodedata, 163
unit testing, 274-275
  Jupyter Notebook, 276
  unittest (Python), 275-276
unittest (Python), 275-276
urllib library, 44, 261
urllib2 module, 194
User-Agent, 262
UTF-8, 134, 147, 150

V
virtual environments
  deactivate command, 46
  Python libraries, 45-51

W
W3C (World Wide Web Consortium), HTML
  and, 9
War Games movie, 23
web crawlers, 71
  blocking, 261
  entire site, 75-78
  Google and, 81
  legal protections, 82
  patterns, 80
  single domain, 71
  structure, 96-102
  undesirable results, 81
web pages versus files, 43
web scraping proxies, 309
  Oxylabs, 314-318
  remote servers and, 301-303
  ScraperAPI, 312-314
  ScrapingBee, 310-312
  Tor, 303-306
  website-hosting accounts, 306-307
  Zyte, 318-320
web servers, redirects, 80
webdriver manager, 210
WebDrivers, Selenium, 216
website hosting accounts, 306-307
  Linux server, 306
  Windows server, 306

websites
  interacting with, testing and, 280-283
  layouts, 91-96
Wikipedia
  server load, 72-74
  testing, 277-279
Wikipedia API, 72
WikispiderPipeline class (Scrapy), 118
Word (Microsoft), 155-157

X

XML (Extensible Markup Language), 8

API response, 222, 224-225
XPath, 215
  text content extraction, 110

Y

Yelp, 39

Z

Zyte, 318-320

About the Author

Ryan Mitchell has been writing books about web scraping and data science since 2013. She has six LinkedIn Learning courses, including *Web Scraping with Python* and *Python Essential Training*—currently the leading Python course on the platform. An expert in web scraping, application security, and data science, Ryan has hosted workshops and spoken at many events, including Data Day and DEF CON.

Ryan holds a master's degree in software engineering from Harvard University Extension School and a bachelor's in engineering from Olin College of Engineering. She is currently a principal software engineer at the Gerson Lehrman Group where she does machine learning and data science with Python on their search team. She regularly consults on web scraping projects in the retail, finance, and pharmaceutical industries, and has worked as a curriculum consultant and adjunct faculty member at Northeastern University and Olin College of Engineering.

Colophon

The animal on the cover of *Web Scraping with Python* is a ground pangolin (*Smutsia temminckii*). The pangolin is a solitary, nocturnal mammal and closely related to armadillos, sloths, and anteaters. They can be found in southern and eastern Africa. There are three other species of pangolins in Africa and all are considered to be critically endangered.

Full-grown ground pangolins can average from 12 inches to 39 inches in length and weigh from a mere 3.5 pounds to 73 pounds. They resemble armadillos, covered in protective scales that are either dark, light brown, or olive in color. Immature pangolin scales are more pink. When pangolins are threatened, their scales on the tails can act more like an offensive weapon, as they are able to cut and wound attackers. Pangolins also have a defense strategy similar to skunks, in which they secrete a foul-smelling acid from glands located close to the anus. This serves as a warning to potential attackers, but also helps the pangolin mark territory. The underside of the pangolin is not covered in scales, but instead with little bits of fur.

Like those of their anteater relatives, pangolin diets consist of ants and termites. Their incredibly long tongues allow them to scavenge logs and anthills for their meals. The tongue is longer than their body and retracts into their chest cavity while at rest. Though they are solitary animals, once matured, the ground pangolin lives in large burrows that run deep underground. In many cases, the burrows once belonged to aardvarks and warthogs, and the pangolin has simply taken over the abandoned residence. With the three long, curved claws found on their forefeet, however, pangolins don't have a problem digging their own burrows if necessary.

Many of the animals on O'Reilly covers are endangered; all of them are important to the world.

The cover illustration is by Karen Montgomery, based on an antique line engraving from *Lydekker's Royal Natural History*. The series design is by Edie Freedman, Ellie Volckhausen, and Karen Montgomery. The cover fonts are Gilroy Semibold and Guardian Sans. The text font is Adobe Minion Pro; the heading font is Adobe Myriad Condensed; and the code font is Dalton Maag's Ubuntu Mono.

O'REILLY®

Learn from experts.
Become one yourself.

Books | Live online courses
Instant answers | Virtual events
Videos | Interactive learning

Get started at oreilly.com.

Printed in the USA
CPSIA information can be obtained
at www.ICGtesting.com
JSHW050026090724
66058JS00007B/90